SYNCOPATIONS

Syncopations

BEATS, NEW YORKERS,
AND WRITERS IN THE DARK

JAMES CAMPBELL

UNIVERSITY OF CALIFORNIA PRESS
Berkeley   Los Angeles   London

University of California Press, one of the most distinguished university presses in the United States, enriches lives around the world by advancing scholarship in the humanities, social sciences, and natural sciences. Its activities are supported by the UC Press Foundation and by philanthropic contributions from individuals and institutions. For more information, visit www.ucpress.edu.

University of California Press
Berkeley and Los Angeles, California
University of California Press, Ltd.
London, England

Library of Congress Cataloging-in-Publication Data

Campbell, James, 1951–
    Syncopations : Beats, New Yorkers, and writers in the dark / James Campbell.
        p.   cm.
    ISBN 978-0-520-25236-3 (cloth : alk. paper)
    ISBN 978-0-520-25237-0 (pbk. : alk. paper)
        1. American literature—20th century—History and criticism.
    2. American literature—African American authors—History and criticism. 3. New York (N.Y.)—Intellectual life—20th century.
    4. Beat generation. 5. Campbell, James, 1951– 6. Authors, Scottish—20th century—Biography. I. Title.
        PS221.C33 2008
        810.9'97471—dc22   2008003978

Manufactured in the United States of America

17   16   15   14   13   12   11   10   09   08
10   9   8   7   6   5   4   3   2   1

This book is printed on New Leaf EcoBook 50, a 100% recycled fiber of which 50% is de-inked post-consumer waste, processed chlorine-free. EcoBook 50 is acid-free and meets the minimum requirements of ANSI/ASTM D5634–01 (*Permanence of Paper*).

To my sisters, Jean, Phyllis, and Julie,
and to my niece, Annie

Contents

Preface

My first magazine assignment was to travel from Glasgow to London, to visit and write about the Scottish novelist, pornographer, and professional drug addict Alexander Trocchi, author of *Young Adam* and *Cain's Book*. The year was 1972. I was twenty-one years old. The magazine was *GUM*—*Glasgow University Magazine*—and the commissioning editor was my best friend, Jack Haggerty.

Neither the editor nor his reporter were students at the university. Jack was an urbane dropout who dressed in a gray herringbone suit and what he called "the Graham Greene raincoat." He had given up an English course for a job on a local newspaper in a dwindling shipyard town twenty miles downriver from Glasgow, but he had a natural aptitude for both the high and low conversations of literature and a liking for stories, including tall stories. I had yet to drop in, having left school at an early age to work in a Dickensian printing factory in the oldest part of the city. When eventually I took up my studies, it would be at the University of Edinburgh, on the opposite coast of Scotland. So far, I had graduated from my busted printer's apprenticeship to a life of guitar-picking and traveling. I was a grade-two picker but a grade-eight hitchhiker, making journeys, more or less according to my own timetable, to Asia Minor, across the Mediterranean, from Tunis through Algiers to Rabat, and south toward Timbuctu. Thumbing lifts in a Moroccan desert at sundown is character-building for a twenty-one-year-old.

Along the way, I made many friends, and in those friends' rucksacks were many books, but it was in the educationally rich bed-sitting rooms radiating from Glasgow University that I took to heart the catechisms of Jean Cocteau, Albert Camus, Hermann Hesse, William Burroughs, and other anti-apostles. I also fell in with a gang of borderline renegades, ragged enough to accommodate big burly guys like John Steinbeck and little skinny guys like Samuel Beckett. Ever since, my intention as a reader—the only decent intention—has been to be open-minded, but I have always felt fortunate to be a receiver of the code of cultural subversion at a time when novels, essays, and poems, not pop music and fashion, still provided the soundtrack to youth.

Trocchi lived in London, four hundred miles away, but Jack was the kind of editor who liked to think big. I should travel down south (paying my own fare, naturally) and bring back the story of the first credible Scottish beat novelist, a writer who had described himself as "a colossus," who had labeled all Scottish writing besides his own "stale porridge."

The interview was arranged from a telephone box—there was no phone in my rented room—outside the Glasgow café in which Jack and I held our editorial meetings. Tape recorders were unlikely possessions in 1972, so I borrowed one with the proportions of a small suitcase. A seat on the overnight train to London was theoretically cheap and could be regarded as giving a bonus ten hours of studious darkness in which to rehearse my earnest questions. When I rang the doorbell at his West London flat, queasy from the first stabs of this new sickness, journalistic anxiety, Trocchi was still in bed. He had forgotten I was coming.

He received me the next day instead and generously filled up my virgin tape with adventures and reminiscence, impossible social projects, extracts from an incomprehensible, never-to-be-completed novel. He lent me copies of scarce books with a touching request for safe return. He apologized for the inconvenience of the previous day and offered to pay the excess train fare. To my protests, he replied with avuncular charm: "I'm short of hundreds and thousands. I'm not short of ones and twos." He asked to be excused while he went to the bathroom to give himself a fix. I remember how his interest was pricked by the news that I was not a student. I was, like him, a freelance writer, from this day on.

Back in Glasgow, my first article was written—four thousand words long—bulging with references to Dada, the Absurd, *la littérature engagée*, and other weapons of disaffection. In the café, I submitted it to Jack, who read it with two Gitanes and a black coffee, and printed it in *GUM* without the editorial surgery a less indulgent friend would have inflicted on it. Twenty years later, I wrote another piece about Trocchi, which is included here, with some recollections of that pioneer assignment.

.   .   .

Travel. A foreign place (London was to me then). A strange but nevertheless familiar face. A notebook to be filled, a story to write. Half the chapters of this book derive from that mixture: not only the profiles, but some of the essays, too. I would never have written about William Maxwell if my wife's mother, who knew him well, had not entrusted me with the errand to deliver a book while in New York. Richard Wright's unpublished last novel would have remained obscure if I had not uncorked a bottle of wine with his widow in Paris, hoping to jog her memory on a different topic.

The interview-based pieces are not celebrity portraits, though the personality of the subject is meant to play a part. The interviewer is not seeking to insinuate a banana skin beneath the interviewee's foot. Sometimes it is the former who is caught by surprise. Shirley Hazzard met me off the Naples ferry at the port on Capri and escorted me to her favorite restaurants and elevated vistas over three days. J. P. Donleavy entertained me for seven hours, asking more questions than he answered, driving us to a deserted pub in a hilltop village for "the best Guinness in Ireland." Afterward, he dropped a line to say that the photograph of him that accompanied the article had been widely admired. Gary Snyder welcomed me to his ranch, a forty-mile drive from the nearest hotel, then put on his backpack for a pedagogic excursion through the neighboring oaks and Douglas firs. When I made noises about getting back to San Francisco, he said, "What—d'you have a date in the city tonight?" Art Spiegelman talked rapid-fire in his French publisher's office for two hours, before going on holiday. William Styron made himself comfortable in a suite at Claridge's in London while his wife went shopping. The basic proposition was the same in every case: let's meet, talk, and generate an article that is accurate and interesting to readers.

Naturally, the writer also wishes to parade a certain style, but I have done my best to be a conscientious literary reporter. One can only depend on past reading, and nifty footwork to skip past the gaps, to take one so far. Preparation is a partner to respect and generally takes longer than the writing of the piece. I have persuaded myself that there is such a thing as being "overprepared"—after all, I reason, eager to close the book and pour a drink—it is they, not I, who have to put on a show.

While having that drink, I will admit that that is only half the story. The best interviews are not those that elicit spicy information, but in which both you and your interlocutor are conscious that you are acting out roles in a playlet called "The Interview." Like actors who take to the stage night after night, you can give a good performance or a bad one, whether playing your part for the first time or the fortieth. As with genuine actors, your performance is abetted or impeded by the movements of those around you. Another half-truth I sell myself is that the ideal interview attains the natural pace of conversation. But an ordinary conversation between two friends in a living room would make a lousy interview. Rather, you want the encounter to seem like ordinary talk, while remaining within the conventions of the playlet.

John Updike was a star performer in "The Interview," generous with his candor, his intelligence, his time, negotiating each of his fellow actor's gambits as if he had never taken to the stage to play such a demanding role before. In my farewell mental snap of him, on Arlington Street, Boston, he is looking back over his shoulder, giggling and waving, hat tipped at a convivial angle, after three hours of good talk and patient posing for photographs. When I telephoned a fortnight later to check a quotation he had drawn up impromptu from William James, he was as remote as if dealing with a cold caller.

What Updike had said that afternoon was: "Somewhere William James talks about, 'If men can believe in gods then they can . . . go to fairs . . . ,' and it's a little like that with me." I tried to verify the quotation, in vain. In "The Interview," Updike had improvised his lines, as good actors sometimes must do. What James actually wrote was: "If men can believe in gods, then the days pass by with zest; they stir with prospect, they thrill with remoter values." Updike would have been displeased to find the quotation diminished and set down wrongly in print but saw no reason at that moment to be grateful for having been prompted to correct it. The telephone call from London had probably interrupted his work, or a duty for the church, or a letter to one of his children. There was no cause to be offended by his offstage chilliness; he was no longer in the cast of that particular staging of "The Interview."

.   .   .   ʼ

Most of the pieces in this book were written in the past five years. The general subject is the writing produced by Americans, mostly since about 1950, though I have smuggled in two chapters about Scots who found a welcome freedom in forming a union with the United States. A companion volume could be filled with essays on Scottish writing and writers. I listen to the great chorus of English literature with boundless pleasure, but the voices sound mildly foreign, and the autobiographical essay here, "Boswell and Mrs. Miller," partly explains why.

The writing that first spoke to me with a modern voice—a voice with "that little twist, that backward-something," to borrow Updike's lovely phrase from our performance of "The Interview"—was generally French or American. When I tired eventually of reading in translation, or was fatigued from tackling originals, I was left with the Americans: the popular Jewish writers who came through in the 1950s and gravitated to Britain in the following decade: Bellow, Malamud, Roth, Salinger; then *New Yorker* fiction editor Maxwell's "three Johns," Cheever, O'Hara, and Updike. Others followed, all bringing colorful American baggage to our sheet metal–gray shipbuilding ports. It was impossible to imagine books like *In Cold Blood, Another Country, Advertisements for Myself, Naked Lunch* being cultivated under British or even European climatic conditions. These were charts of American space, products of the determination to settle unmapped land. They were thrilling as much for their form as for the content—further proof of their originality. Use of the now-hackneyed phrase "nonfiction novel" only dampens the excitement provoked by Capote's book in the years after its publication.

In poetry there were Roberts—Creeley, Duncan, and Lowell—whose experiments in form and utterance made their British counterparts appear bogged down in provincial idiom. (As with many views held at the time, I have refined this one since.) The intrigue of reading Creeley and Snyder, like the first encounter with abstract expressionism, was of seeing an artist make a mark where previously there had been just air. It was—a great thing in literature—unexpected.

At Edinburgh University, I specialized in American literature: two years of intensive reading under the enlightened supervision of Colin Nicholson and Faith Pullin. One Sunday evening on a train, I opened a set text of the coming week, James Baldwin's slim book *The Fire Next Time*. I can still recall the effect of the first pages—"I underwent, during the summer that I became fourteen, a prolonged religious crisis . . ."—and the sensation of being gripped by authority of an "unexpected" kind. I had read books about the blues, had learned to play some of the more basic patterns of Big Bill Broonzy, had heard Martin Luther King. Baldwin's memoir was my first experience of the transmission of that essence from the pages of a book. He was reading from the same script: a spiritual script, but with that little backward-something. Later, at my request, he wrote an article for the literary magazine I edited in Scotland, the *New Edinburgh Review*, initiating a relationship that led to a posthumous biography and to adventures in the U.S. legal system outlined in the essay on that subject in this book ("I Heard It through the Grapevine"). The "grapevine" is the news medium. The news came, and continues to come, from the sources sketched above.

Acknowledgments

This gathering owes many debts, and a few deserve special mention. Nine of the pieces were first published in the *Guardian Review*. The seven profiles are drawn from a larger number written for that paper (the profile of Amiri Baraka was written especially for this book). Its founding editor, Annalena McAfee, and her deputy Susanna Rustin, shaped a routine Saturday arts and books newspaper supplement into a quality literary magazine (Annalena left the paper in the middle of 2006). A single example of Annalena's light touch suggests the benefits of working for her. One afternoon, following some last-minute adjustments to a piece going to press, she said casually, "Suggest something else." I replied that I had been thinking of writing a profile of Gary Snyder, holed up on his ranch in the foothills of the Sierra Nevada. He is less well known in Britain than he might be—a factor which usually moves the minds of journalists in the direction opposite to that in which it ought to: that's to say, "If he's not well known, why are we covering him?"

Annalena and Susanna were exceptions to the rule. On this occasion, Annalena hesitated. "Persuade me." I said, No problem; I'll come up with another. But she meant it. Before the afternoon was out, I sent a message consisting of "Three reasons why you should have a profile of Gary Snyder" and, underneath, "Three reasons why you shouldn't"—which carried the proposal. It took almost a year to fulfill, but in time a four-thousand-word profile of Snyder appeared in the *Guardian Review*. No other newspaper I can think of would have sponsored such an excursion. There are other pieces in this book of which the same can be said. Without the astute enthusiasm of Annalena and Susanna, the work would not have been undertaken.

No less a friend to writers is the fiction editor of the *Times Literary Supplement,* Lindsay Duguid, who commissioned other pieces in the book and who first suggested that I assemble a collection. It owes what coherence it has to Lindsay, to my editor at the University of California Press, Naomi Schneider, who patiently insisted that I aim for something that expresses a special relationship, and as always to Vera Chalidze, who read and often reread every piece before it went to press. I am also grateful for the constructive comments of Marjorie Perloff, Caryl Phillips, and Michael Anderson.

In addition to those already mentioned, I wish to thank the following editors: Lisa Allardice of the *Guardian Review;* Dwight Garner of the *New York Times Book Review;* Neil Gordon of the *Boston Review;* Ian Jack and Sophie Harrison of *Granta;* Wendy Lesser of the *Threepenny Review;* Adam Shatz of *The Nation;* Peter Stothard of the *Times Literary Supplement;* the late William Cookson of *Agenda;* and the late Alan Ross of the *London Magazine.* The essays were first published in the following:

"Sunshine and Shadows: A Profile of John Updike": *Guardian Review,* May 22, 2004.

"Updike's Village Sex": *Times Literary Supplement,* January 28, 2005.

"Maxwell's Lives": *Boston Review,* February/March 2003.

"Notes from a Small Island: A Profile of Shirley Hazzard": *Guardian Review,* July 8, 2006.

"Love, Truman: Capote's Letters and Stories": *Times Literary Supplement,* November 5, 2005.

"Franzen, Oprah and High Art": *Boston Review,* April/May 2002.

"Drawing Pains: A Profile of Art Spiegelman": *Guardian Review,* August 28, 2004.

"Listening in the Dark": *Guardian Review,* March 22, 2003.

"I Heard It through the Grapevine: James Baldwin and the FBI": *Granta* 73 (Spring 2001).

"The Island Affair: Richard Wright's Unpublished Last Novel": *Guardian Review,* January 7, 2006.

"The Man Who Cried: John A. Williams": *The Nation*, September 27, 2004.

"All That Jive: Stanley Crouch": *New York Times Book Review*, April 30, 2000.

"Love Lost: Toni Morrison": *Times Literary Supplement*, November 14, 2003.

"High Peak Haikus: A Profile of Gary Snyder": *Guardian Review*, July 16, 2005.

"Between Moving Air and Moving Ocean": *Agenda*, Autumn-Winter 1999.

"Was That a Real Poem?: Robert Creeley": *Threepenny Review*, Summer 2002.

"Personal/Political: A Profile of Edmund White": *Guardian Review*, January 22, 2005.

"To Beat the Bible: A Profile of J. P. Donleavy": *Guardian Review*, June 26, 2004.

"The Making of a Monster: Alexander Trocchi": *London Magazine*, April/May 1992.

"Travels with RLS": *New York Times Book Review*, November 5, 2000.

"Boswell and Mrs. Miller: A Memoir of Two Tongues" appeared in *The Genius of Language: Fifteen Writers Reflect on Their Mother Tongue*, edited by Wendy Lesser, 2004.

PART I

New York New Yorkers

The writers in this section have or have had an association with the *New Yorker* (with the exception of William Styron, a Southerner who came to prominence as one of a cadre of young Manhattan-based writers and gained force from the alliance). Their grouping here is intended only to display one facet of my literary curiosity—a facet against which the succeeding parts of the book might be viewed contrastingly—and not to set forth a critique of that versatile magazine. The *New Yorker*, through its affluence, its sense of style, its expertise in the skills of editing and presentation, has made itself the salon in which some of the finest talents on the scene may assemble. It is talent of a certain taste and social attitude; talents to offend exuberantly, to utter the remark that outrages the hostess but makes the party memorable, were not welcomed at the salon before the collapse of the ancien régime in 1987.

The best qualities of the old *New Yorker* were personified by William Maxwell, a fiction editor there for decades and the author of delicate fiction himself. John Updike and Shirley Hazzard needed no prodding to pay tribute to Maxwell and his handling of their work at the magazine; Hazzard's development as first a short-story writer and then a novelist is practically inseparable from Maxwell's subtle guidance. He was universally lauded for his intelligence and empathy as an editor, and for his personal kindness and decorum, but he evinced the occasional flash of acerbity. On the morning I first visited his Upper East Side apartment, "over by the river" (the title of his most original short story), he was dressed in collar and tie, with a tweed jacket and flannels, though he had no immediate intention of venturing out. An unsympathetic review of his collected stories in the *New York Times Book Review* the previous weekend had wounded him—the reviewer was an American woman novelist based in London—with the result that virtually the first words I heard from the famously decorous tongue were vituperative.

The pieces that follow on the above writers, and the cartoonist Art Spiegelman, focus on their experiences at the *New Yorker* as one topic among many. The Capote and Franzen essays barely mention it. This might be the place for a story about Capote's relationship with the magazine, which some people thought was distorted and traduced in the biopic *Capote*. In 1989, while researching a book, I asked William Shawn for a brief interview, which was granted over tea at the Algonquin. Capote's name came up. Shawn described him as a wonderful writer, but as for *In Cold Blood*, "He wanted to write this. We gave him some money . . . and he went off . . . and in time he handed it in. It wasn't what we wanted at all." The reputation the book had gathered subsequently had done nothing to mitigate Shawn's annoyance at the memory of his compromise. His face did not relent in its displeasure as he gathered his things from the table. "But we published it."

ONE Sunshine and Shadows

A PROFILE OF JOHN UPDIKE

The name Updike is unusual enough in Pennsylvania to make its bearers self-conscious. It is an "odd name," according to America's most famous Updike, that once upon a time "got a loud laugh in the movie theater." For a chuckle, "Updike" could be parodied as "Downdike" or "Downditch." When he told people his name, John Updike says, they were inclined to think he was being "fresh." The book in which he makes this admission of pain is called *Self-Consciousness.* "Hotel clerks and telephone operators would ask you to repeat it, bringing on (in my case) a fit of blushing and stuttering." Only when he moved to New York City did he find people capable of hearing his name at first try and writing it down "correctly, with a respectful nod."

If Updike's name now commands respect throughout New York and beyond, it is in part thanks to the magazine inseparably identified with the city. He has been a contributor to the *New Yorker* for half a century and shows no signs of drying up. "John is very competitive with the younger writers," says Roger Angell, who has been his editor for fiction at the *New Yorker* since 1976. "For about twenty years he has thought he's on the brink of not being able to write any more short fiction. If I mention that we've got a story by a terrific young writer, he'll say, 'Oh really,' and within a couple of weeks he'll send in a wonderful short story."

The *New Yorker* has been a saving grace for Updike throughout his life. The "little lost pocket" of Updikes in Berks County, Pennsylvania, a ter-

3

ritory characterized by farming and Protestantism, and the gloomy outlook that is apt to attach itself to both callings, was expanded by the presence of a relative who lived within commuting distance of the big city.
Updike's Aunt Mary had once worked as a secretary to the critic
Edmund Wilson. As well as bringing a fashionable "flapper figure" into
the kitchen of her country cousins, she introduced copies of the *New
Yorker*. "The magazine couldn't be bought in Berks County," Updike
says, "except maybe at the railway station. My Aunt Mary bought us a
subscription for Christmas." Her existence suggested a world of cultural
wealth to her nephew. "I wanted to become rich in this way."

Updike is "rich" now in ways he never imagined. He lives with his
second wife, Martha, in a large house at the stringy end of a settlement
called Beverly Farms, some forty minutes' drive north of Boston. The
Atlantic Ocean laps at his doorstep. He can make passing reference,
while picking at a newly discovered hole in his yellow corduroys, to "my
woods." His industry—as a novelist, short-story writer, poet, critic, and
humorist—requires three desks: one oak, one steel, and one veneered in
Formica, where, respectively, he answers letters, writes his first drafts in
pencil, and makes his advance on the word processor. Updike is tall and
trim, happy to smile at the world over his good fortune and to deprecate
his boyish manner. His head is topped by what Tom Wolfe once called a
"great thatchy medieval haircut." Angles of elbows and shins cut sharply
across the laughter patterned regularly throughout his conversation. His
talk flows with a richness comparable to his prose. "Updike is the first
fully harvested, fully expressed American writer since Henry James,"
says Adam Gopnik, a staff writer at the *New Yorker*, who admits to having
"semi-worshipped him since adolescence." Without the nourishment of
the magazine, Gopnik feels, "he might be one touch less completely
expressed than he is. I have a great love for his small, tender things—the
memoirs of Pennsylvania boyhood, for example—and doubt there
would be as many without a magazine to need them. This is as good a
vindication of the *New Yorker*'s existence as any could be."

There have been less friendly reactions to Updike's proficiency. Gore
Vidal referred to him as being "fixed in facility," while Norman
Podhoretz, former editor of the Jewish intellectual magazine *Commentary*,

protested: "I have been puzzled by many things in the course of my career as a literary critic, and one of them is the high reputation of John Updike." Updike's mischievous response was to make his puffed-up Jewish-writer hero Henry Bech—in *Bech: A Book* (1970) and *Bech Is Back* (1982)—a darling of the *Commentary* crowd.

Updike was born in 1932 and raised in the town of Shillington, Pennsylvania. Worship at the local Sunday School, attached to the Lutheran church, began what has become lifelong observance, though he is now among the Episcopalians. His mother's family, the Hoyers, had been farmers, and when John was thirteen, the family moved back to the Hoyer farm to live with his maternal grandparents, an event in which his novel *Of the Farm* (1965) is rooted. Money had been lost in the crash— "Oh no, Johnny, we were poor," Updike's father once protested when the son pluckily claimed to have wanted for nothing. While Updike senior made a living as a schoolteacher, he was laid off each May and could only hope to be rehired in September. During the summer, he worked on building sites.

Updike's initial artistic impulse took the form of drawing, specifically the kind of cartoons he saw in magazines. "Thinking it over, I can't locate another artist in the Updike family. I guess it was my idea. I was an only child, I needed an alternative to family life—to real life, you could almost say—and cartoons, pictures in a book, the animated movies, seemed to provide it." As a boy, he "was not galvanized by the literary ideal." There was, however, one writer in the Updike family. His mother, Linda Grace Hoyer, wrote short stories, which she sent to magazines, including the *New Yorker,* only to have them returned. Disheartening though her failure was to her, Updike reflects that "if my mother hadn't been trying to be a writer, I don't know if I would have thought of it myself." Amid his early memories, he can see himself "crawling up into her lap while she sat at the typewriter banging away at the keys." Later on, his mother had more success with the *New Yorker,* and a collection of her stories was published in 1971 as *Enchantment.* Updike's eldest son, David, a teacher, also made appearances in the magazine and has published several books.

Updike began writing for the *New Yorker* at twenty-two. "They accepted a light-verse poem, and then they took a story. Taking the story was very important to me because that was the *New Yorker,* and here I was on that Pennsylvania farm. I had once thought: how can you get from here to there? And now I had gotten there." His first intention was to be a humorist—"I thought that was a very harmless thing to be"—and to join the suave Algonquin gang whose jokes had given him much pleasure and whose drawings he had traced in imitation. "But of course by the time I got there the gang was gone and the party was over. It's sometimes said that cold war anxieties, atomic bomb anxieties, killed humor, though I don't really buy it. But anyway, the time when facetious writing could attract real talents was over, and the talents were looking elsewhere."

While Updike is seldom identified as the author of "facetious" pieces, the spirit, according to Gopnik, remains. "The secret of his writing lies in his early ambition to be a cartoonist and a humorist. The artisanal high spirits of the humorist have never drained from his hand. Among masters, none is so eager to please. I pick up an Updike story more or less at random every day and find always a high-hearted vein of humor running through everything he writes." This, Gopnik believes, is what lifts Updike's work "out of the normal range of poetic writing into a genial and generous dimension of its own." Angell has found him "a formidable self-editor. He is very critical of his own work. If we've taken something, and I feel that a section doesn't connect with the piece as a whole, I'll bring it up with John. We'll go over it on the phone, and he'll come up with a variation. He often finds something at the very last moment and rewrites it."

Updike majored in English at Harvard, then took up a yearlong fellowship at the Ruskin School of Drawing and Fine Art in Oxford in 1954. He mostly studied life drawing there, but it was while he was in England that he discovered the writer Henry Green, who was to exercise a persistent power over his style. "He showed a new way to use the language. Another writer might have done it, but Henry Green happened to be the one." After holding an office job at the *New Yorker* from 1955 to 1957, Updike retreated with his first wife, Mary, and their two young children, Elizabeth and David, to Ipswich, Massachusetts, where two more children, Michael and Miranda, were born. Living there, not far from his present home, Updike extended himself in novels and experienced critical and financial success. He drove a convertible and came to assume the identity in the mildly bohemian Ipswich community, as he once put it in a typical mock-and-jab aside, of a "mini-Mailer." Updike and his wife separated in the mid-1970s and were granted a no-fault divorce in 1976. He married Martha, thus acquiring three stepsons, the following year.

Updike's first novel, *The Poorhouse Fair* (1959), was, he says, "heavily influenced by Henry Green. Greenisms crop up in later novels, too. In *Couples* [1968], there are a lot of sentences that have that little blur, that little twist, that backward-something, that you find in Green." *The Poorhouse Fair* was a promising debut (Updike had already published *The Carpentered Hen*, a volume of poems, in 1958), but a wider audience greeted his second novel, *Rabbit, Run* (1960), the initial part of what was to become a tetralogy spanning three decades, with volumes appearing at roughly ten-year intervals. When we meet him, Rabbit, or Harry Angstrom (to give him his real name), is a twenty-six-year-old basketball player who is already past his peak. He is in a sour marriage with Janice, which is nonetheless to prove surprisingly resilient. "The character of Rabbit was for me a way into the America I found all around me," Updike has remarked. "What I saw through Rabbit's eyes was often more worth telling than what I saw through my own, though the difference was often slight." When first encountered, Rabbit is having difficulty justifying to his peers his support for the American action in Vietnam. He is nervous of "Negroes" and is about to begin an affair that will rip into his marriage. As a result of his wife's increasing recourse to the bottle, their newborn child is accidentally drowned, an event for which Rabbit will never forgive her, though he himself is partly to blame. The *angst* in Harry Angstrom's name was put there on purpose. In the second installment, *Rabbit Redux* (1971), he will undergo a 1960s reeducation in the subjects of free love and civil rights. Toward the end of his too-brief life, documented in *Rabbit at Rest* (1990), he is overweight and agitated less by angry blacks than by Middle Eastern terrorists, whose representatives have just blown up the Pan Am jet over Lockerbie.

"People ask me what would Rabbit think of 9/11, what would Rabbit think of George W. Bush, and I just can't say. I killed him off. It's strange, you never know when you're going to die, so at fifty-something I thought

I'd better tidy him up before I die and then he's left hanging. I wanted to see him through. I think he would die young, that kind of athlete, sort of old before his time, bad diet and so on, so I wrapped him up in *Rabbit at Rest* and then regretted that enough to at least try to tidy up the children ["Rabbit Remembered," in *Licks of Love*, 2000]. I think Rabbit would probably have the same reaction to the invasion of Iraq that he had to Vietnam, that it may be a mistake but it's our duty to see it through. If he were alive, he'd probably be in Florida most of the year by now and he might have a stars-and-stripes sticker on his car. After 9/11, he certainly would have put the flag up. Janice would have been a little more skeptical." Judith Jones, who has worked at Alfred A. Knopf, the publisher, for more than forty years, shepherding Updike from typescript to hardcovers, was disappointed when Rabbit was laid to rest, "because I liked to read about him. I mean, I wouldn't like to live next door to Harry, or to sit down and have dinner with him, but John always gets an essential compassion for the person. Even with someone so ordinary as Harry, or even so obnoxious, he's always sympathetic. He never has contempt for his characters."

The Rabbit tetralogy is rich in sexual detail, as are many Updike novels. *Rabbit, Run* emerged at a time when books such as *Naked Lunch* and *Tropic of Cancer* were not published in the United States for fear of prosecution. Rabbit, taking eight pages to mount Ruth, the part-time prostitute he met earlier the same evening, had to proceed toward the bookstores with caution. Jones remembers Updike "being worried because *Rabbit, Run* was rather explicit and at that period America was rather conservative. John could see himself having legal suits and ending up with no money and four young children to support. So he said to Alfred Knopf, maybe you should get a lawyer in to look at the obscene parts. Alfred arranged for the lawyer to come in at the weekend, then telephoned John in Massachusetts. And John said: 'Oh no, I can't come down this weekend; I'm teaching summer Sunday school.'"

Updike's faith has remained constant through the changes of venue. Between the Lutherans and the Episcopalians, Updike was a Congregationalist, and the shadow of the Congregational church falls across the adulterous players of verbal and sexual games in *Couples* (1968). Piet

Hanemas in that novel is led to wonder "what barred him from the ranks of those many blessed who believed nothing. Courage, he supposed." Updike claims to "get anxious at 4 AM. I seem to have this need to belong to some church. I get worried on Sunday mornings. Life without religion seems to me to lack a dimension. You may say that dimension's an illusion, but in some ways it's what people have done through these two millennia and many more millennia before that." He feels that his artistic activity "is in some way bound up with my religious faith." Creativity as a gift from God, to be reciprocated via worship, is not a concept he hastens to disavow. "I do think I've been fortunate in life. I've been fortunate to achieve some of my vague ambitions and I'm grateful, when I remember to be grateful. At some point in my adolescence there was an act of faith involved in my setting myself to become an artist. That I have succeeded in doing so is some kind of miracle, as I see it. I think of the boy I was, and I look back and . . . I'm breathless, you know?" He is willing to ask his religion to accommodate earthly pleasures, such as a round of golf on a Sunday morning. "William James says something like, 'If men can believe in gods, then the days pass by with zest; they stir with prospect, they thrill with remoter values.' It's a little like that with me."

Updike stands apart from the ranks of contemporaries in leaning to the right in matters private and political. In 1966, in a symposium dedicated to writers' views on Vietnam, he found himself more or less isolated as a hawk. The *New York Times* pointed this out, without giving proper consideration to his ambivalence. In reaction, Updike wrote "On Not Being a Dove," a fifty-page essay in which he attempted to chart the ins and outs of his resistance to the peace movement and to explain the roots of the untrendy patriotism fortifying his position. "I was sort of embarrassed not to be a dove, since most writers are doves," he says. "It's not my nature to go against the grain. But it was arresting to someone raised in the depression to witness the hatred, venom, fury of those years. In general, I think that these men we elect should be left to do the job, and my guess is that they're doing about as well as they can do, given the problems they face. And I'd be willing to give the benefit of the doubt even to Richard Nixon . . . which maybe is eccentric of me. I find it very hard to believe that the government leaders are villainous, of our democracy or the British democracy. But maybe I've been brainwashed." He is, however, a Democrat, not a Republican, and he finds the situation in Iraq "very troubling. It makes the administration look bad, and I won't be sorry if and when they're replaced."

Gopnik delights in Updike's departure from orthodoxy. "It is the tension between opposed poles in his work that gives it its electricity. He is a patriot, a conservative, a hawk—and an erotic trailblazer, a radical writer of great courage." The critic Zachary Leader, who has written widely on Updike, says, "I always think of that moment in *Rabbit Is Rich*, when Harry leads a Fourth of July parade dressed up like Uncle Sam. His paunch, Updike says, 'in itself must weigh as much as an Ethiopian child.' Updike knows all about American excess and its consequences. He's a clear-eyed patriot, certainly. But he can be cold-eyed too, and defiant, like someone who knows it's wrong to drive an SUV but still does. He'd stand by Harry's conclusion that 'all in all, this is the happiest fucking country the world has ever seen.'"

Updike's ingrained conservatism extends to other matters. In a ten-thousand-word assault on the Updike edifice in the *Times Literary Supplement* in 1996, Gore Vidal wrote: "He is full of Shillington self-effacing gracefulness on what—if any—race problem there might be in the grand old United States." Partly, this was an effect of geography. In the Shillington of his boyhood, there were few black faces, and the same could be said of Harvard in the early 1950s. In "On Not Being a Dove," Updike declares himself a supporter of the civil rights movement in the 1960s and a contributor to the National Association for the Advancement of Colored People, though he goes on to remark that he once "lent a black man we knew some money that he never repaid." (Harry lends a black colleague money in *Rabbit Redux*, which he expects not to be repaid, and is surprised when it is.) There is scant encouragement to integration in Updike's fiction of the period, where black people put in mostly perfunctory appearances, as in old movies. The couple in *Marry Me*, a story of adultery and stubbornly cohesive marriage written in the mid-1960s but not published until 1976 (the year of Updike's own divorce), return to their hotel after lunch to find their bed of passion "stripped and shoved against the bureau, and a slouching Negro was lathering the carpet with a screaming machine," which is pretty much a typical interracial experi-

ence in Updike's work. When a central role was given to a black character named Skeeter in *Rabbit Redux,* the result was heavily burlesque. As
Skeeter is ferried into the wilderness by Rabbit at the end of the novel,
everyone, including the queasy reader, is relieved to see the back of him.

Skeeter is drawn with a large dose of affection, however, and in serving up his desperate psyche in garish tones, Updike is simply following
Rabbit into the America he finds all around him. After his daughter
Elizabeth married a Ghanaian in the 1980s, the author found himself
delighted by two African American grandchildren. In a meditation on the
subject, he counseled Anoff and Kwame that "though exactly half white"
they would be "considered black," and black identity was often uncom-
fortable in a land where "the stereotypical black is a mugger, addict,
dropout and outlaw." Updike ended "A Letter to My Grandsons" by urging them to choose an identity of their own making, and by quoting his
maternal grandfather: "You carry your own hide to market."

Contemplation of skin as the coating of personal identity is something
with which Updike is painfully familiar. Since a bout of measles at the
age of six, he has suffered from psoriasis, a dermatological condition that
gives the victim "the sense of another presence co-occupying your body
and singling you out from the happy herds of healthy, normal mankind."
In a poem in his most recent collection, *Americana* (2001), he refers to himself as a "literary Mr. Sunshine," a piquant description, since it refers not
only to his evident good nature but to his annual effort, over many years,
to obliterate his psoriasis by hammering it with ultraviolet rays, once the
only known remedy. In summer months, Updike was indeed "Mr.
Sunshine," but with the onset of winter his psoriasis flourished again. He
suggests that "having this disability, which was really quite shaming,
forced me to be more adventurous and daring than I ordinarily would
have been. I'm at heart a kind of cautious, conservative person, and without the skin ailment I might not have left New York, but just stayed and
grown old in *New Yorker* harness. It was the need to get to the sun, get to
the beach, that forced me to leave the city and my job, and of course to
earn my living as a freelance writer." He suffers less now—"they have
pills"—but the relentless sunshine to which he exposed himself has
resulted in skin damage. "So I have that to cope with."

Updike is surely the most prolific American writer of serious intent of the past half-century. In addition to thirty novels and collections of stories, he has published six volumes of poetry (his *Collected Poems* came out in 1993), assorted memoirs, and children's stories. His criticism and occasional journalism fills four mammoth volumes, the latest of which he dubbed *More Matter*—an off-putting title which does no justice to the "farraginous" (a favorite word) contents. Yet he observes that he has had only a single number-one best seller, *Couples,* which appeared thirty-six years ago. Judith Jones feels that Updike "doesn't always get his due," but that nevertheless he has "the most consistent sales of any writer we publish at Knopf. He has a distinct audience. It's not huge, but he's read all over the world." To Gopnik, talk of best-sellerdom in the context of Updike's multifarious talent is "absurd." Even though Rabbit is no longer here to grouse about the attacks on New York and Washington, Updike would like to write "a novel about post-9/11. I'm not sure what shape these catastrophes would take, since everything happens so violently and quickly, but I think of the British writers who described the events of the Blitz, Green for one, and I feel I should have a try. I think if you're a writer you try to make something out of everything that happens."

Updike is reluctant to give the impression of preferring the world as it was to the world he finds on his TV screen and in his grandchildren's pop records. Americans, he says, are "trying to figure out how to be happy," but lately "it occurred to me that I have some of my father's depressive temperament. He used to sit in a chair and say, 'I've got the blues.' And I didn't know what the blues was. Why should he have the blues? It might be a tendency of Protestants in general. There's a kind of gloom, fear of death, fear of meaninglessness, and literary activity is one way of staving it off, isn't it? When you're writing something, you're relatively innocent. Time goes by so fast, I find, when I'm writing. It speeds by. When I'm helping my wife in the garden, it crawls by."

TWO Updike's Village Sex

Seventy years old when we meet him, Owen Mackenzie, the hero of John Updike's novel *Villages* (2004), has attained his allotted span without having come of age. The opening chapter of *Villages* is called "Dream On, Dear Owen"; the penultimate section is "You Don't Want to Know." Owen is still addressing his wife in baby talk, still being teased for his "innocent" ways, still going forward under the assumption that the world owes Owen a living, and still not fully awake, even by chapter 13 (helpfully flagged by the author), to the misfortunes he has brought down on others. In a typical joke on innocent Owen, Updike sets him to work during the post–Korean War era on the military computer program SAGE.

The narrative of *Villages* moves smoothly along parallel sets of tracks, switching between the progress of Owen the younger and his wife, Phyllis, in Middle Falls, Connecticut, and the more sedentary life of old Owen in Haskells Crossing, Massachusetts, where he is dependent on the civic efficiency of his second wife, Julia, to guide him through the "threateningly formless" weekends of the retiree. The territory of Updike's twenty-first novel will be as familiar to loyal readers of his fiction as to future biographers, whose notebooks must already be bulging with correspondences between the life and the work. Like Updike, Owen is raised in rural Pennsylvania, the only child in a hard-working household consisting of both parents and grandparents (Owen was born a year after his creator, in 1933). He marries loving Phyllis Goodhue, has four children, and separates from her in the mid-'70s, only to be shepherded, as if by God himself, into the embrace of Julia, the wife of a minister. The details are shuffled, but it's the same pack of cards. Both Owen and Updike left a wife and four children in the mid-1970s, but it was the novelist's first father-in-law who was the clergyman, not the subsequent wife's abandoned husband. The "so-called" village in which old Owen lives, an hour north of Boston, must be just a walk away from the present Updike residence.

A lot of innocence is lost in the course of *Villages*, but it tends to be hymenal innocence, wifely innocence, the innocence of children as they clamber up and down the wreck of their parents' marriage. Owen, whose Scots background points in the direction of J. M. Barrie's famous creation, keeps up his dream of "a life charmed from above." Once, when a small boy, he lost his spectacles and then found them again, as if by the actual grace of an actual God; the perception of himself basking in the Almighty's favor endures into adulthood, even as he does what many in a conservative New England community would consider to be the work of an adulterous devil. When Phyllis dies in a car accident, Owen has it in himself to believe that "God killed Phyllis, as a favor to him," releasing him to marry Julia.

In the 1950s, Owen entered into partnership with the more enterprising Ed Mervine to found a computer business specializing in "contract programming and advisory services." They devote their professional lives to perfecting software rivals to God's omniscience. The company's minor innovations are successful enough to tempt Apple, which swallows the outfit in a deal that enables Owen eventually to leave Middle Falls, with its clamorous memories of sex, separation, and death, and to retire with Julia to Haskells Crossing in comfort. In *Villages,* Updike plays the currently fashionable novelist's game of baffling readers with science. At the same time, one can't help feeling that the writer routinely hailed as "the finest . . . in English today" (Ian McEwan, on the jacket of *Villages*) is up to mischief as he invites us to eavesdrop on the day-to-day chatter of his mathematically minded young couple:

> They no longer shared Introduction to Digital Computer Coding and Logic. She, a senior, disappeared into the counterintuitive exotica of ad-

vanced topology differential manifold, invariant Betti groups embedded in Euclidean space, duality theorems.

Her senior thesis sounded suspiciously like Projective Geometry:
she said it had to do with "the topological classification of manifolds of
dimensions greater than two."

"How far can dimensions go?" he asked.

"To n, obviously."

In opposition to the clean perfection of technological ingenuity that
bulks large in the novel (only occasionally tipping over into verbal exhibitionism), there are periodic meditations on mucky biology, without which
even the cleverest computer programmer would not exist. Returned from
his daily exposure to "blinking cathode-ray tubes" and the "four-storey
concrete eyesores" housing SAGE, Owen the younger is cushioned by the
"abundant down," the "sweaty pale tendrils," of his wife's "hormonally
replete body." The "sexual seethe," though it occupies him hugely, is but
the dramatic, visible part of it. "You ask why do people do the things they
do," his neighbor and lover Alissa begins to explain, postcoitally. "People
don't know, it's deeper than the brain. It's pheromones and all sorts of pro-
grammed behavior, like the nest-building instinct. Haven't you ever
watched birds building a nest and wondered how they do it, all the right
twigs and so on? They don't know either." And then, having "jack-knifed
her flashing legs together around him," the maternal Alissa is suddenly
mindful of the immediate biological needs of her brood: "I must go shopping for Ian's dinner and pick up the cleaning before school gets out."

Owen is equally familiar with the physical imperatives of Faye,
Vanessa, Trish, Karen, Antoinette, and—almost—his partner Ed's
groovy wife, Stacey. The foxy strategies required of an active villager, like
the mind-boggling possibilities of the latest advance in computer tech-
nology, like the science so helpfully, guilt-skipping set out by Alissa,
come to seem labyrinthine in their complexity: "If Owen was going to
make a serious move on Imogene, he needed to be quits with Vanessa."
Dazzled by his own sexual success (we are dependent on Updike's word
for Owen's attractiveness), he withdraws from the light, closeting himself
in a dungeonlike room in the building he shares with Ed. Eventually,
having made his exit from Phyllis and their children—"Phyllis, I'm try-

ing to reform. Julia wants to save me"—he is consigned to "disheveled rooms on Covenant Street," where he awaits the redeeming touch of the pastor's wife.

It is "thrilling for me," Julia says, full to the brim with her own worldliness, "to be associated with anyone so innocent." Yet Owen remains fretful at having robbed God's minister. Moreover, "their relationship is loving, but haunted. He thinks of Phyllis every day." In that early dream ("Dream On, Dear Owen"), Julia was dead and he was responsible. "He yearns to . . . suck back into himself the poison that his existence has worked upon hers." Julia is happily alive downstairs, of course, but Phyllis really is dead. At the moment that he was called to officially identify the body, Owen had to suffer Ed's voice in his ear: "You did this, you fuckhead." Owen knows that it isn't true—Phyllis is the victim of her own reckless driving—and that it is. Notably "passive" to many people, Owen is merely "O" to id-heavy Ed.

The vitality of *Villages* is remarkable in a writer so preoccupied with the depredations of old age (there is an echo of Kingsley Amis's novel *The Old Devils* in the back-and-forth of Owen and Julia's early-morning chat). This is Updike's seventh book since the year 2000. Some readers might start to see it, round about the halfway stage, as a kind of compilation Updike novel, or a novel generated by the computer program UPDIKE. The long section in which Owen keeps his assignation at a nature reserve with Faye, his first mentor in adultery, where lawful and unlawful partners are compared, recalls the opening scene of that brilliant, harrowing novel *Marry Me* (published in 1976, the year of Updike's divorce). The bed-hopping among husbands and wives who have all met one another too often at drink-driven parties is reminiscent of *Couples.* The unhappy collision of the hero's wife and his mother that animates *Of the Farm* and a host of short stories is rehearsed here, as the younger and older Mrs. Mackenzies "make bad electricity in the crammed little house." And whole pages of *Villages,* at a glance, appear to have been transposed from Updike's memoir *Self-Consciousness:*

> Just slightly above the administrators of local order were the national celebrities. They were, indeed, more accessible and familiar: Jack Benny and Fibber McGee cracking their jokes and suffering their embarrass-

ments in the little Philco right in the piano room, next to the greasy-armed easy chair where Owen ate peanut-butter crackers in a double rapture of laughter and mastication; Tyrone Power, his black eyebrows knitted in a troubled frown, and Joan Crawford, her huge dark lips bravely tremulous and her enlarged eyes each harbouring a tear that would fill a bucket, on the screen at the Scheherazade. . . . There was no better way to live, no grander, more virtuous country than America, and no homier state than Pennsylvania.

Minor repetitions crop up here and there: Owen's "ah-shucks way" that pleases Julia rings a bell, because it first sounded some years ago in a first-person piece called "The Burglar Alarm," in which the Julia-like wife is annoyed at her husband's "ah-shucks routine." And if Updike has not depicted the female pudenda as "her cunt, those livid wrinkles looking like lava folds" on at least a dozen occasions before now, one can only say that it seems as if he has.

However, the exuberant prose and quick little perceptions that make almost every Updike novel a pleasure to read (*Brazil* might be an exception) show no sign of abating: "Owen heard the sound of a shot. He had been sleeping. He seemed to awake in the moment before hearing, as if in a dream, the noise that had awoken him." Nor is his ruthless plundering of his own soul and those of his family on the point of slowing down. It may seem impertinent to ask whether the four Updike children from the first union are enjoying yet another fictional outing about a horny old dad and his stricken marriage ("the children, as children must, adjusted"), but it is hard not to. Equally, there may be steep obstacles to the artful disguise of personal details, but the ordinary reader could find it difficult to see what they are. Those impatient to know the sources of the six well-researched chapters of the novel called "Village Sex" and numbered in sequence, will probably have to wait a while before having their curiosity satisfied. In the meantime, they can enjoy puzzling over the encrypted confessions of *Villages.*

THREE William Maxwell's Lives

In 1933, when William Maxwell was twenty-five years old and an aspiring novelist, he decided to go to sea, "so that I would have something to write about." A letter of introduction led him to a four-masted schooner that belonged to the financier J. P. Morgan, at anchor on a bay near Coney Island. When the captain had read Maxwell's letter, he told him that the ship had been in dock for four years; Morgan could not afford to sail her, and the captain was quitting the next day.

Maxwell wrote a brief account of this, his first and probably only stab at being a man of action, in the preface to his collected stories, published in 1995, to acknowledge that "three-quarters of the material I would need for the rest of my writing life was already at my disposal." It was to be an unusually extended writing life: Maxwell's first novel, *Bright Center of Heaven*, was published in 1934, the same year as *Tender Is the Night*; his final book of original fiction, *Billie Dyer and Other Stories*, appeared in 1992, with *All the Days and Nights: The Collected Stories* and a volume of correspondence still to come before his death in August 2000, two weeks short of his ninety-second birthday. (His wife, Emily, whom he married at the end of World War II, had died eight days earlier, and it would seem that Maxwell, frail but not fatally ill, had simply willed himself to follow her.) Neither of these bookends to his career nor any of the four novels and numerous stories published in between say anything about the incident involving J. P. Morgan's yacht; instead, Maxwell returns again and

again to another story, the one that throughout his adult life, to reiterate
his own fraction, occupied about three-quarters of the author's thought
and feeling, certainly of his imagination: the tale of a happy childhood in
the Midwest prematurely disrupted by injury and death.

Maxwell's long span as a writer was matched by a parallel life at the
New Yorker. He began in the art department of the magazine in the mid-
1930s, when Harold Ross was editor, and continued to work three days a
week as a fiction editor under Ross's successor, William Shawn, until a
new union rule on the age of retirement forced him out in 1976. Behind
Shawn himself, Maxwell stands as the prototypical *New Yorker* man:
dedicated to the institution, tactful about its charges, and resolute to the
last in his fidelity to a particular literary standard. An early letter in
Maxwell's published correspondence with the short-story writer Frank
O'Connor, dated March 12, 1948, gives voice to his gentlemanly method
and suggests what a sensitive editor he was:

> I think that, in general, the editing and queries [concerning the short story
> "The Drunkard"] are fairly restrained, sensible and self-explanatory. But
> if there are spots where you feel that none of these adjectives applies, I
> hope you'll point them out. . . . We'd appreciate your making it clear at
> the outset that this story takes place in Ireland, and it occurs to us that a
> good place to plant the locale is in the third paragraph. You could quite
> easily do it by naming the newspaper—the Dublin Times, the County
> Cork Tribune, or some such.

Among other writers whose work Maxwell shepherded onto the page
were Eudora Welty, Mavis Gallant, Harold Brodkey, and the three
Johns—O'Hara, Cheever, and Updike. All were grateful for his attentions. Several of his authors dedicated books to him, as he in turn dedicated his novels to other *New Yorker* writers and editors.

Maxwell was born into a middle-class family in the town of Lincoln,
Illinois, in 1908, with ancestry rooted in the Scottish border country and
the Protestant church. He was proud of his background, though most of
his traceable forebears had arrived in America before the Revolution and
he never visited the "home" country. The family history-cum-memoir
that he published in 1971, *Ancestors,* is peopled by lawyerly grandfathers
and shrewd, kindly aunts, with recollections of favorite toys and houses

with many rooms, each having a distinct atmosphere. He had an elder
brother who lost a leg in a horse-drawn carriage accident but who was
nonetheless sporty and masculine, while Maxwell was bookish and gentle, more at home in the company of his mother and aunts. At the turn of
the year 1918–19, at the height of the Spanish flu epidemic, Maxwell's
mother gave birth to a third son and, within days of the delivery, died.
"My childhood ended," Maxwell wrote.

The death of Maxwell's mother when he was ten years old is directly
present in three of his novels and indirectly in at least one other, not to
mention in several of his stories and in *Ancestors*. For a snapshot of the
resident characters and themes of his writings one might focus on a passage from *They Came Like Swallows* (1937), or alternatively from *The Folded
Leaf* (1945), or from *So Long, See You Tomorrow* (1980), or indeed from
Ancestors or *Billie Dyer*. All converge on the same central event. The short
story "A Game of Chess," published in the *New Yorker* in 1965, will do as
well. Hugh and Amos are brothers, now grown and married. Like
Maxwell's elder brother—like all the elder brothers in his fiction—Amos
is missing a limb but remains the domineering figure he always was:

> "Sometimes I think Mother's death had a good deal to do with it,"
> Hugh said.
> "It was hard on me, too," Amos said.
> The house was like a shell, and the food tasted of tears. And he and
> Amos undressed in the same room and got into their beds, and he
> never spoke to Amos under the cover of the dark about the terror that
> gripped him. . . . "But I was all right," Hugh continued, "until I was
> twenty-five."
> "You were nineteen when you tried to commit suicide."
> "That was part of it," Hugh admitted.

The attempted suicide is also drawn from life. It provides the climacteric
to Maxwell's third novel, *The Folded Leaf*. The reader who approaches his
work in chronological order is likely to be surprised to find the same
events and consequences, even the same incidental details, recurring
time after time. A "new ten-dollar bill" remembered fifty years after it
was withdrawn from his father's wallet, in *Ancestors*, is extracted again
twenty years later in "The Front and Back Parts of the House," from *Billie*

Dyer. Maxwell never denied that the boy who stumbles bemusedly, unhappily through the fiction, eventually in sight of a redemption conditioned by love, was a pen-and-ink version of the man sitting at the desk, urging him on his way. Of *The Folded Leaf,* which turns on an intimate—and, to a reader in the age of "queer studies," startlingly physical—relationship between two students, Lymie and Spud, he said, "the whole of my youth is in it." Writing to O'Connor in 1959 about the preparation of a new edition of *They Came Like Swallows,* the novel which treats the events of his early life most directly, Maxwell said: "I was moved helplessly by the material, which will only cease to move me when I am dead, I suppose." In the introduction to yet another edition forty years later he took up the theme: "Much of the time I walked the floor . . . brushing the tears away with my hand so I could see the typewriter keys. I was weeping, I think, both for what happened—for I could not write about my mother's death without reliving it—and for events that took place only in my imagination. I don't suppose that I was entirely sane." Maxwell's blend of fiction and fact can be seen as the ultimate outcome of the *New Yorker's* disinclination under Shawn to observe any distinction between the two categories, on the contents page or elsewhere.

After his attempt to kill himself, and a first failed effort to make a living in New York (life was "like trying to climb a glass mountain," he wrote), Maxwell began going every weekday to see the psychoanalyst Theodor Reik, who had studied with Freud. By then Maxwell had published two novels, the second of them a modest success, but so powerful was Reik's influence that he appears to have directed the ending for Maxwell's work-in-progress, *The Folded Leaf.* Questioned by the *Paris Review* in 1982, Maxwell conceded that Reik wanted the book to have a "positive" resolution, as if by making things better for his mild young hero, Lymie, following his overwrought relationship with Spud, a boxer, the author might bring into being a better future for himself. When the book was republished by Vintage ten years later, Maxwell rewrote the parts influenced by Reik to accord with his original instincts. For subsequent reissues, however, he reverted to the 1945 edition, the "Reik version." Reik himself enters a story called "The Holy Terror," one of those from *Billie Dyer* that has more the tone of memoir than fiction; he suggests to the narrator, clearly Maxwell with no disguise, that he had made himself "a more tractable, more even-tempered, milder person than it was [his] true nature to be."

To those who met Maxwell and experienced firsthand his old-fashioned courtesy and personal kindness (I did, in 1995, and corresponded with him sporadically until his death), or to anyone aware of his public image, the presence of an overbearing psychoanalyst in his life is at a single glance surprising. He was a man whose outward appearance suggested an inner neatness. Few people are liked by all who encounter them, but Maxwell's benevolence and propriety commanded an unusually high esteem. A friend who knew Maxwell far better than I did—an émigré whom Maxwell had helped selflessly in New York—recalls his "infinite empathy, and uncanny understanding of an alien predicament." In a letter written just over a month before he died Maxwell told me that *War and Peace* was now his "only reading matter." An acquaintance came to his Upper East Side apartment every afternoon to read aloud to him: "Even though I knew it was coming, we barely lived through the amputation of Anatole's leg. And to think that Tolstoy lived through all of it over and over."

There are, not surprisingly, variant readings of his character among those who were closest to him. John Cheever, one of his authors at the *New Yorker,* wrote to a friend about a visit by Maxwell: "Bill, as you must have gathered, is terribly fastidious. He once called to say that he was coming for tea. Mary went wild and cleaned, waxed, arranged flowers, etc. When he arrived everything seemed in order. Mary poured the tea. The scene was a triumph of decorum, until Harmon, an enormous cat, entered the room, carrying a dead goldfish. It seemed to be our relationship in a nutshell." At a time of intense frustration over his dealings with the magazine, Cheever also wrote that his editor "was someone who mistook power for love. If you don't grow and change he baits you; if you do grow and change he baits you cruelly." In a more affectionate mood, however, Cheever dedicated *The Wapshot Scandal* to Maxwell.

·   ·   ·

Alec Wilkinson, in his long friendship with Maxwell, saw nothing of this, or if he did he isn't saying. The two men met when Wilkinson was a child. Wilkinson senior was the art editor of *Woman's Day* magazine. The Maxwells were their neighbors when they lived in Yorktown Heights, and the two men drove to the station together on days when Maxwell worked at the *New Yorker*. Alec Wilkinson later became a *New Yorker* writer himself, but if Maxwell had a hand in steering him there, he does not mention it. His brief memoir of Maxwell, *My Mentor* (2002), is rich in feeling but correspondingly short on circumstantial detail. It is an account of how the author found in Maxwell "the attentive and affectionate father figure my father felt reluctant to be." Maxwell said all sorts of flattering things about Wilkinson's father, which Wilkinson repeats without being able to endorse them. His neighbor was everything his father was not, down to size and manner: "My father was robust and Maxwell's frame was slight. . . . My father was charming and blasphemous and subversive. . . . Maxwell's nature was sedentary." The Wilkinson family home was in a constant state of emotional turmoil owing mainly to the father's adulteries, whereas Maxwell's devotion to his wife, and his desire to rekindle in his New York hearth the lost warmth of his childhood home, was unwavering and plain to all who knew them.

My Mentor jumps around in a disjointed way and lacks a dramatic center, though it is hardly Wilkinson's fault if his relationship with Maxwell was not shaped by torrid reversals. It never occurs to him to wonder if, perhaps at a level deeper than his own understanding, Maxwell "mistook power for love." The book is made of bland devotion. It leads the author toward some odd assertions and pretty corny speechifying: "If we live long enough, our lives make some sort of sensible pattern"—a curious remark in a book about a man whose life was dominated by an absurdity of fate. "Most people are hardly remembered five years after they die," writes Wilkinson, "but I will remember him—his writing, his character, his example, his advice—as long as I live."

The second half of *My Mentor* is largely devoted to Maxwell's decline and death and to the courage with which his wife faced her fatal illness. Maxwell first met Emily Noyes when she came to the *New Yorker* in search of a job in the mid-1940s. She was not hired, but after a year or more of vacillation Maxwell found her and invited her on a date. His determination was provoked again by Theodor Reik. Maxwell saw himself as living in a prison cell, a self-inflicted punishment for having "killed" his mother (he blamed himself for passing on the flu virus). "So I was a murderer," Wilkinson reports him saying in the course of one of their conversations. "And what do you do with murderers? You put them in a cell—no wife, no family. I was in a prison cell, and there was Reik saying, You're in a prison cell, but the door's not locked." His other family was, of course, the *New Yorker* itself.

The sound made by Maxwell's delicate stories is not often heard amid the din of modern American fiction. His novels sometimes float along on a sea of impressions and are apt to turn gooey when love is in the air. The love at the center of *The Folded Leaf* is for another youth, and while it is not quite established as the first postwar gay novel in American literature, the textual evidence is persuasive. Shower scenes in which Spud and Lymie soap each other, hand-holding, even kissing on the mouth might be explained by the customs of a different era; but what degree of innocence produced this scene, in which Spud, having moved out of the room he shared with Lymie, turns up unannounced one night to sleep beside his friend? Lymie at first keeps his eyes shut:

> Lymie waited. He felt the covers being raised, and then the bed sinking down on the other side, exactly as he had imagined it. Then, lifted on a great wave of happiness, he turned suddenly and found Spud there beside him.
>
> Spud was in his underwear and he was shivering. "My God, it's cold," he said. He pushed the pillow aside, and dug his chin in Lymie's shoulder. . . . It was enough that Spud was here, whether for good or just for this once; that it was Spud's arm he felt now across his chest. Lymie lay back on the wave of happiness and was supported by it. . . . All that he had ever wanted, he had now. All that was lost had come back to him.

One of the outstanding qualities of Maxwell's best fiction is its sense of rhythm. The realization of the importance of music in his life—Wilkinson tells us that in middle age Maxwell studied with a concert pianist— makes his insistence on rhythm as a structural element all the more apparent. A good example is "Over by the River" (1974), a story of some sixteen thousand words composed in a fugue-like form with which Maxwell chose to lead off his collected stories, *All the Days and Nights*. As one motif overlaps another—a child's fright at seeing a tiger slipping into the bedroom air-conditioning, a woman seen at a high window, a junkie lurking in the doorway, the malfunctioning of the air-conditioning, the suicide of the woman, a theft from the doorway—a ballad of domestic life, precariously situated between security and uncertainty, unfolds.

The rhythm of Maxwell's novel *The Chateau* is mesmerizing in a different way. No plot, nor even firm storyline, holds the action together. A young couple in France after World War II—based on the newly wed Maxwells and not far removed from the parents in "Over by the River"— are hustled here and there by one misunderstanding and muddle after another. The reluctance of the author to intrude with reasonable outcomes to mundane situations creates a web of feeling and impression that is both humdrum and memorable.

There is a view that Maxwell's reputation ought to be higher than it is, but it is a view held mainly by other members of the family to which both he and Wilkinson belong. The jacket of *My Mentor* is peppered with quotes from *New Yorker* writers, as Maxwell's own books and those of other old-school *New Yorker* writers often are. "Only a saint could have borne with complete equanimity the inadequate recognition he had for years to endure," Shirley Hazzard (herself a Maxwell charge at the *New Yorker*) wrote to Wilkinson after Maxwell's death. But it is hard to agree that Maxwell has been neglected. He received awards and medals and was made president of the National Institute of Arts and Letters. Two of his novels—*They Came Like Swallows* and *The Folded Leaf*—were Book-of-the-Month Club selections. His books have been kept in print faithfully by a number of publishers; Wilkinson says that *They Came Like Swallows* has never been out of print since its original publication in 1937, which is indeed remarkable when you consider that most of the works of Scott Fitzgerald and William Faulkner were deleted in the interim. Moreover, Maxwell was not prolific: between his fourth novel, *Time Will Darken It*, and his fifth, *The Chateau*, was a thirteen-year gap; between *The Chateau* and *So Long, See You Tomorrow,* an interval of almost twenty years. Rare is the author whom readers and critics will pursue through silence.

The view that Maxwell was unjustly neglected is probably shaped by the kind of literary life he led and by the narrow focus of his fiction. His activity seldom led him far from the *New Yorker* orbit, and his friendships tended to be with writers with links to the magazine. The two volumes of correspondence published so far—to and from O'Connor and Sylvia Townsend Warner, yet another of his *New Yorker* authors—contain between them barely anything by way of comment on the work of contemporary writers, particularly of writers unconnected to the *New Yorker.* If one were asked to judge by the evidence of those books—*The Happiness of Getting It Down Right* and *The Element of Lavishness*—the social and accompanying literary changes of the 1950s and 1960s would seem hardly to have touched Maxwell and the Maxwell family. On the Beat Generation, the civil rights campaign and the writers who responded to it, the antiwar movement, and the sexual revolutions—no comment. Writers who for better or worse raised their voices in the public forum— Baldwin, Wright, Mailer, Ginsberg, Vidal—held little attraction for the *New Yorker* (Baldwin's essay "Letter from a Region in My Mind," published in the magazine in 1962 and later made into *The Fire Next Time,* is an exception) or, apparently, for Maxwell. In *The Chateau,* set in Paris in 1948, a time when one of the twentieth century's most talented clusters of writers congregated on the Left Bank, the somewhat affectless hero Harold Rhodes and his wife, Barbara, keep "fastidiously" to the more proper Right Bank. Not a footfall, not a stream of cigarette smoke, not a whisper of an idea reaches them from the cafés across the river. The unwished-for hospitality of a tiresome old lady, on the other hand, must be repaid dutifully several times over. "I know now but I didn't know then," Maxwell wrote in *Ancestors* in 1971, "that the less people have to do with history the better."

There was not a shred of bohemianism in Maxwell (there was, perhaps, a little more in his wife, who was a painter and, Wilkinson notes, a fan of William Burroughs), and yet as a writer he perched on the brink of confessionalism. What he appeared always to be close to confessing was that the orderly behavior he showed to the world, the rigid dress code he imposed on everyday life, were as necessary to him as alcohol and way-ward sex were to Cheever. Beneath them lay a fissure so deep that it threatened to swallow him up. Decorum became a way of life. It was his peculiar literary strategy, the very thing that enabled him to keep in sight "the terror" that lay "under the cover of the dark."

FOUR Notes from a Small Island

A PROFILE OF SHIRLEY HAZZARD

Meetings with three men changed Shirley Hazzard's life in the 1960s. One was with the *New Yorker* fiction editor William Maxwell, to whom she sent a short story in the first year of the decade. "I hadn't ever written a story before. I sent it to the *New Yorker* absolutely cold, not even bothering to keep a copy." Maxwell replied with a check and a note: "Of course we'll publish your story." The tale, "Harold"—it is in her book *Cliffs of Fall*—became the first of many works of fiction and nonfiction to appear in the magazine. Three years later, at a party full of *New Yorker* folk, she met the man who would become her husband, Francis Steegmuller, translator of Flaubert's letters and biographer of Cocteau and Apollinaire. They sustained what appears to have been an exceptionally happy union until Steegmuller's death in 1994, at the age of eighty-eight.

The third significant encounter was with Graham Greene. In the late 1960s, while she and her husband were wintering on Capri, the colorful rock that juts out of the sea in the Bay of Naples, Hazzard found herself sitting near Greene at a café in the island town's compact piazzetta. The novelist was with a companion to whom he started to recite "The Lost Mistress" by Robert Browning—"Mere friends are we—well, friends the merest / Keep much that we resign"—but stalled after six or seven lines. As Hazzard folded her newspaper and prepared to leave, she discreetly supplied the missing words. Later that evening, she and Steegmuller happened to be next to Greene in Gemma's, a well-known local restaurant, and there began an enduring, if turbulent, friendship, as each party returned to Capri (pronounced Cap-ri, like party, not Capree) year after year.

Hazzard relates the story while sitting at the very table in Gemma's, with a view over sheer crags to the neighboring island of Ischia. She is slim with an oval face and birdlike profile, brown hair piled over her head. She is wearing a floral-print blouse buttoned up to the neck. Greene, she says, was apt to throw a tantrum at the most trivial prompting. The memory makes her shiver. "He had something in his makeup: he didn't want to be happy; that was not his desire in life." But Greene remains a commanding presence in her life. She has recorded the relationship in a marvelous memoir, *Greene on Capri*, which serves also as a compressed record of her life on the island with Steegmuller.

Before that ambrosial period, Hazzard's existence had been restless and difficult. The Hazzards were an accidental Australian family. Her father, a chemist, had come from Newport, Wales; her mother, a secretary, from Dunfermline in Scotland. They met, as if symbolically, on a bridge—the Sydney Harbor Bridge, then under construction. Neither had intended to remain in Australia. "My father was the personal assistant to the director of construction; my mother was the secretary to the chief engineer. By the time the bridge was finished, the Depression was coming on and in Britain the relatives were saying, 'No, don't come back, there's no work.'" A reader of Hazzard's first novel, *The Evening of the Holiday* (1967), might be startled at the suggestion that the central character's childhood, "like all childhoods," was unhappy. "I perhaps wouldn't say that now, but I think there is a lot of hidden unhappiness in childhood: not only the terrible dramas at home that emerge from an unhappy marriage, such as my parents had, but a child's sense of mortality, the temporary nature of everything." Although she is keen to stress she "did not suffer as a child," the tone of the household where she and her sister grew up is conveyed in details in her conversation. "My father loved music, but my mother prevented his continuing that interest and said she couldn't stand the sound of the gramophone in the house." Her mother was "very good with words; unfortunately, good with words in an adverse way. She did not ask herself questions. Not asking oneself questions is a source of great trouble in life."

Inheriting the talent for words, Hazzard conquered the adversity. All her heroines are "good with words" and profit not only professionally but morally from being so, just as many of her male characters are at a loss for the words that would clarify a certain vagueness. Some critics were puzzled at the freedom with which Helen, the sixteen-year old at the center of *The Great Fire,* and her younger brother Ben move in the world of Shakespeare and the classics, but Hazzard claims that intimate knowledge of great literature was common among her generation. She is capable of reciting poetry by the yard—not only the Browning that introduced her to Greene, but Wordsworth, Hardy, de la Mare, Auden. "Sometimes people don't know what they're getting into when they ask me to quote a few lines of verse." When asked at a dinner party to name an anthology he would take to a desert island, a friend replied, "I'll just take Shirley."

Hazzard, born in 1930, speaks in winding sentences, enunciating cautiously, treating each word with respect. Throughout the 1950s, she worked at the United Nations in New York—discussion of the experience inevitably leads to words like "awful," "demoralized," "miserable"—having moved to the city with her parents in 1951. Half a century's residence in New York has left no impression on her accent, which is likewise free of Australian notes; from time to time her mother's Scottish voice breaks through. "I seem to be expatriate of so many countries that I can't keep track of them, but in fact I've never felt 'national'— when I was a child in Australia, I never was attached to the chauvinistic view of Australia that was current at that time. I think there were quite a few children who felt this way, who perhaps dwelt in books." She lives most of the year in Manhattan and rents a house from friends outside Naples, but the room-and-a-half on Capri, sixty steps up, with a narrow balcony overlooking tiled roofs and several acres of Mediterranean, is the only property she owns. In the narrow streets radiating from the piazzetta, she is greeted fondly by the Caprese, whose gentle natures she often commends. The attentions of a rosy-cheeked waitress prompt the recollection from Hazzard that she was present at this matronly figure's birth. She was made an honorary citizen of Capri in 2000.

Hazzard's second novel, The *Bay of Noon* (1970), blends her early refuge in Italy with her ordeal at the UN. Like Jenny, the heroine, she was sent on a year's mission to Naples, "as a complicated result of the Suez crisis." She was under the command of men—"there was no advancement for women at the UN"—who were "swaddled up by bureaucracy." The organization reduced the men who worked for it. "Maybe they came in wanting to do something, but they were mesmerized by the idea of getting promoted, or were in rivalry with another for some petty little thing. A more demoralized place I have never met up with since. Especially a place that is claiming that it is doing something to advance humanity." When she first began to write, she had to request permission from the UN to publish, "to prove that there was nothing interesting from their point of view."

Three books came out of her years at the organization: a collection of comic variations on the theme of bureaucracy, *People in Glass Houses* (1967); a full-blown anatomy of the UN and its avowed purposes, *Defeat of an Ideal* (1973); and *Countenance of Truth* (1990), a treatment of the Kurt Waldheim scandal. Hazzard has called the UN "an appalling institution." As for women's lack of opportunity, "of course it changed when the rest of the world changed, but the UN was the last place to change." Typically, she places her reaction in the context of her happiest decade. "When I left the UN, I was astounded to find that there were people who had imagination for other people. That was the last thing I was expecting."

Whereas her first two novels may be described as monothematic, founded on romance leading to self-discovery, her later works are multilayered affairs. *The Transit of Venus* (1980) tracks the postwar lives in Australia, England, and the United States of two sisters, Caroline and Grace Bell, not entirely distinct from Hazzard and her sister. "The atmosphere, the ethos, of our lives are in there, but that doesn't mean that it was just like the lives we had. There is this other part of existence that is to do with observation, and to do with a sense that comes from literature." She does not attribute her love of literature to a particular relative or teacher. "I think I was born with it. I went to a school that was dedicated to teaching literature, however. The two founding headmistresses of the school would not teach domestic science—cookery, housekeeping, and so on—and they took a bit of public flak for this. They stalwartly said: Most of these girls will be doing domestic science for the rest of their lives. This is their only chance to do something else."

It was to be twenty-three years before the appearance of Hazzard's next novel, *The Great Fire,* which won both the National Book Award and the Australian Miles Franklin prize. To the subject matter of love, which drives the earlier books, she brought war—not so much its active dramas as its aftereffects. "I always knew I was going to write about war. My father was in the trenches during the 1914–18 war, as were the fathers of my school friends. It entered into one's imagination, being held up as something glorious, but at the same time—and I think this was especially true for girls—you thought, This is hideous! The terrible sight of the men on the street, the amputees on crutches, this was what the glory had led to." Deep in the texture of these books, a reader might glimpse the shadow of Joseph Conrad, a writer preoccupied not so much with war as with the savagery beneath the civilized skin. Hazzard was rereading Conrad's *Victory* in the Capri cafés this spring. She is curious as to why the affinity has been overlooked, in favor of another, with Henry James, which doesn't exist. "There is this myth that I was formed on Henry James," she says. "I had hardly read anything of him when I started to write. It must be the Italian connection: Northern girl goes to Italy and so on. And also because I take more trouble, perhaps, with words than authors usually do these days. James is a consummate writer, but you do feel that it's like the needle on the old gramophone, that it's got stuck and you want to move it on to the next groove. Also, I have to say, I think I'm funnier than Henry James." If banished to a desert island, she would be happy with Auden and Pearson's five-volume anthology, *Poets of the English Language,* and *War and Peace.*

She would also nourish herself on the cultural conversation with Steegmuller, Maxwell, and Greene that lasted for more than thirty years, and perhaps continues privately. Mention of her late husband is guaranteed to brighten her face. Of the party where they met, she says, almost breathlessly, "He was standing there. . . . and I looked around. . . . It was an extremely cold night. . . . To think, I might not have gone! This accidental factor that governs all our lives. . . ." The two were married in the same year. The hostess that evening was Muriel Spark, who having lately been converted to Catholicism, had a Jesuit priest on her arm. Another friend joked later: "We saw it all. We even had the priest ready."

Maxwell she loved for his transcendent empathy. "Bill wept easily and would do so several times a day, not necessarily out of sorrow. It was as if he always had another layer of tears in his eyes." Greene's eyes, by contrast, were sometimes "popping out" with anger. In *Greene on Capri*, she depicts him "spoiling for a contest," ever berating her for some ostensibly innocent remark. But as a young woman his early books impressed her deeply. "I asked for *The Heart of the Matter* for Christmas in 1947. I suddenly thought, here is this man who can represent ordinary life, ordinary troubles, and make them exciting to read about. After that, I always read his books. Of course, that was a high point, though there were some good books later." When they first knew each other, Greene would compliment her books, "but later on I think he was annoyed by my work. For example, somebody might come up on the street and say to me that they had liked *The Transit of Venus*, and he would say, 'Yes, it had marvelous reviews.' This came up so often it was comical. He had fixed this in his mind as a way to get out of saying anything about it."

Transporting the pages of her new novel from New York to Capri and back again, Hazzard intends to reduce the customary gap between books. "I don't think I have the time for such a long delay." She laments the clamor of modern life (even on Capri), the hollow distractions of television and celebrity, setting them against literature's improving graces. "The idea that somebody has expressed something, in a supreme way, that it can be expressed; this is, I think, an enormous feature of literature. I feel that people are more unhappy, in an unrealized way, for not having these things in their lives: not being able to express something, or to profit from somebody else having expressed it. It can be anything, but it's always, if it's supreme, an exaltation."

FIVE

Love, Truman

You do not have to travel far into Truman Capote's writings to reach the lonely interior; no further, in fact, than the opening paragraph of his first novel, *Other Voices, Other Rooms* (1948), which sets thirteen-year-old Joel Knox on his solitary way to a big house in Alabama to meet the father he has never known. Joel reveals a weakness for telling tall stories ("deceptions"), and he wishes for nothing more intensely than "owning the Koh-i-noor diamond." Capote's uncertain hero—"He was too pretty, too delicate and fair-skinned . . . a girlish tenderness softened his eyes"— need not be taken as a direct representation of the author, but he is minted from the same metal. Capote grew into Joel's grandiose schemes—for the Koh-i-noor jewel, read houses studded across Europe and America, and a collection of expensive crystal paperweights that he claimed (in a "deception," surely) to take on his travels everywhere—at the same time as he tried to put his protagonist's pathetic losses behind him. In a letter written in December 1963 to Perry Smith, one of the killers in the Clutter case that gave Capote *In Cold Blood* (1966), he provided a succinct summary of his heritage: "I was an only child, and very small for my age. . . . When I was three, my mother and father were divorced. My father was a traveling salesman, and I spent much of my childhood wandering around the South with him. He was not unkind to me, but I disliked him and still do. My mother, who was only 16 when I was born, was very beautiful. . . . [She] developed mental problems, became an alcoholic and made my life miserable. Subsequently she killed herself (sleeping pills)."

Like Joel in *Other Voices, Other Rooms,* Capote fetched up in Alabama during his parents' divorce (which in fact occurred when he was seven), being cared for by relatives. He was eventually reclaimed by his mother and her new husband, whereupon Truman Streckfus Persons became Truman Capote and was taken to live in New York. *Too Brief a Treat: The Letters of Truman Capote* contains a series of curt communications with his real father, Arch Persons, which took place in 1962. By now accustomed to the powdered endearments with which Capote showers his regular correspondents—"Malcolm my pet," "Howard dear," "Darling Darling Darling," "Mia Cara," and so forth—the reader is brought up sharp against Capote's father as "Dear A—." The renewal of acquaintance was prompted by a request on Arch's part for financial aid to an uncle. Capote replied: "I can't. All my money (and it isn't so much as everyone seems to believe) is in Swiss francs in Swiss banks." He tells his father that his stepfather, Joe Capote, "has gotten many thousands of dollars out of me in the past nine years," before signing off with "My best wishes to your wife," the sixth Mrs. Persons.

It requires an effort to recall Capote's eminence in the 1960s and early 70s, when he was regarded as a bright star in the constellation that included James Baldwin, Norman Mailer, Mary McCarthy, James Jones, William Styron, and Gore Vidal. Mailer called him "the most perfect writer" of the lot, although he worried over Capote's reluctance or inability to explore "the deep resources of the novel." All of the above writers were friends of Capote, with the exception of McCarthy, whom he disliked, but little in *Too Brief a Treat* beside a handful of letters to Styron testifies to the connections. Vidal, who formed a sparkling triangle with Capote and Williams in the early part of their careers, receives fewer mentions in the index than Audrey Hepburn.

Capote plugged the gap left by the dissolution of his family with a formidable force of friends. His companion for most of his life was Jack Dunphy, a once-married man who was also a writer. There are many letters to Capote's former lover Newton Arvin, author of an acclaimed biography of Herman Melville; to the aspiring writers Andrew Lyndon and Donald Windham; and to older-sister or mother figures such as Mary Louise Aswell, the estranged wife of the Harper & Brothers editor Edward Aswell. There is a chronic addiction to name-dropping, a juvenile habit that was to develop into a middle-aged passion for the superrich. Agnellis, Niarchoses, and Kennedys routinely spice up a dull missive. The parade of notables is so dense that the reader starts to wonder if Capote is joking. "Next week—Peggy Guggenheim," he writes in October 1950, a month after his twenty-sixth birthday. "During a rash moment in Venice I said come on down to Sicily, dear." There was "no one" in Taormina, where he was living with Dunphy, "except Orson Welles"; within a day or two of that news, "Welles asked me to play a part in a movie he is going to make here. Naturally I declined." Over the next few years, Capote flitted from Italy to France to Switzerland to Spain to the Cycladic island of Paros, usually finding it possible to drop into a letter that "Princess Caetani arranged for me to have a private audience with the Pope" (Rome), or that "Greta G. is coming here week after next to stay with us" (Tangier), or "I have a few friends living not too far away—Noel Coward, Charlie and Oona Chaplin" (Verbier), or that "I had dinner with Gide" (Paris). Gide figures prominently, as, later, did Jean Cocteau . . . who engineered a meeting with Colette . . . who set Capote off on his obsession with those crystal paperweights. Most of his celebrity friends had no reason to disavow the link (see, for example, the memoirs of Chaplin and Guggenheim); nevertheless, the cautious reader will bear in mind Gore Vidal, in his memoir *Palimpsest*, inquiring of André Gide, " 'How did you find Truman Capote?' 'Who?' "

No amount of salve administered by a Garbo or a Guggenheim could heal the old wounds, however, as Capote admitted to Robert Linscott, his editor at Random House, in October 1950: "Memories are always breaking my heart, I cry—it is very odd, I seem to have no control over myself." The burden of this letter is the composition of *The Grass Harp* (1951), the short novel that was to be the follow-up to *Other Voices, Other Rooms*. Like the earlier book, it derives from his motherless interlude in Alabama and is dedicated to the elderly cousin Sook Faulk ("Dolly," in the novel) who helped sustain him there. The book disappointed the publishers, as he reveals when writing to Linscott's colleague Bennett

Cerf: "Bob had written to me about your combined reservations . . . which came as a shock because I'd been so certain that what I'd done was right. But there is no point in going into any of my arguments; obviously there must be something wrong or you would not all feel as you do." In the end, *The Grass Harp* was published without changes. The editor of the *Letters*, Gerald Clarke, chips in with a fraternal footnote, "The critics took Capote's side," but the novel is among his less enduring works.

Capote is probably the most prominent American homosexual writer of the postwar period not to "write gay," to use Edmund White's phrase. The love in his love stories is between a man (or a boy) and a woman, though it is frequently unrequited or platonic love. By the time that Baldwin ("I loathe Jimmy's fiction: it is crudely written and of a balls-aching boredom"), Vidal ("If Gore could write, which he can't . . ."), and others had made it permissible to write gay, Capote was preoccupied with the technicalities of the nonfiction novel—a brilliant diversion that turned into a dead end. The letters provide glimpses of his self-discipline as a writer (by his thirty-fifth birthday, Capote had published seven books and made two adaptations for the stage), as when he tells Lyndon that Cecil Beaton is coming to Taormina, "and that would be nice, as long as it didn't interfere with my work, which it would." Letters to the likes of Linscott and Cerf cheer the reader, with their sober attention to manuscripts, proofs, royalty statements, and works in progress; but it's never long before we're back to "Magnolia my sweet" (Lyndon), "Donny lamb" (Windham), "Darling Sister" (Aswell), and advice to Beaton: "You know I seriously think you should solve your servant problem by hiring Italians."

The paradox, as any reader of Capote can see, is that his best work is ignited by contact with people at the bottom rather than the top. His first really impressive piece of writing is "House of Flowers," a story set in Haiti among black prostitutes, their white clients, and the men regarded by both groups as "only natives." One, Royal Bonaparte, captures the heart of Ottilie, the most coveted girl in the Port-au-Prince brothel, and she goes to live with him and his grandmother, "Old Bonaparte," a practitioner of voodoo arts. The headlong pace of the story, written in 1950 and published along with *Breakfast at Tiffany's* in 1958, is sustained with

casual virtuosity. The narrative is laced with cruelty, which is administered without relish or sentimentality but as something inevitable. There
is a hint of Caribbean magic realism *avant la lettre* in the tone, as when
Ottilie is discovered by her friends roped to a tree as punishment for having caused the death of the ancient witch. They all get drunk on rum,
before Ottilie begs them to tie her up again: "Chewing eucalyptus leaves
to sweeten her breath, she felt the chill of twilight twitch the air. Yellow
deepened the daytime moon, and roosting birds sailed into the darkness
of the tree. Suddenly, hearing Royal on the path, she threw her legs
akimbo, let her neck go limp, lolled her eyes far back into their sock-
ets. . . . listening to Royal's footsteps quicken to a run, she happily
thought: This will give him a good scare."

In *Other Voices, Other Rooms,* the liveliest scenes occur when the black
stragglers Zoo and Jesus Fever enter the room (although, in a book so
heavily influenced by William Faulkner and Eudora Welty, that seems
barely worth mentioning). The title of Capote's third and best short
novel, *Breakfast at Tiffany's* (1958), hangs ironically over the tale of a
Manhattan adventuress, Holly Golightly, her assortment of seedy gentlemen, and the innocently besotted young writer in the apartment above
who is telling the story. Even a less well-known nonfiction book, *The
Muses Are Heard* (1956), about the Everyman Opera company's tour of
the Soviet Union with *Porgy and Bess,* pokes fun at the higher-ups in the
project, including Mrs. Ira Gershwin, while generally siding with the
put-upon Negro cast. The best of the stories in Capote's early collection,
A Tree of Night (1949), are about people stranded on islands of loneliness,
threatened by flotsam companionship. There is more than a twist of
Gothic in some of them—"Miriam," for example, in which a macabre,
perhaps imaginary, little girl persecutes an elderly widow—which
appealed to the judges of the annual O. Henry Awards (Capote was a
winner three times) but is less likely to grip the modern reader.

The eight tales of *A Tree of Night* make up just over a third of *The
Complete Stories of Truman Capote,* with a further three having come from
the back half of *Breakfast at Tiffany's.* The best of the uncollected work is
"Among the Paths to Eden," which revisits familiar territory by showing
a widower resisting the advances of a gawky suitor while laying flowers

on the grave of his unlamented wife. It dates from 1960, when Capote
was in his prime:

> Not that he disliked his appearance; he just knew that it was very so-
> what. The harvesting of his hair had begun decades ago; now his head
> was an almost barren field. While his nose had character, his chin,
> though it made a double effort, had none. His shoulders were broad;
> but so was the rest of him. . . . Nonetheless, he did not dismiss Mary
> O'Meaghan's flattery; after all, an undeserved compliment is often the
> most potent.
>   "Hell, I'm fifty-one," he said, subtracting four years. "Can't say I
> feel it."

Capote's talent was so prodigious that he sometimes had difficulty
containing it. The style is frequently on the point of overflowing. What
follows is but a portion of a single sentence describing the film director
John Huston, from *Observations* (1959), a joint project with the photographer Richard Avedon: "his riverboat-gambler's suavity overlaid with
roughneck buffooning, the hearty mirthless laughter that rises toward
but never reaches his warmly crinkled and ungentle eyes, eyes bored as
sunbathing lizards; the determined seduction of his confidential gazes
and man's man camaraderie, all intended as much for his own benefit as
that of his audience, to camouflage a refrigerated void of active feeling,
for, as is true of every classic seducer, or charmer if you prefer, the success
of the seduction depends upon himself never feeling."
    The first act of Capote's brilliant career came to an end in 1966, with
the publication of *In Cold Blood,* the true story, written in the form of a
novel, of the murder of four members of a Kansas family by two small-
time crooks. The crime was committed in 1959. Capote first went to
investigate (in the company of Harper Lee) on assignment for the *New
Yorker.* The conclusion to the case was held up by appeals, and Capote
was reluctant to publish his book without a natural ending. Sympathetic
letters to Perry Smith—"I've only just heard about the court's denial. But
remember, this isn't the first set-back" (January 24, 1965)—sit uneasily
beside complaints to Bennett Cerf and others, such as this, written a few
weeks later: "The execution was set for Feb 18th. But they got still

another stay. However, I do not think the day of reckoning is now too distant." Smith and Hickock were hanged in April 1965, with Capote in attendance, and after publication of the book, he took an extended break. He returned to the United States from Europe, though flitting from house to house as usual. "That caviar!" he writes in January 1968 to Katharine Graham, owner of the *Washington Post*, "I ate the whole pound Christmas day, which I spent alone in the country. Ate it with 3 baked potatoes." His last book, *Music for Chameleons* (1980), is made up largely of dialogues, many of them printed originally in Andy Warhol's *Interview* magazine. Capote also turned his hand to the self-interview, emerging with the disclosure, "I'm an alcoholic. I'm a drug addict. I'm homosexual. I'm a genius."

In 1975, *Esquire* began to publish sections from *Answered Prayers*, an "ambitious novel" which Capote claimed to have started in the 1950s, making comparisons to *A la Recherche du temps perdu*. He promised it would be "triple the length of all my other books combined," but the complete product, published in book form posthumously in 1986, is about forty thousand words long, half the length of the average book. Its interest to readers not driven to pick at the skeletal pages for café society names is practically nil. "Much of Proust, it must be remembered, is gossip," said Arnold Gingrich, the editor of *Esquire*, attempting to defend his author, but it is pathetic to behold the "perfect writer" numbed by his own malice and vulgarity. The title comes from the well-known text attributed to Saint Theresa—"More tears are shed over answered prayers than unanswered ones"—but the subtext to the book, as to much of Truman Capote's work, is better evoked by a prayer uttered by Joel early in *Other Voices, Other Rooms:* "God, let me be loved."

SIX Franzen, Oprah, and High Art

When Richard Wright's first novel, *Native Son*, was selected for the Book of the Month Club in March 1940, both author and publisher were naturally delighted. *Native Son* was not an obvious choice for the Book of the Month Club. One of the selectors called it a "red-hot poker." It deals with life in a poor black Chicago slum, and death, by murder, in a wealthy white household. But the choice rocketed Wright's novel to the top of the best-seller list (displacing *The Grapes of Wrath*) and made him, in the words of his agent, a "fixed star" in the literary firmament.

To obtain untold wealth, it was necessary to sign a pact. The Book of the Month Club dictated the date of publication, delaying the book's release by six months. It also required the deletion of certain passages that the judges feared subscribers would find "objectionable." The main problem concerned a scene in which the hero, Bigger Thomas, and a friend masturbate in a movie theater which is showing a newsreel featuring the girl he will later murder. Wright rewrote it, omitting the raunchy details, without standing on artistic integrity. He regarded his conscription into a more prudish, populist world as part of the gilded bargain.

Book clubs are democratic institutions by their nature. The noncommercial purpose is to spread the word, and because the book club's judges recognize that the target audience is of generally middling education, it had better not be too difficult or disturbing a word. In an echo of the Book of the Month Club's dealings with Wright, the representative of the Oprah Winfrey Book Club told Jonathan Franzen, "This is a difficult book for us," when calling to introduce him, as the author of *The Corrections* himself put it, "to some of the responsibilities of being an Oprah author." Oprah Winfrey's televised book club functions in a similar way to the Book of the Month Club, and it too feels entitled to exact compromises from the difficult book, the red-hot poker. The area of contention regarding Franzen's novel was not going to be sex, which is no longer forced to lurk in the darkened movie theaters of literature; nor was it anything to do with race—*The Corrections*, strangely for a novel talked of as a modern American epic, contains the merest shadow of a nonwhite presence. The compromise, as Franzen understood straight away, involved permitting his novel, and himself, to be adopted by a book club which is part of a project, a concept, that epitomizes everything in "the culture" he ought to be against. A novel by a writer like Franzen is intended as a "correction" to a television program like the Oprah Winfrey Show.

Oprah's Book Club is aware of its own value. The recommendation is worth an actual piece of the books selected. The O-shaped announcement that this novel is an "Oprah pick" comes not in the form of a sticker or wraparound label, each of which could be peeled off by the squeamish reader, but as an imprinted "O." Oprah, by way of her initial letter, shares the billing with the author. While his publisher, Farrar, Straus and Giroux, rejoicing at the prospect of massive best-sellerdom, had a further six hundred thousand copies of the novel printed, Franzen may well have been reflecting that he could set up a character like Oprah, and her hugely appealing effusions, as a target for satire in a future novel. No doubt he recalled his own words of six years before, that the evanescent glamour visited on the "visible" author—"the money, the hype, the limo ride to a Vogue shoot"—was merely a consolation "for no longer mattering to the culture." Those phrases, part of a much-resurrected essay called "Perchance to Dream," published in *Harper's* in 1996, could be taken as the standard intellectual whine. Writers in America complain all the time that they are not taken seriously at home. Some believe that literature is more deeply embedded in the daily life of European countries. Others envy those whose writings provided life support in totalitarian states. So much more pitiful the irony, then, that victory in the Cold War coincided with defeat on the literary front for the sole surviving super-power, that film, or popular music, or television, shape the culture now. The very usage "the culture" is itself an emblem of highbrow demise. The culture is simply mass performance, involving speech, hair dye, footwear, body piercings, choice of diet. It is no longer possible, in the culture, to be uncultured.

What seems to have taken almost everyone by surprise was that Franzen took his own part in this action seriously enough to stand by his word. While the Oprah Book Club considered options for presenting this "difficult book" to its practically captive readership, Franzen complained to Terry Gross on National Public Radio that the way authors were fea-tured on Oprah's show was "sort of a bogus thing," that readers at sign-ing sessions in bookstores had said, "If I hadn't heard of you I would have been put off by the fact that this is an Oprah pick." He told an inter-viewer in Portland, Oregon, that Oprah had chosen "enough schmaltzy, one-dimensional books that I cringe," adding, by way of contrast, "I feel like I'm solidly in the high-art literary tradition."

The striking feature of the Franzen furor is not the author's reluctance to be pressed into the Oprah Empire, the realm of schmaltz, the bogus thing, but the anger and revulsion his remarks set off. *People* magazine pronounced Franzen guilty of "dissing" Oprah. In a similar vein, a jour-nalist with New York University's *Washington Square News*, Shazad Akhtar, wrote that Franzen was not just "a snob" and "a hypocrite," he was also "an elitist" with a "certain strain of sexism running through his beryl-blue blood"—every postmodernist's white-male nightmare. The *Library Journal* preferred the medical approach, perceiving a man "beset by contradictory feelings." Oprah, ever alert to pop therapy, refined the diagnosis to the now-famous judgment that Franzen was "conflicted." It was a perfect summing-up of the whole affair: the superarticulate author of *The Corrections* dismissed by his would-be sponsor in a nonword. By December 15, a month and a half after the story broke, an Australian newspaper, the *Canberra Times*, could describe Franzen as "very possibly the most talked-about writer in the world." Step aside, Salman Rushdie, who blasphemed the Prophet Mohammed and offended his representative the Ayatollah Khomeini. Step forward Jonathan Franzen, who dissed Oprah Winfrey. "Most authors are careful not to offend Ms. Winfrey," wrote David D. Kirkpatrick in the *New York Times*. As are most editors, publicists, and salespeople. Who could afford to? To deploy Franzen's words from "Perchance to Dream" once more: "The dollar is now the yardstick of cultural authority."

Doubtless aware that he, too, is dependent on a healthy balance sheet at Farrar, Straus and Giroux, Franzen tried to recant, disappointing his tiny band of moral supporters (Rushdie attempted to do the same). But "I didn't mean it" never saved a heretic's skin. Oprah proved herself a worthy word queen by recognizing that what has been said cannot be unsaid. What has been invited can be disinvited, however, and Franzen never appeared on Oprah's televised book club.

The Corrections is an enjoyable family saga with five principal characters: Enid and Alfred, an elderly couple living in the midwestern city of St. Jude, and their three children, Chip, Denise, and Gary. Each in his or her own way is trying to cope with personal problems, and not doing it very well. There is no such thing as a plot—just five linear lives twisting in the wind. The writing is extravagantly verbal. *The Corrections* demonstrates an impressive understanding of economic and scientific lexicons—Alfred, for example, an amateur metallurgist, "had clays and gels of silicate. He had silicone putties. He had slushy ferric salts succumbing to their own deliquescence. Ambivalent acetylacetonates and tetracarbonyls with low melting points"—and Franzen relishes long lists of innovative (and unappetizing) gourmet dishes (Denise is a chef). He is apt to spend thirty or forty pages on an incident to which an equally good writer might devote three. Franzen is good on both outward and inward states: the language, which is never dull, has the utmost grip on the characters' inner experience and, additionally, the self-consciousness developing from it—the experience of experience. Here is how we are introduced to Gary, a vice president at CenTrust Bank: "Gary had been worrying a lot about his mental health, but on that particular afternoon, as he left his big schist-sheathed house on Seminole Street and crossed his big back yard and climbed the outside stairs of his big garage, the weather in his brain was as warm and bright as the weather in northwest

Philadelphia. . . . He had a spring in his step, an agreeable awareness of his above-average height and his late-summer suntan. His resentment of his wife, Caroline, was moderate and well contained." Gary's fluctuating self-esteem and the guerrilla warfare he believes his wife is prosecuting against him are typical of the dramas that constitute *The Corrections.* Will Chip be hauled across the coals for sleeping with a student? Will Denise fall in love with her boss or his wife? Will Gary bring his sons to their grandparents' home for Christmas? How long will bottled-up old Alfred endure his humiliating system collapse? Will Enid get her "corrective" drugs?

While these and similar story lines are laced with acute and often humorous observation, the reader of a long novel with upmarket literary aspirations is entitled to ask for more: that the story resonate down among those great everyday themes that touch us all: love, death, iden-tity, fulfillment through work and family, religion or the gap left by its modern absence, and so on. The degree to which a novel is taken seri-ously by a cultivated readership will depend on how profoundly it does this, and it is likely to succeed in proportion to the life that the novelist has succeeded in imparting to his characters. Great fictional characters have a sensibility of their own, above and beyond their actions and their speech. It is about ten years since I read *War and Peace,* but I believe I know not only how Natasha would speak or act in certain situations, but how she would feel about how she is speaking and acting.

The main characters in *The Corrections* are rounded and distinct, but while they change, they scarcely develop. At the end of the book, we feel little different about anyone from how we felt at the beginning. Chip, the failure, was a jerk on page 1, and he stays that way throughout. When I first met his successful brother, Gary, he struck me as a type I would not make an effort to get to know. Four hundred pages later, no change there (which does not make him bad company in a novel, of course).

The Corrections is rather too amused by its own performance for the satire to be effective. Jokes run down into slapstick. The worst feature of Franzen's humorous repertoire is the funny-foreigner routine. Swedes are boring, while Norwegians compete to be more so; Scots say "laddie"; a British author (known only as "the Famous British Author") can achieve nothing more in conversation, during a night out with Philadelphia luminaries, than "cricket-and-darts-related wit." At this point, I wondered if Franzen had ever left America. More dubious than any of these schoolboy larks is the lengthy section of tragedy-as-farce set in present-day Lithuania. Chip, once a college lecturer with a soft spot for Foucault, has failed so badly that he is now cozying down with racketeers in the lawless Baltic republic, a land of warlords, drive-by shootings, chronic coal and electricity shortages, and a heavy dietary reliance on horsemeat.

Is it really that bad? No, apparently not. When Lithuanians objected to the fictional portrayal, a spokesman for Farrar, Straus and Giroux explained that the author just "picked an Eastern European country at random. He created a Lithuania that I assume was largely in his imagination." There happen to be real Lithuanians in a real Lithuania, a distant country of which we know little. But they probably weren't expecting to shift many copies of *The Corrections* over there anyhow.

Franzen draws on news clippings and stock market volatility and modern technologies to move the story along, and in this respect the novel has something in common with another great sweeping saga of "modern times," John Dos Passos's U.S.A. trilogy. The music of *The Corrections* is more in tune with the present day than that of the seven-decades-old work, of course, but in a few years' time Franzen's novel may come to seem the book more tied to its period. It is among the most engaging features of *The Corrections* that, in its tone, its characters, their dialogue, it is phenomenally up to the minute; but nothing dates as quickly.

.   .   .

Each episode of the Oprah Winfrey Show opens with the same clip, in which the hostess declares, "This is Big . . . gonna be Big." She means to spread her blessings widely. In one recent episode, she waited until the applause from the studio audience had subsided, then exhaled gratefully at the wonderfulness of it all. "Ooh. Look at you. Beautiful." Does she mean it? No. Does she believe that she means it? Probably yes. She is extending the frontiers of what Franzen called the "electronic democracy." If you're out of shape and loveless and addicted to pills and the attentions of a therapist (not to mention afternoon TV talk shows), no matter. Look at you. Beautiful. We are all invited, on condition that we play the game and say "beautiful" to each other, or act along with the "sort of a bogus thing" that is Oprah's Book Club. If your highbrow cringe is setting off a bout of nausea, just shrug and say: Well, it sells books, doesn't it?

Oprah Winfrey has the rare gift of being natural in front of the camera. The way she jokes about her dress size makes less confident people feel better about their own size. But her brand of talent and intelligence has nothing in common with that of Jonathan Franzen, or of any other "high-art" writer. His employment impels him to see through Oprah Winfrey, who is "natural" but not real—to understand that her naturalness is an act, and to explain why so many people are content to accept it and are made happy by her anointing: the banal boosterism that persuades them they are involved in something big by being on television. The shallowness of the medium is expertly molded by a "natural" like Oprah into an experience that makes people feel better while they are taking part in it. It's like a pill.

There is a correction to the mass of pap that confronts us every day, the diet of artificially produced pop music, celebrity-focused journalism, and cheap TV: literature. Every decade or so, someone finds a new way to announce the death of literary culture—most recently, it was the "electronic democracy" that brought Jonathan Franzen to such a low point in "Perchance to Dream"—and yet it persists in generally decent health. The codex (a.k.a., the book) appears to have fended off its electronic competitors, the CD-ROM and the e-book, for the time being. It is certainly the book, rather than the film or the television show, that is the first port of call in the narrative-based arts (movies are made from books, not the other way round) and education. Twentieth-century literature's response to the leveling of social stratification, and the culture which feeds it, has been to become "complex" and "difficult," and eventually to demand a separate category—call it "modernism," call it "high art"—hived off from mass-market entertainment. And yet this elitism is still the culture's primary point of reference.

As if understanding this and making a preemptive thrust, the Oprah project embraces tokens of modernist, high-art literature. The Oprah magazine, *O*, makes use of serious writers, in among the numerous photographs of the founder, who is usually smiling broadly (though in a shoot with Mayor Giuliani after 9/11, overlooking Ground Zero, she was caught in a moment of "natural" grief, weeping). The writers in *O* are often those that Jonathan Franzen would approve of. The January 2002 edition, for example, prints poems by Nobel Prize–winning poets Seamus Heaney and Wislawa Szymborska, as well as Grace Paley and Walt Whitman. No great editorial resourcefulness is called for, as all the poems have been published before. The Oprah ingredient is to call the section "The Solace of Poetry," and to provide a preamble: "The poet speaks to us in heightened language, crystallizing an emotion. . . . For the space of the poem, we breathe together." In another section, the magazine offers a "Truth Calendar," with a quotation for selected days of the month of January from authors such as Henry Miller, Simone de Beauvoir, Virginia Woolf, and Vaclav Havel. Paradoxically, the Oprah project can exist, though the project itself is not clear about this, only by subverting the insights of figures such as these. In Oprah's signed editorial for the January edition of *O*, we read: "I have always been a truth seeker. Not a day goes by that I don't look for it, consider how I can use it to evolve into all that the Creator intended for me—and then seek to extend that truth to others." In the world that Seamus Heaney, Virginia Woolf, and Jonathan Franzen inhabit—the elitist world of difficult writing—it is thought best to keep oneself at a distance from people who make this sort of declaration. They may believe themselves, but they are not to be believed. It is such things that "high-art" literature teaches us. It is how things are in Shakespeare, Burns, Balzac, Faulkner. By situating himself "solidly in the high-art literary tradition," Franzen may be understood as saying: If it comes to a choice between her and them, I'm bound to side with them.

Few gave him credit for doing so. After all, Oprah does a great deal for the book trade. Franzen himself acknowledged her beneficence when, like a dissident forced to undergo a show trial—trial by "the culture": he's a snob, a hypocrite, a sexist, an elitist, *he's conflicted*—he tried to take back what he had said. There was no sympathy for him, least of all within the industry. The publishing world is so indebted to Oprah that the National Book Foundation honored her with a Gold Medal on the occasion of that body's fiftieth anniversary in 1999.

.   .   .

The only objection I can see to Franzen's use of the expression "high-art literary tradition" is that it is vague. Most such terms are, but we need them. Imagine: two men meet in a train carriage and discover that they are both writers. One is Dale Carnegie, author of *How to Make Friends and Influence People*, the other is William Faulkner, author of *The Sound and the Fury*. How to distinguish between the two, if not by resorting to the likes of "serious writing," "complexity," "high art"? I think it is fair to assume that in using the last phrase, Franzen had in mind something close to what many readers have when referring to "good books"—books such as *Great Expectations, Madame Bovary, The Princess Casamassima, The Great Gatsby, Invisible Man*.

Jonathan Galassi has already ranked *The Corrections* among them. He called it "a masterpiece." Do we believe him? Do we believe that he believes himself? Galassi used the phrase in the publicity material that accompanied the proof-issue of *The Corrections* (3,500 copies sent to media outlets—more than the expected sale of many novels). He is the book's editor. He is also a poet, a translator of poetry (most recently of the Italian Nobel Prize winner Eugenio Montale), and the former poetry editor of a distinguished journal, the *Paris Review*. It is reasonable to assume not only that he has a firm idea of what constitutes a literary "masterpiece," but also that he is aware that it is generally held in "high-art" literary circles that only the reading public, in its mysterious engagement with time, can reveal a classic, never mind a masterpiece. So much for elitism. There was not even time for Franzen's book to be set before the reading public before the poet, poetry editor, and translator was asserting its imperishable grandeur. But Galassi was talking in his role as a commercial publisher, and not as a writer and editor. He expected us discreetly to distinguish between the two by ourselves—as members of the electronic democracy on the one hand, as readers and critics of "high-art" literature on the other.

Receiving Galassi's pronouncement as the former, I'd be inclined to accept it docilely; as an independent-minded reader of "good books," I'd expect him to calm down. But I suppose he wasn't talking to that half of me. He was talking as Oprah was talking in her role as "ordinary woman," rather than as an ordinary woman, when she said, "Look at you. Beautiful." Both have made an intuitive estimate of their audience and decided they could get away with it. The editor-in-chief of Farrar, Straus and Giroux turns out to be as much a servant of Franzen's electronic democracy as truth-seeker Oprah. The one person in the drama who has proved himself not to be thus conflicted is Jonathan Franzen.

With respect to Galassi, I suggest that he did not mean what he said when he landed *The Corrections* with the judgment "a masterpiece." I believe that he recognizes the glibness of instant verdicts, which publicists and television presenters feel obliged to utter. He was probably thrilled—justifiably—at having an ambitious, well-written, self-consciously contemporary novel on his hands, and wished to promote it aggressively ("This is Big . . . gonna be Big"). When the *Canberra Times* called Franzen "the most talked-about writer in the world," it didn't really believe that either. It simply seemed to someone on the features desk a suitable way to push a big literary story. The next day the leaves of the newspaper would be wrapping Pacific fish.

In his *Harper's* essay, Franzen praised Paula Fox's *Desperate Characters* (1970), a novel which features a character named Otto Brentwood. Brentwood is portrayed as "an unashamed elitist, an avatar of the printed word, and a genuinely solitary man"—he is reminiscent of Franzen himself, in fact, which I think was the despairing essayist's point. Franzen imagined this character, in present-day time, "kicking in the screen of his bedroom TV," as he resiled from "the banal ascendancy of television, the electronic fragmentation of public discourse . . . [the] media jingoism." However, Franzen believed that such an act would be in vain. As an "avatar of the printed word," Brentwood belonged "to a species so endangered as to be all but irrelevant."

Few would be prepared to argue that, in the years since the publication of "Perchance to Dream," the banal ascendancy has been reversed. And yet, how unexpected, how unpredictable, that portrait of the rebel against the all-in performance culture seems when we look at it now. Old Brentwood, the unashamed elitist, has played a trick on us, and specifically Jonathan Franzen. For Franzen succeeded in kicking in the television screen while Oprah was showing, and changing the topic of conversation. Just for a few minutes. Just long enough to make him "the most talked-about writer in the world."

SEVEN Drawing Pains

A PROFILE OF ART SPIEGELMAN

In their familiar modern form, comic strips were introduced to lighten the content of newspapers. They were sometimes called the "funnies" or, in the case of the Scottish *Sunday Post,* which was bred in the same stable as the *Beano* and the *Dandy,* "The Fun Section." Art Spiegelman is among the best-known living cartoonists, but the drawings that have made him famous are not funny, and they are not intended solely for children. Spiegelman and other comic-book artists of the underground renaissance that occurred during the 1960s are inclined to call their work "comix"—the final letter, perhaps subliminally, endorsing them for consumption by grown-ups. His most famous creation, *Maus,* in which the Jews are depicted as mice, tracks the experience of his parents in Poland before and during the Second World War, leading eventually to Auschwitz, or "Mauschwitz." The book was published in two volumes, in 1986 and 1991. The more recent Spiegelman production, *In the Shadow of No Towers,* suggests parallels between the horror suffered by the elder Spiegelmans and that of their son on September 11, 2001, and over the days and months that followed. "Maybe I really want the world to end, to vindicate the fears I felt back on 9/11!" says the Spiegelman figure in one of the *No Towers* strips, dated almost two years after the event. "Maybe it's just my little world that ended."

In person, Spiegelman does not give the least impression that his world has ended, or is about to. His express-train conversation manages to convey wit, paranoia, an obsession with American politics, and a caustic intelligence, all in a single sentence. With his wife and their two children, Spiegelman is about to embark on a three-week holiday in a *gîte* in Provence. "I'd move to France," he says. "I'm just not sure if it's worse to be a victim of Bush's foreign policy than of his domestic policy." The sardonic one-liners roll from his tongue as regularly as the cigarettes from the pack on the table before him. He smokes so much "that I might not live to see the end of the world." An unrealistically sickly looking Spiegelman peers from a panel in *No Towers*, gasping: "Cof!"

The strips in *No Towers* were begun while Spiegelman was working at the *New Yorker*. However, they were declined by the magazine and by other leading American papers, eventually being published in New York's weekly Jewish newspaper, the *Forward*, which had serialized *Maus*. Steve Bell, the political cartoonist of the *Guardian*, is not surprised that Spiegelman had difficulty in getting the new work published in the United States. "It was the climate after 9/11. I've spoken to a lot of cartoonists who had a hard time getting stuff accepted. Self-censorship then comes into play, because you just know they won't publish it. American papers are very careful not to offend—which is silly really, because while you're being careful not to offend, the government is off doing very offensive stuff." Spiegelman describes his acceptance in the relatively humble pages of the *Forward* as being granted "the right of return." He felt obliged to point out to the editor that, unlike *Maus*, his new work would have little Jewish content. "He shrugged and said: 'It's okay—you're Jewish.'" The strips were published, more or less simultaneously, in *Die Zeit* in Germany and in the *London Review of Books* in Britain. Spiegelman resigned as consulting editor of the *New Yorker* at the end of 2002.

In the Shadow of No Towers consists of ten broadsheet plates by Spiegelman and a further seven plates, what he calls "the second Tower," taken from the funnies printed during the early years of the twentieth century in newspapers such as the *New York American*, the *World*, and the *Chicago Tribune*. The latter comics all in some way reflect the themes of Spiegelman's own drawings in the "first Tower." One, dated 1902, shows "Foxy Grandpa" reading the Declaration of Independence on the fourth of July and being interrupted by an explosion, while another depicts the Happy

Hooligan, a popular idiot, assuming the guise of "Abdullah, the Arab Chief" and coming to grief with a thousand-pound weight dropped on his head. In a 1921 cartoon from the *New York American,* a character visits Pisa and, like Spiegelman after September 11, is kept awake by thoughts of the famous tower falling on him. However, the most spectacular of the book's borrowings is in the endpapers, which reproduce the September 11, 1901, front page of the *New York World* with the headline "President's Wound Reopened: Slight Change for the Worse." The story referred to the shooting by anarchists of President William McKinley (he died three days later). The overall effect of Spiegelman's new work is of a synthetic collage, in which the various parts interact in the reader's mind to compose changing wholes. Edward Koren, a cartoonist who has been associated with the *New Yorker* for more than forty years, feels that Spiegelman "has an extraordinary sense of the history of the evolution of the comic strip. It's quite bold of him to put his work next to that of the masters."

The original schedule for publication in the *Forward* was one broadsheet plate per month, but when Spiegelman began work he found that the destruction of the World Trade Center, which he witnessed and which happened close to his daughter's school, had put him into shock and slow motion. Plate 2, for example, took almost three months to complete. "How did the old timers do it?" he asks, in awe at the rapid production of the beautifully executed *New York World* and *Chicago Tribune* strips, featuring the likes of Little Nemo and the Katzenjammer Kids. "I can't imagine. They had to turn out a full-page spread every Sunday, plus lots of work for the dailies. But here, I couldn't always meet my deadlines. And I had a certain kind of urgency. I really thought another attack was going to happen in New York any second."

Small and neat and wearing a black waistcoat like "Artie" in *Maus,* Spiegelman seems every inch the smart New Yorker, although he was born in Stockholm, spent his American infancy in Pennsylvania, and moved to California for six years in the 1970s "after a short stay in a mental hospital." The power of *Maus* derives not just from the atrocious experience of the parents—the betrayal into Nazi hands by smugglers who had promised to save them, the poisoning of their elder son Richieu by a guardian to spare him from the gas chambers, the unspeakable ordeal of the camps—but from the book's subplot, which delineates the difficult relationship between father and son. Vladek Spiegelman is portrayed as selfish and petty. The resources that enabled him to survive Auschwitz have hardened into extreme parsimony. While virtually every other family member perished, Vladek and his wife survived. Then, in 1968, Anja committed suicide. Art was living at home at the time, having been released from a state hospital three months earlier. The suicide is commemorated with shrieking intensity in a four-page strip, "Prisoner on the Hell Planet" (1973), which evokes the artist's imbalanced mind as he speaks from his mental prison: "Well, Mom, if you're listening . . . Congratulations! . . . You've committed the perfect crime. . . . You put me here . . . shorted all my circuits. . . . You murdered me, Mommy, and you left me here to take the rap!!!" Vladek died of heart failure in 1982, four years before the publication of *Maus I*.

Michael Greenberg, a New Yorker who used to work for the *Forward* and now writes a fortnightly column in the *Times Literary Supplement*, says that "a lot of the impact of the *Maus* books came from the fact that Spiegelman didn't sentimentalize the survivor. Like Isaac Bashevis Singer, he showed how destroyed and desperate their post-Holocaust lives could be. There was this sacred, hushed, horrified feeling among Jews toward Holocaust survivors when I was growing up. We were supposed to revere them—they were martyrs of anti-Semitism—but in reality they were often ruined, angry, depressed, impatient people whom you could never figure out." The children of survivors, Greenberg adds, "often had a mordancy that the rest of us didn't have. They had this special knowledge about suffering. And they seemed to resent it. In some cases, there was a need to do something extreme in response to it all. I sense something of that quality in Spiegelman." Bryan Cheyette, the author of *Modernity, Culture, and "the Jew"* (1998), adds: "What does this word 'survivor' mean? What has Vladek survived? He's picking up wire in the street and leaving the gas running all the time to save on matches. At some level, he hasn't survived at all." Cheyette teaches a course in Holocaust literature at Southampton University. "*Maus* has always been a part of the course. I brought it in straight away when the first volume came out in 1986. It very quickly became a canonical text." Students are often "shocked and surprised" at being asked to read a comic book, he says, "but they soon come 'round to seeing the complexity of the work. *Maus* operates on different levels. For example, it introduces the idea of the 'second generation,' that the Holocaust isn't something that's buried in the past but that it flows through the generations."

The use of the first-person narrator in comics is a method Spiegelman popularized, though he credits its development to a fellow cartoonist, Justin Green. "I'm surprised it didn't take off earlier," says Spiegelman, "because comics have that quality of personal storytelling. In a sense it's like an overly developed handwriting. So it seems a natural thing to start using the word 'I' and continue from there." He has been drawing since an early age. At fifteen, he started working for his local paper in Rego Park, New York, "and getting paid for it, so I became a sort of pro. But I really found my own voice as a cartoonist beginning in about 1971, and the first important piece of work was the three-page version of *Maus,* which appeared in an anthology called *Funny Animals.* At that point, autobiographical stories became part of the mix for me."

Spiegelman went to Harpur College (now the State University of New York at Binghamton) to study art. "They told me I would have to take a philosophy foundation course, so then I decided to become a philosophy major to try to figure out why they wouldn't let me be an art major. And shortly thereafter I dropped out of school altogether." (His old university later granted him an honorary doctorate.) In 1968, after "taking LSD as casually as some of my contemporaries now drop antacids," he "snapped" and was stretchered into a padded cell. For many years afterward, Spiegelman worked for the Topps gum company, designing novelty cards and sweet packets, including products familiar to Americans such as Garbage Candy and Wacky Packages.

Spiegelman's drawings are evocative, but they are seldom elaborate. They lack the frenzied inventiveness of some of his contemporaries in the underground comics movement, such as Crumb, inventor of Mr. Natural, Honeybunch Kaminski ("Jailbait of the Month"), and scores of other energetic creations. He describes his "signature way of drawing" as "really a result of my deficiencies." It is partly modesty, but Spiegelman suffers from amblyopia, or lazy eye, "which means that I don't have binocular vision, and have difficulty seeing in three dimensions. This might have been part of what made me a cartoonist rather than a baseball player. I was rotten at sports, but I found that if I could draw good caricatures of the teachers I wouldn't be doomed to be the butt of everybody's scorn." The condition might help to explain the thickset nature of many Spiegelman figures, and their broad-stroked execution. According to Bell, "Art's drawing always impressed me because it was so simple, but I realized it takes a huge amount of work to achieve that simplicity. Some people think it's crude, but Art has developed a style and he can make it do exactly what he wants it to do." Some of Spiegelman's pages are bound together with visual motifs that are not always perceptible on first viewing. One example, which he demonstrates with a copy of *Maus II* open before him, occurs early on in the book. It has a large panel of the artist perched at his desk on top of a pile of emaciated bodies, reflecting on the success of the earlier installment: "At least 15 foreign editions are coming out. I've gotten at least four serious offers to turn the book into a movie." The artist's pride is undermined by a barely visible swastika which, as he points out, "is holding the page together." To Cheyette, this element of *Maus*'s storyline suggests that Spiegelman is "very aware of the commodification of the Holocaust."

Spiegelman claims that each speech balloon in *Maus* was rewritten about forty times "in order to condense it," and he is apt to discuss his work in the manner of a writer. "It's certainly true that I don't draw as my first response. I don't reach for my pen to doodle. To express myself visually, it's a lot of work, because I don't have the feeling in the wrist of total confidence that lets you move forward. It's easier for me to write than to draw, I suppose. Comics are an art of compression. You allow your thoughts to decant, until they achieve their maximum density." An obvious point of comparison for *Maus*, in which the Nazis are cats, the Poles pigs, and the Americans rather genial dogs, is George Orwell's *Animal Farm*. A critic in the *New Republic* compared Spiegelman to "the young Philip Roth" in his ability "to make the Jewish speech of several generations sound fresh and unusually convincing." In 1994, he again took a literary theme when he produced an edition of Joseph Moncure March's epic poem of the prohibition era, *The Wild Party*, with one hundred illustrations. Bell says: "One of the reasons I'm such an admirer of *Maus* is because it's a great piece of writing. 'Graphic novel' is too paltry a term. But I still want to think of him as a cartoonist." Not everyone falls under Spiegelman's spell. In a profile in the *Village Voice* published in 1999, Ted Rall, a cartoonist and graphic novelist, attacked Spiegelman as New York's "undisputed cartoon tsar." The Pulitzer Prize–winning author, Rall wrote, "is The Man: He's managed to triangulate seemingly disparate circles of Manhattan's media elite to gain the power to define cartooning in this town. If you're a cartoonist, he can make or break your sorry ass." Rall also wondered whether he was essentially "a guy with one great book in him."

Spiegelman's methods have done much to bring comics to the attention of an audience that would not normally read them. As he sees it, he is only helping to restore the status of comics to what it was in the 1930s and 40s, when they "tended to appeal to an older audience of GIs and other adults." In 1954, an influential American psychiatrist, Frederic Wertham, published a book called *Seduction of the Innocent,* in which he claimed comics were a major cause of juvenile delinquency. Out of this came the Comics Code Authority, supposedly self-regulating but in effect a form of suppression, since distributors and retail outlets would not handle comics suspected of breaching the code. The result was the domination of the genre by what Spiegelman calls "lobotomized super heroes," frequently engaged in extreme violence while defending America from enemies such as "the followers of Mahomet" (*Arak, Son of Thunder,* 1982) and other exotics. According to Spiegelman, the code practically killed off the "great tradition" of comics, just as the persecution of Hollywood actors and directors by Senator Joseph McCarthy in the same decade wounded the film industry. "There were some very exciting things happening at that time, and some great artists," he says, citing Jack Cole, the inventor of Plastic Man in the 1940s and early 50s. Spiegelman has compiled a book of Cole's comics, with an introductory essay. He is enthusiastic about the period between the first Superman comic in 1939 and the establishment of the Comics Code Authority in 1954, which he refers to as the golden age. "Comics that were very popular during the Korean War were *Frontline Combat* and *Two-Fisted Tales,* edited by Harvey Kurtzman, the same guy that did *MAD*. Those can only be described as, at the very least, humanistic comics—or as antiwar war comics." In the 1940s, Cole was producing hard-boiled pulp fiction comic strips, such as "Murder, Morphine and Me," about a crowd of Los Angeles junkies and hustlers. "The industry was essentially stopped dead in its tracks. It had to rise from its own ashes, and it didn't do so until the underground comics movement of the 60s, led by Crumb, Gilbert Shelton of The Furry Freak Brothers, and so on."

The specter of censorship hovered over Spiegelman's life at the *New Yorker*. In an interview printed in *Corriera della Sera* in February 2003, he was quoted as saying that "the censorship of my work began as soon as I set foot in the magazine, long before September 11." Spiegelman claims not to remember having spoken those exact words, but he acknowledges that "the compromise and self-censorship necessary to play well with others settled in the minute I started working there." He intends to publish a visual memoir of his ten years at the *New Yorker*, "with all the different covers and images I did. It's basically a history of the wrestling matches, of what it means to try to graft an underground cartoonist's sensibility on to the DNA of the *New Yorker*. God bless 'em, they tried. And God bless me, I tried. I guess I got spoiled at an early age. I got used to publishing myself without editorial interference."

Spiegelman was brought on to the staff of the *New Yorker* by Tina Brown, and he raised hackles immediately. In 1993 he caused a furor with a cover drawing that showed an African American woman locked in a kiss with a Hasidic Jew. "People were shocked and upset by it," says Greenberg. "It was the St. Valentine's day issue and Spiegelman was making his statement about the Crown Heights riots and all the depressing shrillness that these powerless groups unleash on one another. I think of him as the political Crumb." Koren recalls that, among certain other artists at the magazine, "there was general lamentation and tearing of hair at that cover. You could look on it as very courageous. You could look at it and say, so what? What are we talking about? The complexity of race relations?"

Spiegelman says he would have been glad to have his *No Towers* work published in the *New Yorker*, "had the *New Yorker* been glad to have it. But

I don't think my tone was appropriate. It was so obvious it wasn't going to be comfortable there. The *New Yorker* sees everything through a certain script, and it has a certain tone to it, but that tone wasn't the one I was striking with my shrill, sky-is-falling voice, cracking at every moment. I say this with no rancor toward the *New Yorker*—it's a wonderful magazine and if I take the right meds I might go back." When the war in Iraq began in 2003 and the editor of the *New Yorker*, David Remnick, published "a reluctant hawk's endorsement" of the invasion, "I told him: 'Gee, I'm sorry I left when I did, because I could have left in protest now.'"

Spiegelman's wife, Françoise Mouly, who is French, joined the *New Yorker* at the same time he did and continues to be the editor in charge of cover art. "Because of that Bill-and-Hillary-Clintonish perception of us, there were difficulties from the beginning." Spiegelman and Mouly have published and edited various cartoon magazines, the best known of which is *Raw*. When they started *Raw*, in 1980, he had been drawing for publications such as *Playboy* and the *New York Times*, as well as working for Topps, and at first was pessimistic about a reentry into the underground scene, which, with its emphasis on mere taboo-breaking—for example, Crumb's story, "The Family That Lays Together Stays Together"—seemed to him "even more bankrupt" than the milieu in which he was employed. But *Raw* proved to be a success, introducing a "fine-art slant" to the comic strip, as Dez Skinn, the author of *Comix: The Underground Revolution* (2004), puts it. "*Raw*'s publishing schedule was erratic, to say the least, with only eight issues published between 1980 and 1986, but what it lacked in quantity it made up for in quality. It launched the careers of dozens of cartoonists and artists, from Charles Burns to Gary Panter." Koren says Spiegelman "has been very generous to other people who are doing the same sort of thing as he does. He has been a helpful mentor to a lot of younger artists, such as Chris Ware, the guy who did *Jimmy Corrigan, The Smartest Kid on Earth*. Selections from *Raw* were subsequently published in the United States as Penguin paperbacks. The Spiegelmans later established *Little Lit*, described as *Raw Junior*. Spiegelman quips: "We were trying to show that comics aren't just for grown-ups." The couple have two children: Nadja, seventeen, who is featured in *No Towers*, trying to talk sense into her freaking-out father, and Dashiell, twelve, who has also been incorporated into comic strips.

In Spiegelman's SoHo studio, described by the *New York Times* as "also a kind of haphazard museum of comic-strip history," he works on a computer for some projects and on paper for others. Beside his old-fashioned drafting table, on which he sketches by hand, is another desk with "all the electronic toys." Sometimes, he draws straight on to the computer, using a Wacom Tablet, a digital graphics pad, "which I find a very great pleasure. It enables you to try things out, make some part of the picture bigger, smaller, yellow, red, or whatever. Then I'll spit that out of the printer, bring it over to the table, put a sheet over it and continue drawing by hand, and then scan that in, and change it again. There are some panels of *In the Shadow of No Towers* that never saw a piece of paper, and some that only saw a computer at the last minute when I scanned them in." He laments, however, that the computer "deprives me of the pleasure of an original."

The slow progress of *In the Shadow of No Towers* is characteristic. The original three-page version of *Maus*, which Spiegelman refers to frequently, saw the light of day in 1973, but *Maus II*, subtitled "And Here My Troubles Began," would not be published for almost another twenty years. "I'm never really satisfied with what I've done. It's not a matter of how long does it take to make that many lines on a piece of paper. It's a thought structure. And comics, at least as I understand them, are very condensed thought structures. It has maybe more to do with poetry than it has to do with narrative prose." With *Maus*, he had "the self-created deadline of chapters in *Raw* magazine, but I was working on all the other contents too, and there would come a certain point when everything else was finished except my damn chapter. As for *In the Shadow of No Towers*, when I did the first few of those plates, I really did believe that I wouldn't live to see them published. Now I feel that the world may be ending, but it's ending slower than I thought."

EIGHT

Listening in the Dark

A PROFILE OF WILLIAM STYRON

"I suppose some of us are cursed with a dark view of life," says William Styron. Tragedy has given him almost all his subject matter, and melancholia has provided the bookends to his career. Styron's first novel, *Lie Down in Darkness*, published in 1951, when the author was twenty-six, centers on the suicide of a young woman in America's Deep South and relates the subsequent damage to those close to her. Almost forty years later, he revisited the territory (and the title) when he wrote *Darkness Visible*, about his four-year clinical depression in the mid-1980s, which he refers to as his "shutdown" and which almost led to his suicide. His best-known work is *Sophie's Choice*, the story of an unhinged Holocaust survivor forced into making a damnable "choice" between her two children while in Auschwitz, which was subsequently turned into an opera by Nicholas Maw for the Royal Opera House in London.

Styron's life appears to have been unusually sunny: successful career, happy marriage, children, prominence in a gilded East Coast society, and wealth. He was born in Newport News, Virginia, a strictly segregated town, into a family he describes with an Anglo-Saxon alertness to social nuance as "semi-upper-middle class." His father was an engineer in the shipyards that line the James River, where many of the workers were black and others had come from Scotland, "straight from the shipyards of the River Clyde." The area is known as "the Tidewater," which, in a small way, he has made into his own version of William Faulkner's Yoknapatawpha County—the province that contains all human life. The clammy atmosphere of the Tidewater pervades *Lie Down in Darkness;* Stingo, the narrator of *Sophie's Choice,* is a Tidewater product, and his background in the former slaveholding territories is used by the novelist and by Stingo himself (they are, to an extent, one and the same) as a counternarrative to the story of Sophie's experience in the concentration camp. Styron's most recent book is a collection of tales called *A Tidewater Morning.*

Styron's literary output is small by comparison with contemporaries of comparable reputation. Even before his 1980s breakdown, he suffered from a "milder depression," which, he admits, "has sapped my creative juices during most of my life." For more than thirty years, on and off, he has been writing a novel set during the Korean War called *The Way of the Warrior.* Styron clings to the hope that it might yet be completed but reacts with a noncommittal smile to the suggestion that the current mood of belligerence could give the work a boost. The expression "the way of the warrior" is a literal translation of Bushido, the samurai code, which stresses unquestioning loyalty and values military honor above life.

Styron's loyalty to the White House is beset by questions, and his concept of honor does not embrace "regime change" in the Middle East. He takes the view that hostility against Saddam Hussein is based more on a desire for oil than for democratic values. Styron once stated that "the concept of tragedy is related to the concept of a nation. The Greeks thought of tragedy as a necessary function in the enactment of cultural events." He cited D. H. Lawrence, who said that what the United States needed to attain maturity was "a death happening." So was September 11 America's "death happening"? "Yes, I think it was the fulfillment of Lawrence's prophecy. America had never had a death happening, and this had led to Americans lacking the tragic sense of life. America has never had a cataclysmic happening. I've been reading about the London Blitz—that type of experience is something Americans are entirely unacquainted with. Virtually every other country you can think of has undergone that sort of experience, except the United States, until September 11. There is this cheery Christian optimism that permeates our society, and part of that emerges from our unacquaintance with catastrophe."

Like other novelists born in the 1920s, almost all of whom came under the influence of Hemingway, Styron took warfare as a given subject. He has already written a war book, *The Long March,* a novella published half a century ago. The story turns on the order made to a battalion of marines to undertake a pointless, grueling thirty-six-mile march from one post to another, while a group of fellow soldiers lies dead, killed in an accidental explosion. The book expresses Styron's dislike of the military experience and must originally have appeared as a reproof to more bullish colleagues such as Norman Mailer and James Jones, who, while exposing the brutality of battle, did so in such a way as to aggrandize it. "None of that Hemingway crap for me," says the hero of *The Long March,* Captain Mannix, with whom Styron has identified himself. Like Hemingway, however, he has remained preoccupied by the imaginative experience of war, and the possibility of its literary expression.

The underlying cause of his "shutdown," he came belatedly to understand, was the death of his mother, Pauline, when he was fourteen. Unlike other writers whose work has been dominated by a similar catastrophe, Styron registered the shock mainly at a subliminal level. "Grief was tightly restrained at that time among members of his social class," says James L. West, who published a biography of Styron in 1998. "As an adult, he couldn't remember much about his reaction to it." Styron says: "Only over the years has it revealed itself as a wound from which I never fully recovered. At the time, I was rather amazed by the coolness with which I accepted it. It bothered me that I could not weep. I could not mourn. This is what caused my later depression, I'm sure. I can see that it was there all along."

The success of *Darkness Visible* brought a bitter consolation, in that it kept Styron's name before the reading public. "His star has faded among critics certainly, yet he remains as famous as ever," says Morris Dickstein, author of a recent study of postwar American fiction, *Leopards in the Temple.* "Some writers get more mileage out of not publishing than others do from being productive. Updike, for one, has taken criticism recently for churning out weaker novels. The books by Styron that get mentioned are nearly always *Sophie's Choice,* because of the movie and the Holocaust subject, and *Darkness Visible,* because that condition bedevils so many people and he was courageous to be up front with it."

In 1952, on a trip to Europe when *Lie Down in Darkness* won the Prix de Rome, Styron met a young department store heiress from Baltimore, Rose Burgunder, with whom he celebrated fifty years of marriage in the spring of 2003. They have three daughters and a son and have lived in the same house, with accompanying acreage, in Roxbury, Connecticut, through most of their married life, with a summer retreat on Martha's Vineyard. Styron is a big man, with an imposing frame and a pleasant face on which the years of depression have left their traces. He walks a little uncertainly, even watchfully. "I had another attack about two years ago, and it mutated into a physical decline," he explains. "I lost about forty pounds. But now I feel safe and sound."

Styron's debut coincided with the flowering of literary talent in and around Greenwich Village in the years after the Second World War. It gives a boost to any writer's career to be part of a group, and Styron had some publicity-conscious people on his team. The late Alfred Kazin, who charted this generation's progress, once referred to the phenomenon of the "super egotist" in modern American letters. "Styron, Mailer and Baldwin fit that category," Kazin wrote. Styron and Mailer had a well-publicized quarrel, which began in the 1950s, over some remarks Styron allegedly made about Mailer's wife's indulgence in lesbianism. Mailer challenged him to a fight "in which I expect to stomp out of you a fat amount of your yellow and treacherous shit." Styron chose not to reply, and the two did not speak for twenty-five years.

While Mailer's large enthusiasms were fueled by the energy of New York City, Styron preferred to remain in the countryside, spending the time away from his desk, walking his dog in the woods (which he owns) or socializing locally. "He is extremely solitary," says West. "His days are strictly patterned. He needs that methodical quality to concentrate on the writing." Styron says that he works very deliberately, needing to get each small section right before moving on, but experiencing occasional bursts of fluency. Parts of some books, such as the final section of *Sophie's Choice*, were written practically without revision.

Unlike Mailer, Vidal, and other contemporaries, he has not been distracted by involvement in politics or tempted by the instant publication offered by journalism. *Lie Down in Darkness* was not just his first novel but practically his first appearance in print. Nine years elapsed before a second book, *Set This House on Fire,* appeared. Styron's mentor, to whom he has frequently paid tribute, was Hiram Haydn, both a publisher and a teacher at the New School for Social Research in New York, which Styron attended in the late 1940s. Under Haydn's guiding hand, *Lie Down* came out and reached the best-seller list (the same list, Styron relates, still proud, on which sat *The Catcher in the Rye* and *From Here to Eternity*). The immediate comparisons were with William Faulkner, the unavoidable genius of Southern writing. The final part of *Lie Down* is given over to a soliloquy spoken by Peyton, whom the reader knows to have committed suicide, a similar device to one used by Faulkner in *The Sound and the Fury.* Malcolm Cowley wrote in the *New Republic,* however, that "the example of Faulkner seems to have had a liberating effect on Styron's imagination."

"The success made him financially solvent," says West, "and he was always successful from then on. He has been uncompromising in his reach and ambition. He has always wanted to have a big theme, and he has always set himself a technical problem, to do with point of view." Styron says of his early success that it was "the perfect sort: good enough to encourage me, but not so great as to distract me from my next book." Apart from a brief spell as an office boy at the publishing firm of McGraw-Hill, from which he was sacked, Styron has never had another job besides writing. Asked if he ever feels the need to "get out of the house" in those long stretches between books, he answers simply: "No."

Styron's follow-up novel, *Set This House on Fire,* was not welcomed by critics in the United States, but it brought him to the attention of a French readership, which has cherished his writings ever since. "The French regard him as in some ways the successor to Faulkner," says Dickstein. François Mitterrand, who later made Styron a Commander of the Legion of Honor, invited Styron to his inauguration. "He actually placed me at his right hand at the banquet table. He also told me that during these days, which represented the apex of his political career, he had spent all his free time immersed in *Le Choix de Sophie,* which had just come out in France. I still remember what he said: 'J'ai plongé'—'I plunged'—into this novel."

The French, and Europe in general, he feels, have been "very receptive" to his work. This has not forestalled a certain degree of anglophobia. "It is always a matter of extreme indifference to me if I am read in England," Styron once stated in a letter to Tom Maschler, his editor at Jonathan Cape, when critical reaction seemed to him unduly harsh. Reminded of that now, following the great fuss about the Royal Opera production of *Sophie's Choice,* he says, a touch sheepishly, that time has mitigated his anger. "But I do feel more at ease in France." Styron was one of the group of young Americans who founded the *Paris Review* in 1953—the others include George Plimpton and Peter Matthiessen—one of the few writers to have been interviewed by that magazine, in its "Art of Fiction" series, on two separate occasions.

The fury in Styron's letter to Maschler in 1968 was triggered by the British publication of his third novel, *The Confessions of Nat Turner,* the story of what the author called "the only effective, sustained revolt in the annals of American Negro slavery." It was Styron's most audacious work, but the real reason for his sensitivity to his British critics surely lay in his shocking experience at home. The novel is a grand imaginative edifice built on a brief pamphlet containing the confessions of the real Nat Turner, who in Virginia in 1831 led a two-day massacre of about sixty whites—slave owners and their families, including his own master. Some blacks regard Nat Turner as a freedom fighter, while to those whites who have heard of him he is more a bloodthirsty terrorist. Turner personally carried out only one murder, of a woman named Margaret Whitehead. Styron, who wrote the book in the first-person voice of the slave, made Margaret the object of Nat's desire.

Styron embarked on the project in the belief that a novel about black history by a white writer would "help effect some kind of reconciliation." His ancestors had owned wide acres in North Carolina, and slaves to work them. His paternal grandmother had lived long enough to tell him the story of two little girls, Drusilla and Lucinda, aged about twelve, like herself, whom she had "owned" in the years before the Civil War. "When the Yankees came, they took them away, and my grandmother never found out what happened to them. She still talked about it with passion. It was like the loss of two sisters. She loved them."

In retrospect, *The Confessions of Nat Turner* has the feeling of something inevitable and commendable. The state of race relations, changing rapidly throughout the 1960s, was one of the most urgent topics of the era, yet white writers have, by and large, neglected the subject, with the result that the black presence in American fiction is shadowy at best. Not all British critics came down hard on Styron's effort. Writing in the London *Evening Standard*, Richard Lister welcomed the book in the spirit in which it was offered: "Here is a novel which digs deep into the roots of one of the worst of our present discontents. Read it, and you will understand as never before the howling resentment every Negro must feel deep in his heart. And . . . all of us, the English no less than the Americans, were guilty of this appalling crime against humanity." In the United States, *Newsweek* described *Nat Turner* as "an act of revelation to a whole society," and the novel won a Pulitzer Prize. James Baldwin, who had been a friend for many years, and who lived briefly with the Styrons at their Roxbury home during the composition of the book, said: "He has begun the common history—ours."

The appearance of the novel coincided with the heyday of Black Power, however, and a decline in Baldwin's own standing among black intellectuals. Within a year, a unique protest against Styron's novel had been organized, with the publication of *William Styron's Nat Turner: Ten Black Writers Respond.* It contained essays with titles such as "You've Taken My Nat and Gone" and "Our Nat Turner and William Styron's Creation." The tone is set by the novelist John Oliver Killens ("The Confessions of Willie Styron"), who wrote that Styron "is in desperate need of emancipation from his slavemaster's psychology." Another contributor to the book was John A. Williams, author of *The Man Who Cried I Am.* In his essay "The Manipulation of History and Fact," he wrote: "I cannot say that Styron's book was honest. I have doubts that even in intent it was honest." Williams declines to withdraw the charge thirty-five years on. "I'm still convinced by what I wrote then," he says. "I would assume it was a kind of a native thing, him being a Southerner. Styron comes out of that seething period of change in American race relations, desegregation in the South, and there's bound to be some baggage you can't get rid of."

Younger African-American writers today are more willing to applaud Styron's attempt to cross the divide. "I suspect that *Nat Turner* may be Styron's best novel," says Michael Anderson, a critic and editor at the *New York Times Book Review*. "The brouhaha over it was disgraceful. Baldwin had one of his finest moments defending him. This country would have been better off if more of its novelists had explored interracial territory. After all, that is what a novelist does." Anderson adds: "Identity politics is stupid enough in politics. In the arts, it is execrable." Darryl Pinckney, who has himself explored biracial subject matter in his novel *High Cotton,* is in broad agreement, though with reservations: "Styron did do something rather silly and gratuitous with his Turner: that it had to be because of a white woman. Something psychological. The distressing thing is that a white writer did not think the wish to be free a strong enough motive in itself for a character. Even so, Baldwin was right to defend Styron's right to the subject."

Styron still finds it extraordinary that in his lifetime he has been in touch with slavery. He says that his grandmother's story about the two slave girls had a "tremendous effect" on him, and it is evident that it did, for the themes it embraces—love, war, the ambiguities of justice and injustice, the revolt against tyranny—are the themes that have dominated his fiction. "I was disappointed. In fact, I was outraged," he says now of the fuss over *The Confessions of Nat Turner.* "It was a low-grade attack. Nowhere in these essays was there even a glimmer of recognition that I might have portrayed slavery as the horror that it was. . . . It was very painful to be attacked, in the most odious terms, by people who in many cases I knew had not read the book." Styron says that it is still "very hard to write or even speak about race in this society. Even when we speak the truth about history, we are branded as racists. The whole thing soured me in being a friend of black people . . . and I hate to say that." He also insists that the "ten black writers" who claimed Nat Turner as a folk hero had "never heard of Nat Turner before I wrote that novel." This suggestion is laughed off by John A. Williams. "I most certainly had heard of Nat Turner. It's silly of Bill to make that kind of remark. A lot of the people in that collection of responses to his novel were well set up to talk about Nat."

Styron retreated into his customary gestation period, emerging in 1979 with *Sophie's Choice*. "I think there is a natural historical link between the two novels. The link is slavery." Slavery is almost as much the dominant theme of *Sophie's Choice* as the Final Solution is. "It is important to regard Auschwitz as the recrudescence of slavery, the first in Western civilization since the American Civil war," Styron says. He has always emphasized that non-Jews suffered and died in great numbers in the Holocaust—Sophie is a Polish Catholic with an anti-Semitic father—believing that "this has never been acknowledged as much as it should have been."

Dickstein feels that since the novel "gives full play to Styron's ambivalence toward Jews, he might have realized he couldn't do a Jewish heroine." He enlarges the point to touch on what he sees as Styron's own insecurity: "In the very first paragraph, Stingo finds himself plunked down in a strange and exotic Jewish city, New York. He befriends a mad Jewish intellectual who tells him that the star of Southern writing has set and the hot young Jews, typified by Bellow, are about to take over. Stingo's resentment at this—the idea that his train has arrived too late, that his huge literary ambitions may be for naught—is one of the authentic emotions behind the book." Sophie's case, Dickstein believes, "has enabled readers to see the Holocaust as a universal story, not strictly a Jewish one. And this would-be correction is grounded in Stingo's initial resentment and ambivalence."

Styron had nothing to do with the opera *Sophie's Choice*, leaving the libretto to the composer, Nicholas Maw. However, classical music has been a great source of consolation to him over the years. His mother studied singing in Vienna and accompanied herself on the piano. "I don't think I would have been able to write a single word had it not been for music as a force in my life," he once said. The other companion to his literary endeavor was alcohol, or as he puts it, "hard liquor." Until the mid-1980s he drank what he describes straightforwardly as "a lot." Alcohol was "a friend whose ministrations I sought daily," he wrote in *Darkness Visible*, "sought also, I see now, as a means to calm the anxiety and incipient dread that I had hidden away for so long somewhere in the dungeons of my spirit." Quite suddenly, his body refused to tolerate any more. "When I drank I felt horrible." His "comforting friend" had abandoned him. Styron traces the onset of his depression to this abandonment. It was during a trip to Paris in 1985 that he first sensed his mind losing its grip. His book on the subject provides a moving account of his decline, one which, with its clear discussion of causes and cures, is intended to be helpful to others. At the nadir of his illness, his daughter Polly visited him in his bedroom at dawn. Later, in her journal, she wrote: "When I went upstairs to his room he was lying there, with his long grey hair all tangled and wild. I took his hand, which was trembling. 'I'm a goner, darling,' he said, first thing. His eyes had a startled look, and he seemed to be not quite there. His cool, trembling hands kept fumbling over mine. 'The agony's too great now, darling.'" The next day he was admitted to hospital, and he gradually got better.

Styron is prepared to admit that he might have done all he can do in the novel form. "He wants to do something different from what Mailer or James Jones did," his biographer James West says of *The Way of the Warrior*. "He has to have in mind the central metaphor of a novel before he can proceed with it, and he hasn't yet been able to bring that into focus for the war novel."

PART II

Through the Grapevine

William Styron was a good friend to James Baldwin, and one of a small number of so-called white American writers to have taken on black-and-white life, black-and-white history—as Baldwin put it to Styron, "the common history—ours." In 1968, Styron received a unique "Keep out" notice, in the form of a book, *William Styron's Nat Turner: Ten Black Writers Respond,* an early warning of the division of literature into separate fiefdoms based on the modern construction of "identity"—mostly racial and sexual—that later became widespread. As Styron explained during the interview which led to the article in the foregoing pages, the experience disappointed and embittered him. It is difficult for the grandson of former slave owners to stand on his pride as "a friend to black people" without seeming to be mighty patronizing, but what Styron wanted to say, I think, was that he had accepted the challenge, had done the good deed— even allowing that goodness is subjective—only to be bullied and vilified for making the effort. Similar bullying, on a smaller scale, has made others cautious about establishing contact with African American writing. A lamentable effect of the hesitancy is neglect of one wing of American literature by the inhabitants of another (i.e., neglect of black by white); a second is uncritical adulation.

I myself have been told to keep out more than once—to my face—by people who might not have read a word of Baldwin, Wright, or Morrison but whose cultural identity was understood (not only by them) to validate their every utterance. This was the last area on which a traveler expected to find banning orders. Turf wars in the arena of art are obnoxious—and surely seem so to all but those who confine themselves to their own spiteful patch.

The attraction for me was eloquence generated by the heat of action. The experience of black writers in the United States, especially the generation that came of age before the civil rights era, gave the work they produced a special tension in the eyes of readers overseas, not unlike the tension emanating from the work of writers from the Soviet bloc. But these writers were not on the opposite side of the Iron Curtain—they were in living rooms decorated and supposedly sheltered by drapes of a style and design familiar to us. Their subject, at a remove, was our subject, too.

An aftertaste of bitter paradox lingers from the work of writers such as Baldwin, Wright, and others who followed: desiring to be released from their core subject—race—they inevitably recognize that the topic is their raison d'être as artists. Meanwhile, writers who stick to "blackness" as a source risk becoming imprisoned in a cage, the cage of "race," which, as Amiri Baraka of all people said to me, does not exist.

NINE I Heard It through the Grapevine

JAMES BALDWIN AND THE FBI

I

At the turn of 1962–63, James Baldwin was regarded as a writer with the power of healing. He spoke across chasms: male-female, father-son, straight-queer; most of all, Baldwin seemed capable of locating the hurt good white Americans felt at being separated, by crimes too ancient and convoluted to contemplate, from their black countrymen—neighbors, school friends, wet nurses, lovers, even children. The passage most often quoted from Baldwin's work is the one which occurs near the end of "Down at the Cross," the essay which forms the larger part of *The Fire Next Time*. It spread over eighty-five pages of the *New Yorker* in November 1962: "If we—and now I mean the relatively conscious whites and the relatively conscious blacks, who must, like lovers, insist on, or create, the consciousness of the others—do not falter in our duty now, we may be able, handful that we are, to end the racial nightmare and achieve our country." And, he added, "change the history of the world." The rhetorical flourish was unnecessary, though it was becoming a common feature of his style, as the urgency of his message increased. "Change" was Baldwin's text. He grew up in Harlem tenements in the 1920s and 30s literally praying for change, and he embraced it in the storefront churches which still dot uptown New York streets today. At the age of fourteen, Baldwin became a Young Minister in the Baptist church, urging Harlem denizens to change their ways. *The Fire Next Time* was his secular sermon, addressed mainly to whites, but its moral ardor was equal to that of the boy preacher: "Change, or your sin will find you out." Baldwin had long since lost his Christian faith, but not his conviction that the soul hovered dangerously between redemption and damnation, depending on a mere human action to determine its fate.

The Fire Next Time was published as a book in January 1963. By June, it had entered a tenth printing. Everything changed for Baldwin that year. Two other books he had written—a novel, *Another Country,* and a collection of essays, *Nobody Knows My Name*—were already best sellers. In May, *Time* magazine paid tribute to his influence by putting his face on the cover, which led in turn to a personal invitation from the attorney general, Robert Kennedy, to hold a meeting to address the widening chaos in the South. Bombs were exploding in black leaders' houses, churches were being set on fire, civil rights workers and all who followed them walked in constant fear for their lives. When Martin Luther King led the March on Washington in August, Baldwin fell in behind the leader, expecting to be among the key speakers (we will get to the reasons why he was not). A writer known for his delicate examinations of private themes had suddenly become a public figure, or to use the term he disliked so much, a "spokesman."

Something else happened to Baldwin that year. He lost his faith for a second time, a humanist faith. The moment can be traced back to the meeting with Robert Kennedy, which took place in the attorney general's New York office on May 24. Baldwin brought along a troop of friends, colleagues, and show business personalities—Harry Belafonte, Lena Horne, and the playwright Lorraine Hansberry were among those present—and Jerome Smith, a young man from the Deep South who had been badly beaten during the Freedom Rides of 1961, the efforts to integrate Southern waiting rooms and lunch counters by traveling in buses from town to town. To Baldwin, Smith's broken bones gave him a greater authority than anyone else in the room. During the increasingly heated exchanges, Smith waved a finger in the attorney general's face and declared that he would never fight to defend his country, since his country had noticeably failed to defend him (in trying to use the same waiting

rooms as whites, the Freedom Riders were only acting within their con-
stitutional rights). According to eyewitness accounts, Kennedy recoiled
visibly at this. He was more shocked by it than by anything else said during the meeting. Baldwin was shocked, too, but for a different reason.

Smith's bleak comment, and that made to him by another young black
man at the same time, "I got no country, I got no flag," would chime in
Baldwin's mind a few days after the encounter with Kennedy, when he
announced to a reporter from the *New York Times* that "22 million black
people cannot be negotiated with any more." He added: "There is no possibility of a bargain whatsoever." It chimed again, some months later,
when he accused the Kennedy administration and the FBI of a "lack of
action" following the bombing of a church in Birmingham, Alabama, in
which four little black girls were killed. And again, when he told a rally
in Washington, D.C., that he knew of "many people, even members of
my own family, who would think nothing of picking up arms tomorrow."

These remarks and many others, more despairing than belligerent,
were copied down, typed up on headed notepaper, and logged in
Baldwin's new FBI file. A card marked "baldwin, james arthur, 1924– ,
negro, male . . ." had been filled out in 1960, after Baldwin signed a petition organized by the pro-Castro Fair Play for Cuba Committee. Now,
following the affront to Robert Kennedy, his status was to be upgraded.
Four days after the meeting, on May 28, Clyde Tolson, associate director
to J. Edgar Hoover, circulated a newspaper report of the meeting among
FBI colleagues at Washington headquarters, together with the query
"What do our files show about James Baldwin?" The following day, the
Crime Records division requested "a check of the New York indices for
any information [on Baldwin], particularly of a derogatory nature." The
summary was required "for dissemination to the Attorney General."
Although Baldwin continued to regard the attorney general as an ally,
Kennedy had ordered FBI reports on several of those who had humili-
ated him in his own office, and he authorized a wiretap to be installed on
the telephone of at least one, Clarence Jones, a lawyer who worked for
Martin Luther King.

A forty-five-page report on Baldwin was drawn up, the basis of a
dossier which would soon grow to over a thousand pages. The report

included details of Baldwin's education, military status, residences past and present, criminal record ("subject was arrested on September 3, 1954, on a charge of disorderly conduct"), publication history, bank records, and every other detail of his behavior and opinions that could be unearthed. His name was placed on the Security Index, the list of "dangerous individuals" who posed "a threat to national security," who would be rounded up first in a state of emergency. A link was made, via sinuous logic, to the Communist Party: "In 1961 he sponsored a news release from the Carl Braden Clemency Appeal Committee distributed by the Southern Conference Educational Fund." Braden had been "identified as CP member" and the fund was "the successor to the Southern Conference for Human Welfare cited as a Communist front by the House Committee on Un-American Activities." Two years later, Baldwin would quite likely have been unable to remember the "news release"—a petition bearing his signature, among many others—and almost certainly would never have heard of the defunct Southern Conference for Human Welfare, allegedly a "communist front." But from now on his card would always be marked communist, whereas, in fact, he had no formal affiliation to any political organization, not even among civil rights groups. In keeping with the spirit of Baldwin's sudden visibility in the news media, the FBI made no distinction between private and public affairs.

.   .   .

After Baldwin's death, in November 1987, I began to write a book about him. In the course of my research, I applied for access to his FBI file, under the United States Freedom of Information Act (FOIA). Baldwin often referred to his "friendly file," sometimes in my presence, and was certain that on more than one occasion his telephone had been bugged. Friends and relatives would allude to the same thing, and amid the natural outrage, you could sense the feeling of continuing importance it induced. Late in life, Baldwin's literary reputation had taken a drastic fall, and his public image shrank with it; but he retained the belief that he was being badgered by government agencies. The most recent persecutor was the Internal Revenue Service. Baldwin told me that he intended to arrange his tax affairs in the neatest possible order, "and then I'm going to sue them." I have the clearest mental picture of the fury in his face— an anger deeper than resentment at fiscal bullying could explain. "I got no country, I got no flag," the reproach that triggered an internal change in 1963, had become his own bitterly unwelcome banner.

In cases where the subject is no longer living, the procedure for requesting an FBI file is simple: "May 10, 1988. Dear Sir/Madam, I request access to the FBI file on James Baldwin, under the Freedom of Information Act." An acknowledgment that there existed "investigative files responsive to your request," together with a plea for patience, came back within two weeks. I was patient. Eighteen months later, all I had received on Baldwin was a few documents in which his name was mentioned in passing; whole paragraphs, even entire pages (except the words "james baldwin," peeping through the black veil), had been deleted according to "subsections of Title 5, United States Code, Section 552." Mostly, these "exemptions" concerned the protection of the privacy of informants, or of other people mentioned, including friends of the subject. Or else they refer to "national security." So wide-ranging were the exemptions that the agents responsible for reviewing the documents believed they were entitled to delete every item of information, together with its context, concerning even an unwitting informant, or any person who is not dead (or whose death has not come to the attention of the FBI) or who has not specifically waived the right to privacy. "National security," it hardly needs saying, is an elastic term.

On the advice of an experienced user of the Freedom of Information Act, I wrote to a lawyer in Washington, James Lesar, who, it was promised, could speed up the process of review. A friendly, overworked attorney in private practice who single-handedly puts to death the caricature of the avaricious American lawyer, Lesar advised that the only way to obtain substantial "disclosure"—a word he uses often—without a further long wait, was to file suit against the FBI. This sounded alarming to me, but it was action Lesar was used to taking, and so, after settling on a fixed fee, we duly went to court on the grounds that an author was being hindered in his pursuit of an honest living.

Soon afterward, a large box thumped onto my doorstep. It contained a thousand pages, including many duplications and useless copies of index cards, from the records that FBI headquarters in Washington, and field offices in New York, Los Angeles, and San Francisco, had compiled on Baldwin. Smaller batches of records came from the CIA and from army and air force intelligence services. The huge black squares of "exemptions" were everywhere; in places a form had been interleaved, stating that a number of pages had been withheld.

Many documents were accessible, however, even when they had not evaded the dead hand of the censor, enough for me to see that Baldwin's political engagement had been answered, in proportion, by secret and continuous surveillance, in New York, Hollywood, and the American South, in Istanbul, Rome, and elsewhere. Spies had gathered information from unwitting neighbors and relatives, either by telephone or in person. Among them were FBI agents "posing as a newspaper reporter," "posing as a publisher," "using the pretext of being a foreign auto sales representative," "posing as a college student," "on the pretext of being an American Express representative," and so on. Agents would attend any meeting at which Baldwin was advertised as a speaker, and the organization which had invited him would be scrutinized for links to the Communist Party. Afterward, a report would be written up of what had been seen or heard, and so a substantial "investigative" file on James Baldwin, a "person likely to pose a threat to the security of the United States," was compiled. I gleaned what I could from it and finished my book.

Lesar, however, has spent twenty years nipping at the heels of the investigative agencies in order to obtain greater disclosure. "I get personally incensed every time I see stuff being withheld, where it has not been adequately explained to me why. I recognized at the outset that it would be bad practice to go score a quick victory, declare victory, and hang it up. The agencies would take advantage of that situation. They had to know and understand that I was going to be there as long as possible." Lesar is a specialist on the assassination of John F. Kennedy in Dallas in 1963 and is president of the Assassination Archives and Research Center. We agreed that he would proceed with the case in order to attempt to extract more information about the surveillance of Baldwin, and so began *James Camp-*

bell, plaintiff v. U.S. Department of Justice, defendant, a nine-year legal slog, which came to a head on December 29, 1998, at the Court of Appeals in Washington, the second most powerful court in the United States, with what Lesar calls a resounding decision. Although the case bears my name, the victory is Lesar's. The Court of Appeals judges decided three to zero in the plaintiff's favor, giving us victory on almost every front. Judge Judith Rogers, who delivered the forty-five-point Opinion of the Court, issued a series of stern rebukes to the FBI, over its past conduct and its present manipulation of the Freedom of Information Act. After the sitting, Lesar overheard a bureau supervisor saying of Judge Rogers: "She trashed us." Baldwin would have been interested to know that and to learn that Lesar counts *Campbell* among the most important decisions in all his years of FOIA litigation.

.   .   .

My acquaintance with Baldwin began in the late 1970s, when he agreed to write an essay for the *New Edinburgh Review,* of which I was then the editor. I would say that I was friendly with him in a respectfully distant way—but it was impossible to be distant from Baldwin once a friendship had begun. I stayed as a guest at his house outside the village of St-Paul de Vence, near Nice, on several occasions, and I chaperoned him around London—with Baldwin, there was always the role of Man Friday to be filled—and later on he visited Edinburgh, where I interviewed him in front of a live audience at the Edinburgh Festival. I was proud of our working relationship, and he, sensing that I did not like to be counted among the hangers-on, would introduce me to others, with an avuncular wink, as "one of my editors."

The essay, which was ostensibly a review of a book about jazz, was called "Of the Sorrow Songs," echoing W. E. B. Du Bois's famous chapter on Negro folk song in *The Souls of Black Folk.* Baldwin improvised relentlessly in the course of the piece, dissecting his theme, then restoring it, in a tone entirely his own: "This music begins on the auction-block. Whoever is unable to face this . . . whoever pretends that the slave mother does not weep, until this hour, for her slaughtered son . . . can never pay the price for the *beat* which is the key to music, and the key to life." Many baleful changes had occurred since his appeal to the "relatively conscious" in *The Fire Next Time*. The reply, it seemed to him, was like the crack of a repeating gun: in June 1963, Medgar Evers of the National Association for the Advancement of Colored People was shot outside his home in Jackson, Mississippi; two years later, Malcolm X was killed in Harlem; then Martin Luther King in Memphis in 1968. A new generation of young radicals emerged, and some of them were killed too, in battles with the police or prison officers.

The middle and later years of the 1960s were not prolific ones for the writer. Between 1963 and 1973, Baldwin produced only one novel, *Tell Me How Long the Train's Been Gone*, a sprawling first-person tale, bedeviled by flashbacks and bearing a more ponderous racial burden than his previous work. To critics who asked if politics had edged out literature in his life, Baldwin would reply, with studied coolness, that he had been "trying to write between assassinations." In his "Open Letter to My Sister, Angela Davis," in 1970, he indicated where the bright hopes of the early part of the decade had led: the day had come "to render impassable with our bodies the corridor to the gas chamber. For, if they take you in the morning, they will be coming us that night." Another sermon for another time. When critics or journalists, or just well-meaning friends, asked, "Gas chamber?" Baldwin stared back and repeated: "Gas chamber."

The murder of King, in particular, froze his heart. In an interview conducted two years after the assassination, Baldwin was asked about current projects. He replied that he was writing "a long essay on the life and death of the civil rights movement." Taken aback, the interviewer asked: "It died?" "Yes," said Baldwin. "It died with Martin. . . . We've marched and petitioned for a decade, and now it's clear there's no point in marching or petitioning. And what happens I don't know, but when they killed Martin they killed that hope."

By the time I first arrived at the old farmhouse on a hillside just beneath St-Paul de Vence, he had written and published his essay on the movement, but it was an incomplete diary-style account (*No Name in the Street*, 1972), and the subject continued to preoccupy him. He was trying to get started on a "triple biography" of Medgar Evers, Malcolm X, and Martin Luther King, and he wore a watch with King's face on it, a portrait in cartoon colors of the martyr with head raised, mouth open, as if in midflow. King, though five years younger, was his mentor, and the watch strapped round Baldwin's wrist was a band of fidelity to King's crusade, which was, in essence, a biblical crusade: the deliverance from the land of bondage. Baldwin gave the impression of living every hour at the crook of optimism and despair. To spend a day in his company meant traversing his entire emotional territory. His mood determined the mood of every gathering at which he was present. Writing to his brother David in 1969, he characterized a self divided into three: a "mad-man," determined to change the world; a "fragile, gifted child"; and a "superbly paranoiac intelligence." All three were actively competing at all times.

My first sight of him was across the village square, on a Tuesday afternoon. At the conclusion of the long and sometimes comical sequence of telephone calls required to coax him into fulfilling his commission for the *New Edinburgh Review,* Baldwin had invited me to "drop by," as he put it, "if you ever happen to be down this way." He probably issued many such invitations, but I took him at his word. During a sojourn in Paris, I rang to say I was thinking of dropping by. He said: "I'd love that." I offered to call again before boarding the train for Nice, but the suggestion was brushed aside. "I look forward to meeting you," he said in the smoky baritone which bobbed in and out of French and American intonations.

In spite of all that, he forgot that I was coming. "Oh, baby," he said, when I rang from outside the station in Nice, "I wish you'd let me know." But it was said without annoyance, and when I crossed the square in St-Paul, where men were playing boules, he raised the shades above his eyes, took my hand, and said: "Are you him?" It is rare, Baldwin wrote about his first meeting with Martin Luther King in 1958, "that one *likes* a world-famous man—by the time they become world famous they rarely like themselves." Yet, he continued, in a phrase which I would apply to him, his hero was "immediately and tremendously winning, there is really no other word for it."

I stayed five days. Baldwin rose around noon. After his second coffee, he would move on to Johnnie Walker Black Label. The menu varied throughout the day, beer in the afternoon and wine with meals. At about one in the morning, he would cast a glance at the whisky bottle and say: "I'm going to have a last drink and then go downstairs to do some work." I would join him in that drink, and we would talk until four or five.

A moral force drove everything he said, even his witty, frequently self-effacing small talk. Every one of us was living on the Redeemer's account. "People pay for what they do, and they pay for it very simply— by the lives they lead." His huge, searching, vulnerable eyes shone their lights on every conversation. When his assistant, Bernard Hassell, a tough, likable New Yorker, complained about some righteous hip type, who had called on Brother Baldwin a month before and left with a fistful of money which would never be repaid, Baldwin simply shrugged. Only the miscreant could suffer, in that transaction. It was up to him to foresee the desert to which his actions would lead him.

The piece he wrote for the *New Edinburgh Review* came out in the syncopated "blue" style which had become his mode, replacing the lovely logical elegance of his work from the years spanning 1953 to 1962, a decade which produced three novels, *Go Tell It on the Mountain, Giovanni's Room,* and *Another Country,* and three books of essays, *Notes of a Native Son, Nobody Knows My Name,* and *The Fire Next Time;* work which led to Baldwin being crowned, in Lionel Trilling's phrase, "the monarch of the current literary jungle." The triple biography, though, would never get written. Nor would a novel, *No Papers for Mohammed,* for which he signed a contract in the early 1970s. Somewhere at the base of my esteem, I was aware that a trauma had occurred to separate the writer I admired so strongly that I continued to read his books over and over, and the writer sitting opposite me. Baldwin flashed brilliant remarks across the table, and had immense generosity and humor, but he was less and less inclined to think in a dialectical manner. "She is a victim, therefore she is my sister," he said of Angela Davis. As a young writer, he had possessed natural gifts perhaps unequalled among his contemporaries; he had superb control over rhythm, phrasing, the structure of an argument, and the poise proper to its resolution. But the years of harassment, culminating symbolically in the assassination of King, permanently affected his balance. "Since Martin's death . . . something has altered in me," he wrote in *No Name in the Street*, "something has gone away."

II

The decision of the court meant that the FBI had to go back and review all files relating to Baldwin again, to reprocess them in line with the judges' directions. "The record suggests that the FBI made an abstract attempt to identify possible public interests in disclosure and accorded these interests surprisingly little weight," said Judge Rogers, in what Lesar regards as one of the most censorious public scoldings administered to the FBI by a legal figure. "This attitude is troubling given the presumption of openness inherent in the Freedom of Information Act." The adequacy of the bureau's search for documents, she said, was insufficient. In the view of the court, the FBI had resorted to the pesky exemptions—specifically those governing National Security (Exemption 1) and Law Enforcement (Exemption 7)—too zealously and too frequently. The present administration was reminded of "the obvious historical value of documents describing the FBI's role [in the cold war and] in the civil rights movement." The privacy of individuals deserved consideration but ought to be balanced against historical interest in a case in which the documents date back more than thirty years. The three judges of the Court of Appeals concluded that the FBI had treated "the balancing process in the instant case as somewhat of an empty formality." The following gives a taste of the opinion (164 F 3d 20, DC Cir 1998):

> The Department [of Justice] has identified only two facts to establish that documents relating to James Baldwin were compiled for a law enforcement purpose. First, the FBI relies on a declaration from Special Agent Regina Supernau, in which she lists the names of the files containing withheld information. The relevant labels are: "Interstate Transportation of Obscene Material," "Security Matter—Communism," and "Internal Security." The fact that information is stored inside a folder with an official-sounding label is insufficient standing alone to uphold nondisclosure. . . .

Second, the Department relies on a statement in the declaration of Special Agent Debra Mack that "the FBI investigation of James Baldwin was predicated upon the fact that established security sources of the FBI had indicated that James Baldwin was associating with persons and organizations which were believed to be a threat to the security of the United States." . . . The FBI appears to maintain that once it can justify its investigation of a person, all documents related to that person are exempt from FOIA, even if the documents were collected for a different reason.

And so it continues, "issue after issue," as Lesar delightedly said to me. "The rulings are not the only measure of the significance of the *Campbell* decision," he added. "Its tone and attitude will be extremely helpful to a host of FOIA requesters." More than a year after the verdict, a new edition of Baldwin's file arrived on my doorstep, significantly augmented in comparison to the one I'd received almost ten years earlier. According to an enclosed letter from the chief, FOIA Section, John M. Kelso, it included "108 pages released for the first time and 625 pages now released in full." It was not crammed with sensational revelations, but it gave a more ample, detailed picture of the global surveillance to which Baldwin was subjected while attempting, as he would put it, to bear witness, or more simply, while exercising his right to freedom of speech.

.   .   .

The wiretap placed on the telephone of Clarence Jones, King's lawyer, after the meeting with Robert Kennedy, was to be the conduit for a great many conversations between Jones and others, including Baldwin, concerning the overall strategy of King's Southern Christian Leadership Conference (SCLC). No record has been released of a similar authorization for electronic surveillance of Baldwin, though many of his conversations were recorded via bugs on the telephones of others. He himself was certain that an attempt had been made to install a device, and he complained to journalists—and to the FBI—that three days after the Kennedy meeting two men had turned up at his apartment on East 18th

Street and tried to gain entry, only to be refused by the doorman. Hoover took swift action to deny this, in a letter to President Kennedy's special assistant, Kenneth O'Donnell: "It should be noted that an allegation has been made that Agents of the New York Office had attempted to enter Baldwin's apartment on May 27, 1963, and the further allegation has been made that persons attending the conference [with Robert Kennedy] had been interviewed by Agents following the conference. Both allegations are completely false. . . . Baldwin has not been harassed in any way by agents of this Bureau." The assistant attorney general, Burke Marshall, later admitted to a *New York Post* journalist, Fern Eckman, that the two men were FBI agents (though he denied that their purpose was to plant a bug). In any case, harassment by other means had begun. According to Natalie Robins, author of *Alien Ink: The FBI's War on Freedom of Expression* (1992), "For Hoover, those who were anti-FBI were as dangerous as those who were pro-Communist." Baldwin's name was already linked to communist-front organizations—which, in Hoover's mind, might be a left-leaning body such as the National Lawyers Guild—but now attention focused on his attacks on Hoover himself. After the bombing of the church in Birmingham, he told a journalist: "I blame Hoover." An article in the *Washington Post* ended with a quotation from another interview: "First of all . . . you've got to get rid of J. Edgar Hoover and the power that he wields. If you could get rid of [him] . . . there would be a great deal more hope." There followed many more assaults on the integrity of the director—Hoover was "not a lawgiver [nor] a particularly profound student of human nature"—and they all passed through FBI memos to be incorporated into Baldwin's Security Index file, as proof that he posed a threat to national security.

An example of how persistent the FBI could be in tracking down statements unfavorable to the director concerns the case of a television program made by the U.S. Information Agency (USIA) on August 28, 1963, the day of the March on Washington. Through the wiretap on Jones's phone, the FBI learned that Baldwin had made "remarks regarding the FBI and Mr. Hoover" while being filmed for the broadcast. "The substance of his remarks . . . were 'Part of the problem in the civil rights movement is J. Edgar Hoover.'"

This section of the program had been edited out before transmission. Still, Hoover wrote personally to the director of the Office of Security at the USIA, Paul McNichol, to inquire about the situation. McNichol dutifully replied (October 11, 1963) that "the portion of Mr. Baldwin's remarks which were removed contained attacks on you and Senator James Eastland." It was USIA policy, however, that "if an individual is attacked by name, some answer to the attack must be included." Since there was no answer, Baldwin's comments had been cut.

The bureau would not leave it there. The Domestic Intelligence division contacted McNichol and demanded a verbatim account of Baldwin's remarks—remarks which were never broadcast. On October 25, McNichol furnished a transcript: "It will be a matter of attacking, really, J. Edgar Hoover, and asking very rude questions such as why the FBI can find a junkie but cannot find a man who bombs the homes of Negro leaders in the Deep South. They still have not found anyone."

Concern over Baldwin's criticisms increased as it began to be suspected that he was engaged in writing about the bureau. In the letter to President Kennedy's assistant (June 6, 1963), Hoover said that "a confidential source, who has furnished reliable information in the past," had advised that Baldwin was preparing "a statement" on the FBI and that he intended to release it to coincide with King's prospectus for "political action this summer." Hoover did not reveal, though the Baldwin file does, that the "source" in this case was a wiretap on the telephone of Stanley Levison, one of King's most senior aides ("a confidential source" is frequently, but not always, code for a listening device). The eavesdroppers heard Clarence Jones tell Levison: "I have seen some statements on the FBI, but I have never seen one like this. He is going to nail them to the wall." Levison agreed: "It really will, because Baldwin is a name in the news." The FBI also learned that Baldwin had told Jones, his main link to the King camp, that the SCLC had a "blank check to do whatever they wanted" in his newsworthy name. Jones informed Levison proudly that he had "spent all day Sunday going into some detail" with Baldwin on a program of political action.

The FBI took a keen interest in Baldwin's putative "statement." Just by dwelling on it, they made it grow. Within a few weeks, it had swollen to become an "article," and by early in the new year it had sprouted into a full-length book. Another wiretap, this one on a civil rights foot soldier, revealed that Baldwin intended to use information given to him by Annell Ponder, a woman who, like Jerome Smith, had been badly beaten while taking part in the Freedom Rides in 1961. Ponder had been taken to jail and assaulted by a Negro prisoner at the direction of white policemen. The "source" (i.e., wiretap) conveyed Ponder's opinion that "anyone who tells you the FBI is really interested in Mississippi is full of junk."

Progress on the book continued—even without the participation of the author. It was mentioned in the *New York Herald Tribune* (July 14, 1964), and shortly afterward an FBI memo stated confidently that "Dial Press will publish next Spring," a fact discovered "through established sources at Dial Press." An informer at the firm, which had been Baldwin's publisher for eight years, said that the book was to be called *The Blood Counters* and that galley proofs could probably be delivered to the FBI "in November or December."

The precise content remained a mystery, but in an interview with the theater magazine *Playbill,* Baldwin let drop that, like *The Fire Next Time, The Blood Counters* would first be serialized in the *New Yorker.* This begat an FBI summary report on the *New Yorker.* The words "communist front" were withheld, but "over the years [it] has been irresponsible and unreliable with respect to references concerning the Director and the FBI."

When, in 1988, I asked William Shawn, then editor of the *New Yorker,* if he had ever planned to publish an article by Baldwin about the FBI, he replied that he had never heard of it. Likewise, Baldwin's editor of the time at Dial Press, Jim Silberman, had no recollection of such a project. No additional detail about *The Blood Counters* appears in any book about Baldwin. The main source of information about it is the FBI file.

·   ·   ·

No action was recommended to be taken against Annell Ponder's torturers in the memo which recorded her beatings. The moral dimension of the black struggle was not the stuff of which FBI reports were made.

Hoover frequently reiterated that the FBI was not a police force. "Stick to the facts," he wrote in his book *Masters of Deceit* (1958). "The FBI is not interested in rumor or idle gossip." Morality, in the civil rights context, would have seemed to him to tend toward the latter category, as something intangible, subjective. However, he was constantly on the lookout for evidence of "immorality," in the shape of "facts" which could be used to undermine significant figures, perhaps even dislodge them. The most notorious example concerns the release of details of Martin Luther King's secret sex life, gathered on tapes from the many listening devices planted around King. The recordings were used in 1964 to try to blackmail King into committing suicide. William Sullivan, the head of Domestic Intelligence, later admitted in his memoir, *The Bureau* (1979), that the FBI was responsible. Sullivan himself arranged for the compilation tape to be sent to the King household on the eve of King's departure for Stockholm to accept the Nobel Peace Prize.

Efforts to smear Baldwin in a similar fashion would prove more difficult, as Baldwin was relatively open about his homosexuality. The qualifier is necessary: in the early 1960s, the fact of homosexuality was unspeakable in public life and was often left unspoken even among friends. The concept of "coming out" could not exist, for it had no context (Baldwin played a part in creating it). The subject of homosexuality, linked to the quest for identity, was at the core of his two most recent novels, *Giovanni's Room* and *Another Country*, and to that extent his sexual preferences had been made public. In the mind of Hoover, though, proof of deviance in Baldwin's private behavior could still be a useful weapon in destroying public confidence, or in setting others in the civil rights movement against him. Within the FBI, there was no questioning the legitimacy of such intrusion. Once a person was on the Security Index, it followed that this was a "dangerous individual" (or a "master of deceit") and that every item of "derogatory" information was ammunition for the fight.

At the foot of a memo on the phantom book to the director from one of his assistants, in July 1964, Hoover scrawled a query: "Isn't James Baldwin a well-known pervert?" It may have been prompted by the memory of a separate investigation of Baldwin which had taken place in 1962, under statutes relating to "Interstate Transportation of Obscene Material." The material at issue was the novel *Another Country*. After some dillydallying, no action was taken against the author. Or the question may have arisen as a result of a more recent memo, which recorded a conversation between Baldwin and Hunter Pitts ("Jack") O'Dell. In a deal involving Hoover, and brokered by the Kennedys, O'Dell had been fired from King's SCLC in 1963 because of his left-wing past. The trade-off was, supposedly, that his removal would make it easier for the president and the attorney general to mediate between civil rights groups and the FBI.

O'Dell was now working for Baldwin, as part of an ever-expanding, fluid staff of assistants, accountants, secretaries, lawyers, all helping the ever-more-prominent writer to weather the storms of fame. O'Dell's duties in the spring of 1964 involved negotiating with Broadway theater management over Baldwin's play *Blues for Mister Charlie*, a civil rights drama set in a racially divided town in Mississippi—the first, though not the last, politically motivated work which Baldwin had produced. O'Dell's telephone was tapped, and the confidential source threw up some rich reports. "It is noted that in greeting O'Dell, Baldwin stated, 'Hello, baby, how are you,' and in closing the conversation stated that 'It's good to hear from you, baby.'" A check on the FBI's "Obscene Log" confirmed the suspicions to which this gave rise. Baldwin mentioned to O'Dell that he had a dinner appointment that evening, with someone (whose name is withheld) whom the log revealed to be "another degenerate."

Of more immediate interest to the bureau was an earlier conversation between Baldwin and Jones, who only recently had been singing Baldwin's praises to Stanley Levison, right-hand man to King. Through the wiretap on Jones's phone, it was learned (October 10, 1963) that "Jones told [name withheld] that he had a falling out with James Baldwin, Negro author, last night. . . . Jones said he has been critical of Baldwin's activities and mentioned that Baldwin's sexual propensities have become known." The SCLC, which staked all its civil rights demands on nonviolent action within the law and on a general aura of respectability, could hardly afford to have candid homosexuals close to the seat of power.

In answer to his scribbled question about Baldwin being a pervert, therefore, Hoover received a carefully researched reply:

It is not a matter of official record that he is a pervert; however, the theme of homosexuality has figured prominently in two of his three published novels. Baldwin has stated that it is also "implicit" in his first novel, *Go Tell It on the Mountain.*

The *New York Post* published a series of six articles about Baldwin in January 1964. . . . He criticized American heterosexuality, saying it isn't sex at all but "pure desperation." He claims American homosexuality is primarily a waste which would cease to exist in effect if Americans were not so "frightened of it." . . .

These remarks are similar to others Baldwin has gone on record with regarding homosexuality. While it is not possible to state that he is a pervert, he has expressed a sympathetic viewpoint on several occasions, and a very definite hostility toward the revulsion of the American public regarding it.

This memo could now be set beside another, from late the previous year, when "a confidential source" advised that Stanley Levison had ridiculed Baldwin's attempts to mount a boycott of department stores over the Christmas shopping period, in protest at white mob violence in Birmingham. Baldwin's idea was that damaging the commercial sector would lead to pressure for stronger government action in the South. Levison didn't agree. King, the FBI learned, was put off by the "poetic exaggeration" in Baldwin's approach to race issues. Levison's own view was that Baldwin and Bayard Rustin, a King aide with whom he had become friendly, were "better qualified to lead a homo-sexual movement than a civil rights movement." Should a strong alliance between Baldwin and King threaten to emerge in the future, Hoover now knew where to attack it.

.   .   .

Baldwin had a repertoire of responses he would draw on when faced with a crisis too many: he could "collapse" (a favorite term of self-diagnosis by this stage in his life); he could refer all requests and responsibilities to one of his assistants; or he could flee.

It was flight that he chose at the end of 1964, as his outer obligations multiplied and the inner world, where writing began, seemed to shrink to the dimensions of a miniature ivory tower. In an interview with a West

German newspaper in September 1964 (interviews by now far outnum-
bered written articles), Baldwin threatened to "emigrate" should Barry
Goldwater win the election that year. The interview was clipped and
filed by an FBI agent. Goldwater did not win, of course—Lyndon
Johnson was returned in a landslide victory to the White House—but
Baldwin left anyway.

The FBI went, too. "On 11/27/65 [name withheld] met James Baldwin
at the Hotel Boston, Rome, and shared a room with him." (They were still
sharing, the memo noted, two days later.) Baldwin was booked to speak
at the Italian Cultural Institute during the same week, and his comments
were monitored. In 1966, he began to spend long periods in Istanbul, having gone there originally five years earlier at the invitation of a Turkish
actor, Engin Cezzar, and his wife.

> NY T-2 advised that James Baldwin . . . arrived at Istanbul, Turkey, by
> ship on March 29, 1966. During his stay, Baldwin resided with Engin
> Cezzar, Ayapasa Saray Arkasi 32/3, Istanbul.
> NY T-5 advised . . . during the summer of 1966, Baldwin rented an
> apartment in the Bebek Section of Istanbul. She found out later that
> Baldwin was evicted by the landlord for having homosexual parties.

"Turkish Police records" were searched to establish further addresses. By
now, Baldwin was the subject of an FBI F#1 Stop Notice, which meant
that bureau sources within the Immigration and Naturalization Service
(INS) were obliged "to immediately notify the FBI if [Baldwin] passes
through the area." Journeys from the United States to Mexico, Canada,
France, and other destinations were duly logged. Each time a report was
filled out, it was likely to be marked "communist," though no further evidence of Baldwin's membership of any communist organization, or sympathy for communism, had been put forward. Quite simply, the FBI saw
no need for it. Even ex-communists who left the party and spoke out
against it—such as the novelist and former friend of Baldwin, Richard
Wright, a vehement anticommunist who had contributed to the anthology *The God That Failed* in 1949—were not permitted to disavow their former allegiance, in the eyes of the bureau.

The nomadic pattern of life, a reaction to the heady political engagement of 1963–64, continued for the rest of the decade. By now, Baldwin's

absences from the United States were so frequent and lengthy that FBI interest in him was dwindling, though he remained on the Security Index. The global surveillance involved pestering his personal associates under false pretences. When he flew from Istanbul to Paris on December 23, 1966, an FBI man attempted to establish his precise whereabouts by calling his literary agent Robert Lantz and pretending to be "a member of a peace organization soliciting a statement." (However, "Mr. Lantz would not divulge Baldwin's address.") When he returned to New York for Christmas the following year, the FBI first learned of his arrival from sources within the INS and then attempted to confirm that he was staying at his usual address by means of a similar "pretext telephone call." They got his sister Paula, who was referred to as "Mrs. Baldwin, subject's wife," only one of many basic errors in the reports. At various times, Baldwin was described as a "former professor," as the author of the novels "*Go Tell It to the Mountains*" and "*Another World*," and as living at "Horation Street" (that is, Horatio Street) at a time when he had already moved out.

The news that Baldwin had been contracted by Columbia Pictures to write the screenplay for a film based on the life of Malcolm X triggered a new investigation, with spies from the Los Angeles field office making "discreet inquiries" at the studio to see if a copy of the script could be obtained, and the undercover questioning of mail carriers and friends (including Truman Capote) to find out about addresses, travel plans, and associations with militant groups on the West Coast. Each of these people then became a "confidential source" entitled to legal protection under the FBI's view of the Freedom of Information Act. "When people think of informants, normally they think of paid informants," says Lesar. "But the FBI had traditionally regarded anyone who provided it with information as a confidential source. If the FBI calls up James Baldwin's landlord and says, 'Hey, is Baldwin in the country?' that guy becomes an FBI informant."

The Hollywood project ended acrimoniously, and no film about the life of Malcolm X based on Baldwin's script was ever made.

Toward the end of February 1968, Baldwin took part in a rally at Carnegie Hall, with Martin Luther King among other speakers, to mark the one-hundredth anniversary of the birth of W. E. B. Du Bois, a guiding spirit of the modern civil rights movement. In a sober suit bought especially for the occasion, Baldwin was photographed with King, looking like a small boy next to his hero. It seems likely that he was never aware of the extent to which he had been deliberately sidelined by the SCLC, which briefly, in the middle of 1963, had regarded him as a prize. Levison, in particular, was hostile toward him; his view that Baldwin was not "too deep intellectually" (stated in a telephone conversation recorded by the FBI on October 22, 1963) was not shared by King himself, who nevertheless wished to see him distanced from the organization. According to a taped conversation between Levison and King, the SCLC leader felt that "Baldwin was uninformed regarding his movement. King noted that Baldwin, although considered a spokesman of the Negro people by the press, was not a civil rights leader."

The FBI had several informants in the audience that night, all of whom filed reports. "Dr. Martin Luther King said [*sic*] tribute to Dr. W. E. B. Du Bois and stated that Dr. Du Bois would be with him when he and others go to Washington in April." With him in spirit, the informant meant; or perhaps he or she was unaware that Du Bois had died five years before. In any case, King did not march on Washington for a second time, as planned, to make a renewed appeal to the nation's conscience. He and Baldwin shared a belief that the continuing degradation of blacks demeaned whites as well. "It is a terrible, an inexorable law," Baldwin had preached at the beginning of the decade, "that one cannot deny the humanity of another without diminishing one's own." King was shot dead in Memphis just a few weeks after the Carnegie Hall rally, on April 4. Baldwin wrote in *No Name in the Street* that he wore the same new suit to the funeral, adding, with a touch of the very poetic exaggeration which had caused King to separate himself from Baldwin, that it was "drenched in the blood of all the crimes of my country."

III

Appearing on television with David Frost not long after the assassination, Baldwin displayed the odd, riddling manner which was now his accustomed style, in both writing and speech:

FROST: Are you more conscious now of being black than when you
were a child?

BALDWIN: I think you should ask that question of our president.

FROST: Pardon?

Overcoming his puzzlement, Frost mentioned King's assassin, a drifter
and small-time thief. He began to say that "for every James Earl Ray"
(who, after the shooting, had flown to England, where he was arrested)
there are "a hundred thousand other" whites who feel differently, but
Baldwin interrupted: "I don't think we want to discuss James Earl Ray,
because I don't believe—speaking in my persona as Sambo—that he
could have swum across the Memphis River all the way to London by
himself."

The conversation ended there, with Baldwin hinting at the collusion of
powerful people in King's murder. At the time, it was not known publicly that the FBI had sent King the tape containing recordings of his bedroom exploits (mainly with white women), accompanied by the suggestive letter: "King, you're a fraud. . . . You know what to do." But in his
"persona as Sambo"—the intuitive fool—Baldwin would have known of
government attempts to destroy public confidence in prominent black
figures, including himself.

These efforts were given renewed impetus in an intensive campaign
which Hoover began in August 1967, eight months before the assassination, officially known as Counterintelligence Program [COINTELPRO],
Black Nationalist—Hate Groups. It was remounted in the spring of 1968,
when the FBI in Washington issued a memorandum (March 4) urging
action to "prevent the rise of a messiah who could unify and electrify the
militant black nationalist movement." King and Stokely Carmichael were
singled out for attention. King was "a very real contender" for the position of "messiah," should he "abandon his supposed obedience to white
liberal doctrines (nonviolence) and embrace Black Nationalism."

King's influence had been severely reduced since the mid-1960s, but
Hoover could think only of stepping up the campaign against him.
According to Sullivan in *The Bureau,* "Hoover believed that King was a
Communist and he went after him with his biggest guns. No one, not the

Kennedys and certainly not anyone at the Bureau, could stop the surveillance and harassment to which King was subjected until his death in 1968." The "messiah" memo was distributed to forty-four FBI field offices (including Memphis), with the instruction that "imagination and initiative" should be used in action taken against black groups and their figureheads. And action was expected. In a novel strategy, Washington headquarters directed local field offices to respond within thirty days. Thirty-one days after the memo was issued, King was shot.

This little sample of syllogistic presentation does not, of course, prove that the FBI murdered Martin Luther King. Numerous investigations by journalists and lawyers (including Lesar, who was once part of James Earl Ray's legal team), and by a Department of Justice task force, have failed to establish concrete connections. The task force, which was set up in 1975 to examine the FBI's harassment of King, and his assassination, found that "the COINTELPRO campaign was . . . very probably felonious," but not that Ray had FBI backing.

A House Select Committee report, published four years later, threw up some startling new details about the Lorraine Motel in Memphis, where King was killed. During a visit to the city to support a strike by garbage workers in the week before the assassination, King had had to make a quick exit from a demonstration that turned violent. He and his entourage took refuge in a nearby Holiday Inn, remaining there until they left town. When the FBI learned of his decision to return to Memphis the following week, to try to repair the bad publicity caused by the riot, Sullivan's Domestic Intelligence division arranged for the release of a "news item" (initialed by Hoover) to sympathetic press agencies: "The fine Hotel Lorraine in Memphis is owned and patronized exclusively by Negroes but King didn't go there after his hasty exit. Instead, King decided the plush Holiday Inn Motel, white owned, operated, and almost exclusively white patronized, was the place to 'cool it.'" King had stayed at the Lorraine on visits to Memphis since the 1950s, and it is likely that he would have returned there anyway, without the bureau's insidious encouragement. The gunman was certainly expecting him. He trained his sights on the balcony on April 4, confident that King would walk across sooner or later, as he did just after 6 P.M.

Speaking to David Frost on television in 1968, Baldwin knew nothing of COINTELPROs, or directions to use "imagination and initiative" against black "messiahs," or of FBI coercion to guide King back toward the hotel in which he was murdered; but "Sambo" did. Sambo relied on—one of Baldwin's favorite lines from scripture—"the evidence of things not seen."

.   .   .

After the assassination, Baldwin appears to have been subject to what medical people call "sympathetic identification" with the victim. Just a few days after King's death, he wrote to Engin Cezzar in Istanbul that he was now "the black elder statesman" and, more puzzlingly, that he was "the only mobile black American left." It is hard to see what he meant, but meaning was all off balance in Baldwin's inner ear. He told the *New York Times* that "white America appears to be seriously considering the possibilities of mass extermination," and again and again he raised the specter of the Reichstag Fire and the Holocaust. He told Cezzar that the FBI had his every change of direction covered and that his telephone conversations were being taped. In fact, at this time, what little interest the FBI had in Baldwin concerned the ill-starred project to make a film based on the life of Malcolm X.

The following year, Baldwin wrote to another friend that he had been ill: "first the stomach—then the eyes—I never really believed that any of it was physical. . . . I simply panicked, or, in effect, fainted." After a spell in the American Hospital in Paris, he surfaced in St-Paul, first renting and then buying the old farmhouse on the hillside, which would be his base for the rest of his life. A further perplexing scan of his nervous system shows up in an interview given at the time to the black magazine *Essence*. Baldwin had always had a tendency to mythologize his own past. In the conversation with Ida Lewis, the editor of *Essence*, he makes a number of gnomic comments, punctuated by a flagrant rewriting of the story of his life in Paris on first landing there, broke, in 1948. In the new version, Baldwin lived among "Algerians and Africans," rather than the young and mostly white Americans and Europeans who sustained him socially and financially. He then uttered the remark which was to become a refrain ever after: "I loved Medgar. I loved Martin and Malcolm. We all worked together and kept the faith together. Now they are all dead. . . . I'm the last witness—everybody else is dead."

He believed there was still a role for him, though it was not the traditional writer's role. Passing over the curious claim to be "the last witness," Lewis pressed him to distinguish between a witness and an observer. "An observer has no passion," Baldwin said. "I don't have to observe the life and death of Martin Luther King. I am a witness to it."

.   .   .

In October 1963, Baldwin had made a trip to Selma, Alabama, to encourage black citizens to register to vote. The people who turned up were kept in baking heat outside the county courthouse all day long, forbidden to leave the line, surrounded by policemen who carried on a charade of treating Baldwin and his co-organizers as if they were interfering with the rights of would-be voters. "I will not have these people molested in any way," the county sheriff kept repeating when Baldwin or one of the others tried to bring refreshments to the queue. After an all-day wait, about twenty, out of three hundred, were admitted to the courthouse. The others were told to try again.

On his return to New York, Baldwin kept an appointment with Fern Eckman, who was writing a profile of him for the *New York Post*. In a state of nervous agitation, he described what he had witnessed in Selma. "And all of this is happening, by the way, under the eyes of the FBI. Who are taking *pictures*."

The pictures were developed and stored in Baldwin's file, turning up twenty-five years later, in Xerox form, on my original FOIA request. He is visible, indistinctly, arguing with the sheriff on the steps of the courthouse, in the company of his brother David and the Student Nonviolent Coordinating Committee leader, James Foreman. The FBI had many of the details of his trip to Selma, including flight number, the name of the person who was to have met him at the airport, the fact that he or she did not turn up, the name of the hotel at which Baldwin was staying, and what telephone calls he had made from there. The incident, together with the earlier one involving the agents who tried to enter his apartment, shows that Baldwin was aware that he was under surveillance almost from the moment it began.

The precise weight of this burden can be measured only by the impression it makes. After 1963, Baldwin began to deteriorate as a writer. Five years later, he would tell Engin Cezzar that he was being shadowed permanently, when almost certainly he was not. In this state of mind, every conversation is at risk of being overheard, even when no one is listening. Friends may appear to act in unfriendly ways, appeals from eager college students are confused with pretext telephone calls, and every passer-by taking innocent snapshots is working for the FBI.

The writer works out of a private conversation with himself, but the game of shadows makes it likewise difficult to decide which sentence is a true sentence and which a "poetic exaggeration," which radical creation is a second-hand stereotype, and whether the novel five years in the making, but too often interrupted by the urgencies of politics, is a mirror to the soul or a garrulous shambles. It is hard to write between assassinations, and even harder when everyone—or so it seems—is listening to the writer's private conversation with himself, except the writer.

.   .   .

The FBI formally wound up its investigation of Baldwin on March 25, 1974. No reports had been filed since Hoover's death two years earlier. The campaign was grounded in personal affront, sustained on a misapplication ("communist"), and was probably "felonious." In James Lesar's opinion, virtually everything for which the FBI targeted Baldwin was "protected free-speech activity" covered by the First Amendment to the United States Constitution. "These files were not compiled for law enforcement purposes. They are a compendium of every piece of gossip that the FBI picked up through wiretaps and other sources that relate to Baldwin, but none of it relates to illegal activity."

In the most ruthless reading of the facts, it is possible to conclude that Hoover succeeded in his campaign against Baldwin. Baldwin left the country at the height of his influence and at a crucial turning in the struggle for civil rights, when King's power was slipping among a people impatient for change. To several of Baldwin's contemporaries, including Norman Mailer and Jim Silberman, his editor at Dial Press, his decision to leave was misguided. "I felt that he was wasting his substance being in Europe," Mailer told me. "He spent too much time in Europe, when there was so much to write about in America at that time. If he'd gone to Europe and written great books about America, it would have been all right. But he didn't. He went to solve problems in his own life." (Mailer was not as severe as he might sound. He added: "One affinity I've always felt with Baldwin is that each of us could be faulted for having spent too much time solving our personal problems.") The FBI was neither happy nor unhappy to see him go, but merely recorded the facts in the neutral tone which characterizes the bulk of FBI paperwork. Sure evidence of his diminishing importance is to be found in the tapering off of his file; only a few memos date from the late 1960s, and a report of June 1971 states that Baldwin is now "removed from the mainstream of Black Power activities." There was a brief revival of interest when an interview appeared in *L'Express* in August 1972, in which Baldwin talked about "making the cities uninhabitable," but that was conducted in Paris, printed in a faraway country in an inaccessible language.

Despite his attempts to align himself with the more militant Black Panthers, and to offer Stokely Carmichael the support of an "older brother"—so wrote one of the informants at Carnegie Hall that night—Baldwin was left behind when the movement entered its new phase. This was a young, fast-talking, gun-toting leadership; it included Huey Newton, Rap Brown, and Eldridge Cleaver, who published a fierce attack on Baldwin in his book *Soul on Ice* in 1968: "There is in James Baldwin's works the most grueling, agonizing, total hatred of the blacks, particularly of himself, and the most shameful, fanatical, fawning, sycophantic love of the whites that one can find in the writings of any black writer of note in our time."

When History changed the tune, Baldwin was still dancing the old step. But History changes tunes unpredictably. The FBI of those years continues to be exposed as an organization which regarded itself as being above the law, run by a director who was obsessed by the communist menace and the sexual peccadilloes of others, and who operated, as his assistant director Sullivan later wrote, "in fear of blacks and social change."

Baldwin's second act as an American writer was not a happy one; nor, despite the fact that he continued to be productive after 1970, writing two more novels and several works of nonfiction, was it successful. History, though, will refer to something else in him, a quality he himself raised in that conversation with Ida Lewis: "I always felt that when I was talking publicly . . . I was talking about people's souls. I was never really talking about political action."

TEN The Island Affair

RICHARD WRIGHT'S
UNPUBLISHED LAST NOVEL

In the spring of 1988, I went to Paris to meet Ellen Wright, the widow of the American novelist Richard Wright, at her home in the heart of St-Germain des Prés. The purpose of the visit was to discuss James Baldwin, about whom I was writing a book and with whom Richard Wright had had a fractious, father-and-son relationship. The Wrights had moved from New York to Paris in 1947, and Baldwin, fourteen years Wright's junior, arrived the following year. Whereas Wright was the author of several outstanding books, including the novel *Native Son* and the memoir *Black Boy*, the story of his grueling Mississippi childhood, Baldwin was practically unpublished. One of the first things he turned his mind to, on settling in Paris, was an essay ostensibly about Harriet Beecher Stowe and *Uncle Tom's Cabin*, which ended by attacking the continuation of "protest" fiction in contemporary black literature. The prime example of the sterility cited by Baldwin was *Native Son*. Wright never forgave him.

The talk in Mrs. Wright's living room that afternoon turned naturally to the friendships within literary circles in Paris in the 1950s, when many other African American writers and artists followed Wright to France, and to the climate of suspicion and resentment that gradually dissolved those alliances. The subject arose of a novel Wright had left behind when he died in 1960, set amid a fictionalized black community that congregated at the Café Tournon, in the rue Tournon, between Odéon and the Luxembourg

Gardens. *Island of Hallucination* is mentioned in biographies—Michel Fabre offers an account in his excellent book *The Unfinished Quest of Richard Wright* (1973)—but it has never been published.

Mrs. Wright spoke vivaciously about most things as we drank a bottle of what she delighted in calling "plonk." She briefly flattered me with the notion that I might write an introduction to a reissue of one of Wright's books. But when it came to *Island of Hallucination* she frosted over. The book would "never be published in my lifetime," she said, her eyes rising toward the ceiling as if a copy were stored in the attic above our heads. The story involved characters based on people still alive, who might view their presence in the novel as defamation. The Wright estate had fought, and lost, an expensive legal action over the use of unpublished material in a biography by Margaret Walker (*Richard Wright: Daemonic Genius*, 1988). Ellen Wright did not say so outright, but I left rue Jacob with the impression that the presence in *Island of Hallucination* of a character based on one member of the Café Tournon circle, an African American writer and journalist called Richard Gibson, was largely behind her decision to withhold the novel.

Island of Hallucination, begun in 1958, represented a late departure for Wright: it was the first time he had written about Paris, his home for the past eleven years. Dispatching a completed draft to his agent, Paul Reynolds, at the beginning of 1959, he sounded pessimistic about its chances: "I can readily think of a hundred reasons why Americans won't like this book. But the book is true. Everything in the book happened, but I've twisted characters so that people won't recognize them." Wright's most recent published novel, *The Long Dream* (1958), had had a poor reception, with critics repeating the charge that he was out of touch with the subject matter that paradoxically most inspired him, the "Negro problem." He had recently turned to nonfiction, producing books about the Far East, Spain, and the newly independent Ghana, for the title of which he coined the term "Black Power." *Island of Hallucination* is a sequel to *The Long Dream*, in which a character from the earlier novel, Fishbelly, flees to Europe to escape the racial nightmare in his homeland, as Wright had done after the war. By the time he mailed the typescript to Reynolds, he was in frail health and living apart from Ellen and their two daughters. His financial affairs were in a bad way, each book having made a poorer show than the one before. If *Island of Hallucination* should "get the same press that *The Long Dream* did," he told Reynolds, "then I must seriously think of abandoning writing for a time. One has to be realistic."

Apart from a brief stopover on his way to Argentina to make a film of *Native Son* at the end of the 1940s, Wright never returned to the United States after moving to Paris. The reasons for his estrangement are not hard to illustrate. Shortly before leaving the United States, the couple—Ellen Poplar was from a Polish immigrant family—had been obliged to form a bogus property company to buy the house they desired; not in Mississippi, where Wright was born in 1908, the grandson of former slaves, but in bohemian Greenwich Village. Paris would spare them such bruising indignities. In the letter to Reynolds that accompanied *Island of Hallucination,* in which he brooded on his hobbled career, Wright endorsed his decision to live in France, which had brought him "such a bad press in the United States." His daughters would become "emotionally ill" if he were to take them back across the ocean. "I'd be a criminal to do so."

The motives behind Wright's departure from America were not exclusively racial. At the time of his success with *Native Son,* he had been a member of the Communist Party. Although he broke with his increasingly oppressive comrades in 1942 and wrote a well-publicized account of his reasons ("I Tried to Be a Communist," included in Richard Crossman's anthology *The God That Failed*), the allegiance was neither forgotten nor forgiven at home. Almost every entry in Wright's FBI file after 1944, when the essay was first published, makes reference to his party membership, continuing into the mid-1950s, by which time he was a committed anticommunist.

In Paris, on the other hand, where literary life was flourishing in the new conditions created by the liberation, and where modern American fiction was widely read, Wright was welcomed as the representative "Negro writer." Parties arranged in his honor were attended by Albert Camus, André Gide, and others. Publishers competed to obtain his books. Jean-Paul Sartre and Simone de Beauvoir befriended the Wrights, and Ellen became de Beauvoir's literary agent, a position she still held at the time of our meeting. Wright's stories were translated by the mischievous writer and musician Boris Vian, and *Native Son* formed the thematic base of a scandalous *roman policier, J'Irai cracher sur vos tombes* (I Will Spit on Your Graves), written by Vian under the guise of being a black American.

However, Wright soon began to feel he was under threat from an unexpected source: the black American writers and artists who had traveled to France in his footsteps. The first blow was struck by Baldwin's essay about *Uncle Tom's Cabin* and *Native Son*, to which he gave the title "Everybody's Protest Novel," publishing it in the first issue of a Left Bank magazine called *Zero* (spring 1949) and shortly afterward in *Partisan Review*. Wright's pain at the assault could only have been exacerbated by the fact that the accusatory piece appeared directly after a short story by Wright himself. "The Man Who Killed a Shadow" is the tale of a black cleaner who murders a white schoolteacher and hides her body after she attempts to seduce him and falsely accuses him of rape when he refuses her. Baldwin argued that fiction such as Wright's—including, by implication, the story that readers had just read—perpetuated a self-spinning web of "lust and fury" which, instead of unshackling the black spirit, continued to imprison it. Because of its grisly action and tangled moral outcome, Reynolds had failed to place the story in the United States, but it was welcomed by the editor of *Zero*, Themistocles Hoetis, who relished the idea of launching his magazine with a spat between "the old black writer and the new black writer," as he put it to me during an interview at his home in southeast London.

Hoetis recalls receiving "The Man Who Killed a Shadow" in person at Wright's apartment on rue Monsieur le Prince, close to L'Odéon, where the successful author was once photographed with his family at the dinner table, while a uniformed maid waited in attendance. Wright was "a bit staid, but very friendly," Hoetis says. "I remember thinking at the time that he seemed pleased that a Yank would even come and visit him." Baldwin did not visit Wright at home, in Hoetis's recollection. "He was going to chop him down."

"Everybody's Protest Novel" was followed by even more withering attacks from Baldwin's pen. Later, Wright quarreled with another African American writer and one-time friend, Chester Himes, after seeing himself portrayed in what he considered to be an unkindly light in Himes's novel

A Case of Rape. A younger novelist, William Gardner Smith, author of *The Last of the Conquerors* and *Stone Face,* was alleged by Wright to be in the pay of the CIA, for whom he was supposed to be spying on what Wright called the "black church" at the Café Tournon. Wright himself was not above suspicion of a similar kind. In 1956, the American writer Kay Boyle, a veteran of Paris of the 1920s, wrote to tell him that "there is a story, a rumor, about you that is going about . . . that you give information about other Americans in order to keep your passport and be able to travel." Wright must have blushed when he received this, for there were grounds for the rumors. Two years earlier, he had had difficulty in obtaining a passport from the American embassy to cross the Pyrenees to research his book *Pagan Spain.* After a visit to the embassy on September 16, 1954, when he provided or confirmed the names of more than one person "known to him as a member of the communist party," the passport came through. (A record of the interview is in Wright's FBI file, available under the U.S. Freedom of Information Act.) The English poet Christopher Logue, who was in Paris in the 1950s and was friendly with William Gardner Smith, says of the atmosphere at the Tournon: "Everybody thought everybody else was spying on someone or other for somebody."

This was the situation Wright set out to dramatize in *Island of Hallucination,* representing in fictional form the web of false friendship, deception, corruption, and betrayal that increasingly threatened to ensnare him, or so he believed. By the time he entered the Eugène Gibez clinic, where he died of a heart attack at the age of fifty-two on November 28, 1960, the project was in abeyance. Reynolds had forwarded the manuscript to Wright's editor at Doubleday, who had asked for cuts and changes that appear to have been beyond the author's energies. After his death, Ellen permitted a small section to be printed in an anthology, but then withdrew the manuscript. It now sits among the Richard Wright papers at the Beinecke Library at Yale. For many years, Wright scholars were not permitted to read it. One biographer, Addison Gayle, stated in a footnote in his book *Ordeal of a Native Son* that his request to read *Island of Hallucination* "was denied."

.   .   .

Ellen Wright died in 2004 at the age of ninety-two. Not long before, a photocopy of *Island of Hallucination,* more than five hundred pages in Wright's typescript, came into my hands by an unexpected route: it was lent to me by Richard Gibson, whose presence in the novel is thought to have been behind its suppression. Now in his seventies, Gibson, who was born in Los Angeles and raised in Philadelphia, has lived in West London for many years. He talks readily about a colorful past that involves various political affiliations and adventures, disgraces, and protestations of innocence. In the early 1960s, he was head of the Fair Play for Cuba Committee (FPCC) in the United States, in which capacity he met Fidel Castro and Che Guevara on several occasions. When John F. Kennedy was assassinated in 1963, Gibson was approached by the CIA for information on Lee Harvey Oswald, who also had links with the FPCC. He is the author of the book *African Liberation Movements* and was for a time English-language editor of the Algiers-based magazine *Révolution Africaine,* run by the French lawyer Jacques Vergès, who later denounced Gibson in the magazine (July-August 1964). Since his Paris days, when he was a regular at the Café Tournon, Gibson has had to fend off suggestions of egregious activity, including spying for the U.S. government, allegations he has consistently denied, sometimes in the law courts and sometimes with humor. "If I'm CIA, where's my pension?" he once quipped to me.

Of the many things that vexed Wright in Paris in the 1950s—Baldwin's perceived treachery, Smith's snooping, Himes's unfaithfulness—it was the sequence of events that became known as the "Gibson affair" that exercised him most. In 1957, Gibson and Smith, acting in concert, sent a letter to *Life* magazine criticizing French policy in Algeria. Such a gesture could only be seen as foolhardy on the part of an American, provoking the risk of deportation from France. Gibson wrote the letter, but signed it in the name of the newspaper cartoonist Ollie Harrington, a popular figure at the Tournon and one of the few members of the "church" whom Wright did not regard with suspicion or contempt. Wright and Harrington were furious when the letter appeared over the latter's signature in *Life* (October 21, 1957). Gibson was questioned by French police and admitted his part in the forgery. He was released without charge but lost his job at Agence France Presse and returned to the United States to take up a post with CBS News. Gibson claims he wrote the letter as part of a scheme concocted with Smith, involving a series of communications to various publications, each signed in a false name by a different member of the black community.

A version of the Gibson affair, and the related disagreement between Gibson and Harrington over the lease to a Left Bank apartment which led to a violent fight between the two men, features prominently in *Island of Hallucination.* There is an unpleasant character in the novel called Mechanical, who reflects certain aspects of Baldwin, notably his homosexuality, which disgusted Wright. At one point, in a nightmare, Fishbelly opens a coffin to find Mechanical dressed as a woman. Other composites display fragmentary resemblances to Smith, Harrington, Gibson himself, and figures more peripheral to the black literary scene in Paris, such as the West Indian writer C. L. R. James, who appears to have been used as the basis for the character called Cato. When I first met Mrs. Wright, James was still alive.

Island of Hallucination is not the roman à clef that admirers of Wright who know of its existence might expect, however. As with the characters, events are distorted. There are story lines that appear to be pure products of the imagination, such as the opening scene involving Fishbelly and his entrapment by French con artists who rob him of two thousand dollars on the flight to Paris. There are many examples of the "lust and fury" that Baldwin objected to in Wright's fiction. And there is ample evidence of the numbing of his talent that Wright himself feared, in thumping dialogue among characters that are two-dimensional personifications of various vices.

The novel is at its strongest in dramatizing the psychology of the black exile. On arrival in Paris, Fishbelly sits in a boulevard café and marvels at the lack of attention from surrounding whites: " 'I've been toting a hundred-pound sack of potatoes on my back all my life and it's goddamned good to get rid of it,' he told himself." A woman called Irene, who has tricked guilty whites out of thousands of dollars by begging money to enable her to feel "the good old sweet ground of the United States under my old black feet," is said, in a brilliant phrase, to be "bitter, but completely happy about it." Only one figure, Ned Harrison, based partly on Harrington, rises above the moral swamp, acting at times as a sane chorus on the insane action. "No man can stand absolutely alone and make any meaning out of life," Ned says at one stage, speaking for the author as much as for himself. "When you begin distrusting the images that make your world, you're standing alone. Soon you'll begin to doubt everything. Your world turns into a dream. It's as though you were having a hallucination." The action comes to a close with Mechanical hurling himself off the tower of Notre Dame cathedral, only to be caught in a net spread by the police below, in which he succeeds in hanging himself.

Wright had always been a writer with a preference for the broad brush, but his early books emerged from a conviction that he was in possession of an original subject matter: the fiery passage of the "black boy," striving to become a man in a society bent on suppressing his masculinity. In Wright's hands, the odyssey was likely to have a bloody outcome, as Baldwin perceived. In an unpublished letter to his New York publicist Bill Cole about Wright's novel *The Outsider* (1953), which attempts to yoke the tenets of French existentialism to the psychic state of emergency of the black male in pre–civil rights America, Baldwin said it struck him "as though Native Son had read a few books which, far from changing him, simply affords him some kind of half-assed intellectual justification for his unhappy brutality."

Gibson has had to wait for more than forty years to read the novel in which he and others were assumed to feature so significantly that the author's widow chose the safe course of deferring publication (Gibson preferred not to say how he came into possession of a copy of the manuscript). "I turn up as Bill Hart, the 'superspy from Rome who spied on spies,'" he told me. While he believes that "the motor of the book's plot comes straight from the Gibson affair," he was surprised to discover that Bill Hart is cast not as the forger of the offending letter to *Life*, but as the person in whose name the letter is signed. The fraud is ascribed to Mechanical, the Baldwin figure, though when the events of the Gibson affair "rocked the African American community in Paris" in 1957, as Gibson puts it, Baldwin was on his way to the American South to report on the civil rights movement.

In Gibson's opinion, *Island of Hallucination* should now be published. "It's a curiosity. It would attract attention as a document, even if not for its literary value. Anyway, Wright wanted it published." Asked if aspects of his personality in the character of Bill Hart would be likely to prompt him to seek legal redress, Gibson scoffs. "You wouldn't even know it was me. All the characters are composites." In his view, the book "is a reflection of the nightmare that Wright was living in by then."

It would not be the first posthumous publication of a book by Wright. In 1963, the estate released a lively novel set in the offices of the Chicago post office, *Lawd Today!* Written in 1935, it makes use of the "newsreel" technique pioneered by John Dos Passos in his U.S.A. trilogy in the same decade. Near the end of his life, Baldwin, who had long since played down the old enmity, cited *Lawd Today!* as his favorite among Wright's novels. Ellen Wright told me he had agreed to provide an introduction to a new English edition, but he died in 1987, before he could fulfill the promise. Plans to reissue the book subsequently collapsed.

Two years before *Lawd Today!* a collection of short stories appeared, under the title *Eight Men*, which Wright had prepared for publication during what turned out to be his final weeks of life. It contains "The Man Who Killed a Shadow" and is dedicated to friends "whose kindness has made me feel at home in an alien land."

ELEVEN The Man Who Cried

JOHN A. WILLIAMS

In the spring of 1960, the year of his death, the novelist Richard Wright wrote from Paris to his friend and Dutch translator Margrit de Sablonière: "You must not worry about my being in danger. . . . I am not exactly unknown here and I have personal friends in the de Gaulle cabinet itself. Of course, I don't want anything to happen to me, but if it does my friends will know exactly where it comes from. . . . So far as the Americans are concerned, I'm worse than a Communist, for my work falls like a shadow across their policy in Asia and Africa. . . . They've asked me time and again to work for them: but I'd rather die first." This letter contains the essence of John A. Williams's roman à clef, *The Man Who Cried I Am,* first published in 1967 (reissued 2004). Wright, an ex-Communist who had turned his back on the party and moved to France in 1946 but had never succeeded in throwing off the attentions of the American government, died unexpectedly in a Paris clinic eight months after writing those words to Sablonière in Leiden, Holland, and their eerie prescience has kept speculation about his death smoldering ever since. *The Man Who Cried I Am,* which opens in Leiden, brings a heavy load to the fire. It charts the journey through the 1940s and 50s of Max Reddick, a black novelist and journalist, leading up to the death of Reddick's friend and mentor, Harry Ames. Harry is an expatriate former Communist living in Paris with a white wife and a career on the slide. "I'm the way I am, the kind of writer I am, and you may be too," he tells Max early in the novel, which proceeds by way of flashbacks and a jigsaw structure, "because I'm a black man; therefore we're in rebellion; we've got to be. We have no other function as valid as that one."

This repudiation of writing that is not politically committed sets the tone of *The Man Who Cried I Am*. In the parallel real-life story that runs a few feet below the surface of Williams's novel, Harry's remark also serves as a dismissal of James Baldwin's famous attack on Wright as the author of "protest fiction" in his precocious essay "Everybody's Protest Novel," published in 1949. Harry Ames is decisively committed, or as his French friends would have said, *engagé*. Harry has long been a thorn in the flesh of the American government, and Max suspects that someone—even someone from among their own café circle—was deputed to kill him. For Max, Harry's very existence was a challenge to white power; so his death is one more deferment of the dream of racial justice. The consequences, as set out here, are likely to be apocalyptic. Williams was surely in earnest in predicting a bloody reckoning, for he followed *The Man Who Cried I Am* with *Sons of Darkness, Sons of Light*, a story written in the late 1960s but set in the next decade, with the uprising about to begin.

In his journal in January 1945, a year before his migration, Wright described Paris as "a place where one could claim one's soul." That Harry Ames is a dead ringer for Richard Wright nobody would deny, least of all John A. Williams. When I asked him if it was fair to make the connection between Ames and Wright, he said it was. When asked if Wright might have been assassinated by the American security services, Williams replied, "I would say his death was highly suspicious" (he added, "I wouldn't put it any stronger than that"). His suspicions arose from conversations with people who were in France at the time of Wright's death, most notably the novelist Chester Himes, who had been close to Wright though the two were by then estranged. Asked why the government would risk murdering a writer who was no longer a force in the civil rights movement, Williams said, "I do believe there is such a thing as teaching people a lesson."

The official cause of Wright's death on November 28, 1960, was the obstruction of a coronary artery—a heart attack. His body was cremated, without a postmortem. Almost immediately, rumors began to circulate that he had been poisoned. A mystery woman was said to have visited his bedside an hour before he died. There was talk of an urgent telegram dispatched from the clinic. In his memoir, *My Life of Absurdity,* Himes named a "soul brother" by whom Wright felt he "was being persecuted." More than thirty years later, a friend of Wright from Paris days, the cartoonist Ollie Harrington, told me, "I *know* Richard Wright was assassinated" (despite promptings, he remained vague as to how he knew). Speaking on a BBC radio program about her father in October 1990, Julia Wright put it more subtly, giving credence to "a CIA plot to isolate him, in order to make him more vulnerable," thus fatally undermining his health. After a poorly attended service—Wright's wife, Ellen, had wished to keep it closed—the author's ashes were interred in Père Lachaise cemetery. In *The Man Who Cried I Am,* Max attends Harry's funeral in Paris: "Charlotte, Harry's wife was there, a few Americans. . . . There were some Africans, a few Indians. And it was only twenty hours after Harry had died."

The Man Who Cried I Am is the kind of novel that many novelists dream of writing—a bulging bag that seems to contain everything the author knows about life. It is a book that hums with sound and smell, and a good deal more hate than love. Its greatest strength is in making the reader feel the height and solidity of the oppressive wall that Max, Harry, and others must negotiate daily, just to hoist themselves up to safety, to be able to say, "I am." In his introduction to the new edition, Walter Mosley compares it to *The Odyssey* and Max to Odysseus. "And the journey home is more dangerous than Odysseus could ever imagine," he writes with reckless abandon. The minutiae of Max's existence are crammed in, from his talent to his paranoia, down to his culinary skills. An odd touch of authenticity is added by the graphic descriptions of a rectal illness that plagues him throughout. *The Man Who Cried I Am* takes lungfuls of breath from the author's angry energy, and from his ability to convey to the reader his belief that he is uncovering hidden truths.

While Williams succeeds in bringing Max Reddick to life, he fails to make him likable. Max is a bristling bundle of conspiracy theories, glued together with hatred for white men and desire for white women. The latter seems at times closer to sadism than affection. Nothing good happens to Max—a job at *Pace* magazine (for *Pace*, read *Time*), a White House speech-writing assignment—that is not the product of white men's cynical maneuvering. There is scarcely a white male character who isn't a creep, and hardly a white female character who is not the target of the "cocksman" Max fancies himself to be. From one point of view, it is a bravura depiction of a peculiar pathology. From another, it feels as if Williams, intending to create a hero, has brought into being an emotional Frankenstein.

Williams emerged as the patience of the civil rights movement was hardening to anger, and he has always been an angry writer. His books are apt to take rage as a viable substitute for morality. His first novel was called *The Angry Ones*. In 1962 he edited a collection of writings called *The Angry Black*, to which he himself contributed a story about a writer, Wendell, who tries to seduce a white woman in her own home. She first welcomes his advances, then tries to disengage herself as her son is heard approaching, but Wendell holds her in a clinch just long enough for the nine-year-old to see them. By any standard of decency, Wendell's rationale is tantamount to child abuse: "no matter how his mother explains it away, the kid has the image for the rest of his life."

It is a form of revenge that Max Reddick could as easily have taken. In Max's eyes, bad luck is a stranger to whites—"What have you got to be nervous about?" he teases an associate. "You're white"—whereas almost every misfortune in a black life is traceable to color. Such an apprehension is enough to drive someone mad, and at times, rereading this novel, I felt that Max had taken leave of his senses. "Dying violently was a European habit," he reflects at one point, thinking of a French friend: "All other deaths were commonplace. A European learned by his condition to expect catastrophe and invariably that was exactly what he received. In Europe, a winner was one who bested those common deaths arbitrarily assigned to others. You crawled, kissed behinds, ate *merde*, and grinned like you loved it. Living was everything. The final act of death was of no consequence; it was the living while everyone around died that counted."

Max's sexual politics are likely to seem equally unappetizing to a present-day readership (and probably did to many in 1967). Women are there for the taking. Max is the kind of fellow who passes the time in his office making lists of those he has slept with. He and Harry keep up a running joke about the unique delights of "redheads." The novel is shot through with reflections such as this, on Max's Dutch girlfriend, Margrit: "Time sped by. Now, she was almost thirty. In Europe that made you an old maid or a lesbian. Or a whore. Managing an art gallery hadn't helped. She had gone through a couple of painters, or more correctly, they had gone through her."

To what extent the reader is expected to accommodate Max because, as he says, "it was bad when I was born" (i.e., "born black"), is unclear, but I suspect that Williams feels he should be indulged quite a bit. Max certainly does. He lacks the faculty of self-examination. For example, he is said to be unpopular at the houses that have published his novels because "he . . . liked white women." Presented this way, it sounds like blatant racism, but might not the publishers simply be collating the observation about his love life with an insight Max provides into his own character: "Max had already given himself a name; he was a pimp without briefcase. . . . you borrowed money from the girl and the girl knew you'd never pay it back, and chances were, every time you met you'd borrow more money"? In Max's endlessly self-justifying hatred of the outside world, his tireless generalizing, there is no need for self-scrutiny, for every personal criticism can be deflected by the countercharge of racism.

Various figures who circled in Wright's orbit during his fourteen years in France are depicted under light disguise in *The Man Who Cried I Am*. A scene in a Left Bank café involving Max, Harry Ames, and a young disciple of Harry's called Marion Dawes is a rough rendering of a meeting that took place in the spring of 1953 between Wright, Himes (the character of Max contains elements of Himes), and Baldwin. It was during this stormy encounter, recorded by all three principals, that Baldwin gave warning to Wright, "The sons must slay the fathers." In the first volume of his memoirs, *The Quality of Hurt*, Himes described the incident, adding that he thought at the time that Baldwin had gone crazy; "but in recent years I've come to better understand what he meant."

No such empathy is extended to the Baldwin character, Marion Dawes, who is treated unkindly. Baldwin and Williams, almost exact contemporaries, were never close, and it's hard to imagine that Baldwin would have been amused to see himself as Marion Dawes, whose homosexuality makes him a target for Max's disgust and ridicule. (It is suggested that Dawes gained a fellowship by means of which he moved to France by sleeping with certain people; in real life, Baldwin got a Eugene F. Saxton award on the recommendation of Wright.) Crucially for Max and Harry, Dawes is not a "writer in rebellion." The young Baldwin's concerns were more aesthetic than political, and he spent his nine years in Paris coaching his heart to exorcise the outrage that he feared would kill him if left to fester. Max, on the other hand, is consumed by anger. He cannot pick up the telephone without seeing it as "another one of the white man's inventions" and reflecting that it was "ironic that one must inevitably come to use the tools of the destroyer in order to destroy him, or to save oneself."

Near the end of the novel, Max is trying to relay to a Malcolm X figure, Minister Q, the contents of a file discovered among Harry's papers, which outlines the King Alfred Plan, an FBI- and CIA-designed scheme to "terminate, once and for all, the Minority threat" and to consolidate the league of nations known as the "Alliance blanc," or White Alliance. In an afterword to the novel, Williams compares the King Alfred Plan, his own invention, to intelligence programs devised by J. Edgar Hoover in the 1960s to monitor the movements of black militants, which did not become public until much later. Harry is already a victim of the King Alfred Plan, and Max fears that he is about to become another.

The Man Who Cried I Am is driven by a furious beat and constantly illuminated by the real-life drama behind the fictional one. It is let down by loose writing and a lack of generous characterization. The latter may be ascribed to Max's solipsism, and no doubt there are powerful psychological reasons for that, but a solipsist is hardly a trustworthy guide. Walter Mosley's ingenious classical comparison must be tested against the objection that Max is not a tragic hero but a pathetic one, wounded as much by vanity and self-pity as by racism.

Does the conspiracy theory about Wright's death have any basis in reality? No one has provided a shred of forensic evidence to support the notion that he was murdered. From another angle, however, it is possible to argue that Wright's premature death was willed by the state. Wright's widow, Ellen, spoke to me about his quarrels with Baldwin and others and said how futile it all seemed to her now that these great men were gone. "My husband lived with tension all his life," Mrs. Wright said. "Every day, awful tension." If there is an alternative cause of death to be inserted beside the official entry on Wright's records, then that is surely it.

TWELVE

All That Jive

STANLEY CROUCH

Stanley Crouch refers to his study as "the war room." As a cultural and political contender, he has much in common with the Norman Mailer of *Advertisements for Myself*. Both are energetic polemicists, driven by a desire to speak from "the middle of our time," in Crouch's words, combined with a tendency to go against the grain. In Crouch's time, the grain is identity politics, the cult of victimhood, the race, class, and gender industry bedeviling academe, and the all-around "politics of narcissism" that corrupts the democratic morale. Few contemporary writers, black or white, have the gumption to trace the origin of those "divisive categories" to the door of the black power movement of the mid-1960s. But the contrary gesture is Crouch's signature punch: he has damned the work of Toni Morrison and James Baldwin, written off the later recordings of Miles Davis, and described Malcolm X as "boneheaded," accusing him (and Baldwin) of "selling out to hysterical alienation." At the same time, he writes more thoughtfully than most about what he insists on calling "Negro culture." His essays (collected in *Notes of a Hanging Judge, The All-American Skin Game*, and *Always in Pursuit*) read like dispatches from a battlefield. The impression is confirmed by the motto that Crouch has posted at the entrance to his two most recent collections: "Victory is assured."

Fiction, however, is not a form of combat. Generally speaking, it depends on more pastoral virtues, among them dispassionate observation and a temporary suspension of moral judgment—not habits that come easy to a hanging judge. It depends, above all, on the ability to tell a story, and while the characters in *Don't the Moon Look Lonesome*, Crouch's first novel, play fast and loose with anecdotes—usually told at some unenlightened black or white fool's expense—there is but a threadbare story, and almost no plot whatsoever. Most of the characters are bundles of moral certainty, variously deficient in the skills of conversation but prolific in assertion, declamation, and opinion—opinion that will seem largely familiar to readers of his nonfiction.

Crouch's boldest stroke is to make his main character a white woman. Carla Hamsun is a jazz singer in the Peggy Lee mold. She is approaching forty, childless, and in love with Maxwell Davis, a black tenor saxophonist. Maxwell is at the forefront of the New York jazz scene, and Carla is coming up. Although the story is told in the third person, Carla is the focus of consciousness; the narrative unfolds through her memories, feelings, responses to friends and colleagues both black and white, her desire for Maxwell, and her wish to bear his child before it is too late. When we encounter them, however, on their way to Houston for Carla's first meeting with Maxwell's parents, the couple have hit stormy weather. Maxwell appears to be losing interest. It is not that he is being lured by another woman—though we are invited to believe he could have his pick—but that he has been distracted by what Crouch elsewhere calls "the decoy of race." At a jazz club one night, a black woman took a gold handkerchief from his breast pocket, wiped her face and then returned it, saying, "You brothers need to come home." Maxwell appeared affected, and Carla was duly mortified. In the novel's own terms, her song has ceased to be "Easy to Love" and become "You've Changed."

Jazz determines the structure of *Don't the Moon Look Lonesome.* The basic tune is a familiar standard—can Carla succeed in protecting their love from the predators who surround them?—with the modern twist provided by racial obsession. Dispensing with linear narrative, Crouch develops his themes through improvisation, in the form of flashback and stream of consciousness, working one recollection into another as a way of deepening the texture of the story. The catch, though, is that while impromptu development in jazz is adventurous by its nature, a dependence on flashback risks rendering narrative inert. Crouch is no Proust. Crucially, for someone presenting "a novel in blues and swing," he keeps bad time: as memory melts into further memory, the reader is apt to be confused as to which layer of her own experience Carla is inhabiting. By page 200, barely a single dramatic action has occurred in present time.

Carla is, nevertheless, Crouch's most successful creation. The portrait he draws is genuinely tender, showing a talented, nervy woman, lacking in self-confidence, though endearingly so, except when on the bandstand or in Maxwell's arms. Her roots are far from the world of hip: of Norwegian stock, she was raised in South Dakota; her sister is a dyed-in-the-wool racist. Maxwell's pedigree, on the other hand, is deep blue. His father is a deacon in the church, and his mother delivers a sermon whenever she speaks: "Three's not a crowd when it comes to having babies," she tells Carla almost before they've shaken hands. "Birth is always a full house. When you pregnant, then one's a crowd. A crowd inside you, swelling up and turning over and all that mess, until you lay down and give birth to that darling child." This prompts Carla to consider her "another of those thinkers whose intellect rises out of common experiences." Maxwell's brother is gay and is living with AIDS, while his sister has retreated into crack addiction.

Unlike Carla, who comes to life off the page, Maxwell exists only in the author's description of him. "There was also his sense of humor," we are told. "He could make her laugh." But humor fails to show up in Maxwell's conversation, except in rather low forms. Here he is showing appreciation of Carla's shape: "Say, is this here the palace of the crown princess of the posteriorotti? . . . How is that blond Hottentot institution? I'm talking about that rump roast, which also offers hot velvet courses in marine polyrhythms." Likewise, the information that his apartment is stocked with books is not reflected in his speech. Among the other leading characters, Carla has a special affection for Leeann, "her favorite girlfriend," a black model who comes as close as anyone she knows to living "a perfect life." Leeann is "always on the guest lists of the very best parties and openings and private lectures and dinners with exceptional people." Judging by the status notes that ornament the tale, Crouch relishes this exclusivity at least as much as Carla does. The awestruck regard for the lush life becomes comical when one of her friends, rushing into the bathroom of Leeann's town house, is imagined to be "muffling her crying in a monogrammed towel."

A notable lacuna in a novel in which there is so much coupling, so much appreciation of "boody," is an absence of eroticism. The beautiful Leeann speaks in a continuous scatological flow and mistakes exhibitionism for candor. Crouch has a taste for bad taste, which he appears to believe is sexy. A description of the stain left at a woman's crotch after riding, "when the inside of the jodhpurs had been sweated through, leaving an embarrassing outline of . . . private parts," is developed over two pages. At one point, Maxwell upbraids his brother for talking dirty in Carla's presence: "She didn't have to hear that." This is rich, since she, and we, have to hear a great deal of it, and mostly from Maxwell. After a short time, the use of taboo words—*nigger* crops up frequently, usually in conversation between blacks, but often as a provocation—becomes tiresome, and they lose what power they have to shock. Far more shocking, in "a novel in blues and swing," is the author's overall insensitivity to language. Sentences such as "When Carla first declared herself as completely available to him, body and soul, was about six weeks after that spring day in Brooklyn," or "Bad luck had fallen like a storm of excrement," do not swing at all.

The intention behind *Don't the Moon Look Lonesome* is a sympathetic one. Crouch sets out to dramatize his conviction that not only does the melting pot contain everyone in America, but it belongs to everyone, too, and that the idea of separate "white" and "black" categories—in culture, in politics, even in race—is misguided. It is the friction caused by various elements rubbing against one another that creates the special American rhythm.

THIRTEEN

Love Lost

T O N I   M O R R I S O N

There is an arresting moment in Toni Morrison's second novel, *Sula* (1973), in which the heroine is said to be "guilty of the unforgivable thing—the thing for which there was no understanding, no excuse, no compassion. The route from which there was no way back, the dirt that could not ever be washed away." What is this dirt, this sin for which there is, so emphatically, no forgiveness? We know that Sula has a secret in her life that, with a friend, she has caused the death of a little boy—but that is not it. "They said that Sula had slept with white men. . . . There was nothing lower she could do, nothing filthier."

Interracial friendship (mostly male) is part of the mythology of America, embracing Huckleberry Finn and Jim, Leatherstocking and Chingachook, even overlooking the territory run by the Lone Ranger and Tonto. Some commentators have held it to be the essential New World story. Morrison would object that that story is told from "the center, which is white" (although readers might find extensions of it in novels such as *Another Country* by James Baldwin). At any rate, as a reliable guide to the "free republic," or even the contents of a melting pot, it terminates with *Sula*.

The cross-racial bond is all but impossible, certainly undesirable, in Morrison's fiction; evil hangs about such unions because evil hangs about whites, or "whitepeople," as they are sometimes styled. The most vigorous expression of this feeling appears in *Tar Baby* (1981), which fea-

tures a copper-complexioned model, Jadine, who has become the pro-
tégée of a degenerate, wealthy white couple on a Caribbean island. Light-
skinned black characters in Morrison's novels are objects of loathing: the
distinguishing mark of Maureen Peal in *The Bluest Eye* (1970), for example, is her "long brown hair, braided into two lynch ropes"; a girl in *Jazz*
(1992) is cursed by a "creamy little face" which, if cut open, would show
"nothing . . . but straw." The comfortable setup in *Tar Baby* involving the
"inauthentic" Jadine is disrupted by a dark stranger, Son, who first
breaks into the house and is then invited to stay by the amused owner.
When a pair of black servants are dismissed for petty theft, Son consid-
ers his unlikely host and hostess at table:

> They had not the dignity of wild animals who did not eat where they
> defecated but they could defecate over a whole people and come there
> to live and defecate some more by tearing up the land and that is why
> they loved property so, because they had killed it soiled it defecated on
> it and they loved more than anything the places where they shit. . . .
> That was the sole lesson of their world: how to make waste. . . . One
> day, they would all sink into their own waste and the waste they had
> made of the world and then, finally they would know true peace and
> the happiness they had been looking for all along.

After more of the same, Son delivers a lecture to Jadine, soon to become
his lover: "White folks and black folks should not sit down and eat
together. . . . They should work together sometimes, but they should not
eat together or live together or sleep together. Do any of these personal
things in life." Jadine, who is after all integration made flesh, can only
"smile a tiny smile" and rejoice in Son's sexual athleticism while it lasts.

Son's views are not to be taken as the author's, of course; it is, however, his moral brinkmanship that drives the action of *Tar Baby* forward.
Coming some forty years and a revolution in civil rights after *Sula,* whose
debasement occurred in 1939, he would still condemn her as righteously
as did her peers. It is perfectly possible to see what has driven Son into
such a corner, while at the same time hoping to coax him out of it, but
Morrison shows no inclination to do so. One of the strategies of her fiction is to put the reader on the spot in this way: You expect Son to show

more "humanity"? What is the basis of your expectation? The integra-
tionist appeal of Baldwin or Richard Wright, not to mention Martin
Luther King, scarcely gets a look-in. When the whites of white eyes glint
at the edges of Morrison's stories, they are quickly extinguished not by
violence but by a force identical to that which has for so long excluded
blacks: culture.

Morrison, who was awarded the Nobel Prize for Literature in 1993,
has said that she writes out of a consciousness of living in a "wholly
racialized world." Her response has been to create a world which is
almost wholly African-Americanized, in which separate existence is presented as not only inevitable but good. A central cultural reference of her
fictional realm is terror, inspired by the shared memory of unutterably
cruel deeds committed by whites, and its sublimation into beauty, at the
fingers of a Duke Ellington or a Paul Dunbar. We should not expect
Morrison to say, as Baldwin repeatedly did, "There is one race and we are
all part of it," nor to try and draw her artistic effort to within touching
distance of that at once hopeful and hopeless observation. Dependent for
her huge popularity on the tendency toward multiculturalism, Morrison
remains determinedly monoculturalist, concerned to give written form to
the taste and texture of African American life, in a span reaching roughly
from the last days of slavery to a nation reshaped by the civil rights
movement.

The project is the outcome of a considered choice, but there may also
be a failure of imagination to take into account. In *The Bluest Eye*,
Morrison's first novel, the narrator relates an incident which is every bit
as striking as the condemnation of the racially promiscuous Sula. A little
girl, Pecola, enters a shop run by a Mr. Yacobowski. As she gets out her
pennies and points at some sweets, "the grey head of Mr. Yacobowski
looms up over the counter": "He does not see her, because for him there
is nothing to see. How can a fifty-two-year-old white immigrant store-
keeper with the taste of potatoes and beer in his mouth . . . see a little
black girl? Nothing in his life even suggested that the feat was possible,
not to say desirable or necessary." As posed here, the question is rhetorical—no way he could see her. But to some people, and surely not only
"whitepeople," it should be possible to answer it differently. Mr.

Yacobowski must at some stage in his pre-American, pre-"wholly racial-ized" life have encountered the elementary tenet that there is one race and we are all part of it, and, who knows, he might have found some-thing "desirable or necessary" in the suggestion. He might see Pecola just because he is a man with feelings and she is a child. But no; no way. Anyway, he will soon understand that Pecola is culturally directed to "see" him as belonging in a category of souls than which "there was nothing lower . . . nothing filthier."

The editorializing tendency ("How can a fifty-two-year-old white immigrant . . .") is much in evidence in Morrison's fiction, one factor in her prevailing moral one-upmanship. Her female narrators are weary experts in the arts of head-shaking and sarcasm of the "good luck and let me know" variety. Her dialogue at times seems cut to fit soap opera. Stanley Crouch, the awkward squad of contemporary African American letters, has remarked that Morrison's characters "rarely . . . exist for any purpose other than to deliver a message," which contributes to the air of implausibility hanging over so many dramatic encounters in the novels. Morrison has a job putting two people in a room and making them talk like folks. How can characters breathe when the effort to correct the bal-ance of history is using up all the oxygen?

The dominant literary presence behind all Morrison's work is William Faulkner. From the start, she has employed Faulkner's method whereby the narration proceeds under a shadow, only gradually admitting the detail that casts light. "Quiet as it's kept, there were no marigolds in the fall of 1941." The cryptic introduction to *The Bluest Eye* has been repat-terned in almost all her books. With its jigsaw structure and claustropho-bic atmosphere, her new novel, *Love* (2003), is her most familiar nod to Faulkner yet. Told front-to-back, the story would go something like this: In the years before and after the Second World War, Bill Cosey was the owner of a fashionable "Hotel and Resort," the "best vacation spot for colored folks on the East Coast"; his wife bore him a son; she died, and the son followed, leaving behind a young wife and a daughter, Christine; Cosey had long been entangled with a mystery woman, but for his sec-ond wife he chose Heed—aged eleven—the best friend of little Christine; the two women are now grown up and living in hate-fueled isolation in what remains of the Cosey property, each claiming it as her own; into their lives, trailing echoes of Joe Christmas from *Light in August,* comes Junior, a girl who has known nothing but trouble; Heed wants her to forge a will, but her mind is on the teenage grandson of a couple of local worthies, whom she coaches into a rampant stud; out of the chaos Junior creates come redemption and healing.

Of course, the tale is not told like that. There are several points of view, switching from first to third person, from italic to roman, past to present. Morrison scatters fragments before her readers, inviting them to trace the significant fact a paragraph or a chapter down the line. The story is framed by the ruminations of a woman known as L, who, like the others, has had her life shaped by the overbearing hotel owner: "The ocean is my man now. He knows when to rear and hump his back, when to be quiet and simply watch a woman. He can be devious, but he's not a false-hearted man. His soul is down there and suffering. I pay attention and know all about him. That kind of understanding can only come from practice, and I had a lot of that with Mr. Cosey."

At times, *Love* reads like notes for a novel—"Christine accepted his invitation to dinner. By dessert they had plans. . . . As couplehood goes, it had its moments. As marriage goes, it was ridiculous"—at other times like notes for a by now predictable lecture: "It comforts everybody to think of all Negroes as dirt poor, and to regard those who were not, who earned good money and kept it, as some kind of shameful miracle." Whatever happy "couplehood" there is about the place is of the sisterly type, or else is given to the salt-of-the-earth grandparents, Sandler and Vida, copies of Sydney and Ondine from *Tar Baby.* Morrison's world is not only wholly racialized, but as she said at the same time (in her non-fiction book *Playing in the Dark,* 1992), "genderized, sexualized." Men here mostly occupy themselves rearing and humping, looking handsome in hats, and abusing small girls.

Morrison is good at delineating youthful female desire, though that too has been repeated in one novel after another, but grown-up hetero-sexual partnership is rare and fleeting in her books. The brief interlude in *Tar Baby,* in which Jadine and Son take refuge in a Manhattan Hilton before a difference in skin tone forces them apart, is about as close to a successful match as any Morrison characters are likely to come. What love affair could survive prose like this? "He looked at her face in the mirror and was reminded of days at sea when water looked like sky. She surveyed his body and thought of oranges, playing jacks, and casks of green wine. He was still life, babies, cut glass, indigo, hand spears, dew, cadmium yellow, Hansa red, moss green and the recollection of a tree that wanted to dance with her."

The reader of a disassembled story reasonably expects to come across something solid around which it coheres. What is there in *Love*? Homilies galore, of both the pragmatic and metaphorical kind: "You can live with anything if you have what you can't live without"; "He didn't understand: a dream is just a nightmare with lipstick," and so on. Twists in the tale, including a final one concerning the Cosey will. Lyrical rumination on the part of L, the first-person storyteller. A wholesale renunciation of "looking for Big Daddy" ("We could have been living our lives hand in hand instead"). Lots of unbridled lust, and the usual association of "floods, white people, tuberculosis, famine and ignorance." Near the end of *Love*, with that air of smug self-regard often heard in Morrison's narrators, L tells us that "most people have never felt a passion" as strong as that between Heed and Christine, but "if your name is the subject of First Corinthians, chapter 13, it's natural to make it your business." Her business, like her name, we are invited to deduce, is "Love," though there has been little of it in evidence in the tale of sex and greed that's gone before. Readers of the King James version of the Bible will recall the subject of 1 Corinthians 13 as charity ("Charity suffereth long, and is kind") but, as Sula will tell you, there is not a lot of that here either.

FOURTEEN

The Rhetoric of Rage

A PROFILE OF AMIRI BARAKA

Springfield Avenue in Newark, New Jersey, is a sloping drag of shops and dismal dwellings, lined with telegraph poles and pitted with vacant lots, a street familiar even to those seeing it for the first time. Springfield does not figure much in literature, but in *The Autobiography of LeRoi Jones* it holds a central place in the action as the area where the city riots—what the author calls the "rebellion"—began. It was 1967, the year that Jones changed his name to Amiri Baraka. The poet and some friends were eating a late afternoon meal at the "Spirit House," the name given to the community center which doubled as the Baraka residence, "when some of the young boys who came in and out of the Spirit House rushed in. 'They're breaking windows on Springfield Avenue' was the word." Outside, it seemed to him as if "the sky had a long, wide reddish streak to it. It was low and wanted to burn. It sizzled and carried images and words, buzz turning to roar."

With two other men, Baraka boarded a Volkswagen camper van, heading "straight up Springfield, not fast, not slow, but at a pace that would allow a serious observer to dig what was happening." Looting and burning were under way, both activities meeting with the approval of the camper crew. In Baraka's Black Nationalist way of conceiving the turbulence that ensued, the Newark rebellion was an expression of black people's demand for a better life, for release from under the yoke of white supremacy, for freedom, in a word. The uprising was not only inevitable but necessary, an instrument in the process of liberation, "an evolution that can only be brought about by *fire!*"

The evening ended with Baraka in the Essex County Prison, beaten up by a (black) policeman, bleeding, semiconscious, in solitary confinement. The fire continued for six more days. Baraka was given a three-year sentence for illegal possession of two firearms by a judge who concluded his summing up by quoting an inflammatory prose poem by the defendant: "What about that bad jewelry on Washington Street, and those couple of shops on Springfield? . . . All the stores will open if you will say the magic words. The magic words are: Up against the wall mother fucker this is a stick up!" The text continues by exalting the colonial struggles of "our brothers . . . all over, smashing at jellywhite faces. We must make our own World, man, our own world, and we cannot do this unless the white man is dead. Let's get together and kill him my man." The judge's extravagant gesture, which was intended to clinch the charge, led to Baraka's conviction being overturned on appeal.

The Autobiography of LeRoi Jones is a work of momentum and narrative energy, springing organically from a life packed with incident. Baraka wrote the book during a subsequent detention. In 1979 he was arrested for assaulting a police officer outside a movie theater in Greenwich Village. "Arrested for what?" he says, apparently still puzzled, though more than quarter of a century has permitted a measure of amusement to blend with frustration and anger. "I don't know until this day. I was arguing with my wife, she was sitting in the car, I was standing outside, my head poked through the window. And suddenly somebody's got me by the back of the neck. I turn around. 'What the—,' and this guy starts arresting me. It's a cop. So I wound up in the jail." Again he was beaten up, again by a black policeman—again a knowing smile as he says so— "trying to be more vicious than the white policemen." He received a sentence of forty-eight consecutive weekends in the Harlem Correctional Facility. This time he served the term in full, and wrote his autobiography. "I call it my Harlem Literary Fellowship. They gave me a room with a desk, two beds and a shower, and a closet full of paper. I had a little portable. I would go there at 9 A.M. on a Saturday and get out at 5 P.M. on a Sunday. It was grueling, nevertheless, looking toward that each week."

Baraka is pint-sized, pugnacious, wiry. At seventy-two, he is slightly bent-backed, with close-cropped gray hair but a youthful face. The face is the advanced guard of his personality: challenging from one angle, it is fetchingly ingenuous when caught from another. It lights up, to the accompaniment of hiccupping mirth, as he recalls one of the ironies or self-generated mishaps that have beset, and directed, his life. Unlike school-of-hard-knocks characters such as Chester Himes, Claude Brown, and Malcolm X, Baraka did not graduate to the black American literary tradition direct from prison, but from Greenwich Village, where he studied under a sophisticated bohemia. Supplementary education was provided by Rutgers and Howard Universities, followed by a three-year spell in the air force, where he attained the rank of sergeant (he was eventually discharged "undesirably" from the service). In the autobiography, Baraka mentions one high school friend who became a lawyer, another a government advisor, yet another a general.

While the label "black Beat" does not stand much scrutiny—Jones was serving in the American military when Allen Ginsberg's *Howl* was prosecuted—he was a strong team player in the downtown New York literary scene. In the late 1950s, Jones started the little magazine *Yugen*, followed by another journal, *The Floating Bear* (with Diane DiPrima), which between them represented the avant-garde chorus of the period. In 1959, he founded Totem Press, later merged with Corinth Books, publishing seminal work by Charles Olson (*Projective Verse*), Frank O'Hara (*Second Avenue*), Edward Dorn (*Hands Up!*), Jack Kerouac (*The Scripture of the Golden Eternity*), and Gary Snyder (*Myths & Texts*). Ginsberg and Dorn were "close friends," and he was close, too, to O'Hara, whom he describes fondly as "a boulevardier of New York, who could talk about contemporary life with a certain sweep." Jones features in O'Hara's "Personal Poem," about a lunchtime walk around Manhattan:

LeRoi comes in
and tells me Miles Davis was clubbed 12
times last night outside Birdland by a cop

The publishing and editing activities were offshoots of a furious productivity. Between 1961 and 1967, LeRoi Jones wrote some fourteen plays, as well as poems (*Preface to a Twenty Volume Suicide Note; The Dead Lecturer*), short stories (*Tales*), a novel (*The System of Dante's Hell*), jazz criticism (*Blues People*), and essays (*Home*). It was the last book, published in 1967, that prepared his readership for an individual evolution, involving political and literary beliefs, and a change of name to catch the tone of the new character as it slipped the prison of the old. The title essay, "Home," ended: "By the time this book appears, I will be even blacker." In the same year, LeRoi Jones, born in 1934, was folded away, with a farewell to the "bitter bullshit rotten white parts" of the son of Coyt and Anna Lois Jones; Amiri Baraka, consisting of the "useful parts, the sweet meat of my feelings," was born.

The new name was bestowed on him soon after the Newark riots by a cohort of Malcolm X, Heesham Jaaber, and a half-Italian friend of Jaaber's—"a kind of gangster," Baraka says in the autobiography—who had assumed the identity Kamiel Wadud. "It was Heesham who gave me the name Ameer Barakat," which in Arabic means "blessed prince." He jokes now that, since his parents had had him baptized LeRoi, the princely designation represented a demotion. Later, he changed the name again, "Bantuizing or Swahilizing" it to Amiri Baraka. His wife, known in the old world as Sylvia Robinson, became Amina, "faithful."

"It was the influence of the African liberation movement then," Baraka told me, "the anticolonial movement. We were very much impressed by that. And remember that for a long time to be called an 'African' for a black American was insulting. So we began to take pride in that, and to say, Well, we don't want to have our slave names, that is, the names that had been given us."

In 2007, Amiri and Amina Baraka celebrated forty years of marriage. They have had five children together, in addition to several others from previous relationships on both sides. LeRoi Jones's renunciation of white society in the mid-1960s involved leaving behind his "white" wife, Hettie Cohen, whom he met while she was business manager of *Partisan Review*, and the couple's two daughters, Kellie and Lisa. Hettie still lives in Manhattan, where she writes poetry and children's books.

The Barakas live in a three-story Victorian house off Springfield Avenue. Nailed to a notice board outside is a poster urging voters to elect

Ras Baraka as mayor of Newark. Between 2002 and 2006, the Barakas' second-eldest son served as deputy mayor. In 2005, Ras published a first book of poems, *Black Girls Learn Love Hard,* a memorial volume to his sister Shani, who was shot dead in August 2003 by James Coleman, also known as Ibn El-Amin Pasha, along with her female partner. Coleman, who had served time for drug-related offenses, was the husband of Shani's half-sister Wanda Pasha. She had previously reported him to the police for violent and threatening behavior. "There could be nothing worse than this / No amount of pain," Ras Baraka writes. Amiri Baraka endorses his son's achievement on the back cover of the book: "Ras is one of the finest of the new generation of poets. If you think this is nepotism you are probably illiterate."

When I arrived, the Baraka household was in minor turmoil. The furnace in the basement was malfunctioning, on one of the coldest days of the winter, and the man who could fix it had failed to turn up. Baraka had postponed our appointment from early to late afternoon, and then had been delayed at Chicago's O'Hare Airport because of the freezing conditions. There seemed also to be a problem with the electricity. As I stood in the vestibule after being admitted by Amina Baraka, he emerged out of the gloom on the stairs, bespectacled and behatted, staring, an almost spectral figure.

In a lyrical, heartbroken memoir, *How I Became Hettie Jones,* Baraka's first wife wrote that the poet's Greenwich Village colleagues were startled to read in his second book of poems, *The Dead Lecturer,* lines such as these, from "BLACK DADA NIHILISMUS":

> Come up, black dada
> nihilismus. Rape the white girls. Rape
> their fathers. Cut the mothers' throats.

The poem goes on to exhort black dada nihilismus to "choke my friends / in their bedrooms with their drinks spilling." The book was dedicated to the poet Edward Dorn. Hettie reports how the first copy was presented during a happy period the Joneses spent with Dorn and his wife, Helene, in Buffalo.

Notwithstanding the grisly setting to which it is adapted, "BLACK

DADA NIHILISMUS" is a striking verbal creation. The work of Jones, often written in a fast, improvisational fashion, has a dexterity that marks him out as a natural writer. It was Jones, not his Greenwich Village friends or "the white man," who had to be killed. Amiri Baraka would not have achieved his own distinction—a distinction based mainly on talk of "fire!" and the glad embrace of a new ideology even before the last is sloughed off—without choking LeRoi Jones to death in his bedroom. From the outset, Baraka endeavored to set himself apart from whatever literary refinement his former avatar might have possessed: "What was you doing down there, freakin' off / with white women, hangin' out / with Queens." The queens are Ginsberg and O'Hara, the white women his old self's wife and lovers. From Greenwich Village, Jones looked proudly across the Hudson to New Jersey, envisioning the radical example of his home-state bards: Walt Whitman, William Carlos Williams, Ginsberg. As Amiri Baraka, now home in the ripe-for-revolution Newark ("If you're not home, where / are you?"), he looked further afield, drawing black-nationalist inspiration from Franz Fanon and Malcolm X, and from the Mau Mau of Jomo Kenyatta, of which "BLACK DADA NIHILIS-MUS" is but the Harlem harlequin version. If it meant jettisoning what he repeatedly refers to in the autobiography as the "petty bourgeois" way of life and artistic traditions, then good riddance to them. Jones was a writer, a colorful, precipitate branch of an old tradition; Baraka, throat-cutter of the tradition, redefined himself as a "cultural worker."

After a brief session with a photographer in the living room, Baraka led me into the kitchen, where the heat was holding up better. With the photographer, a young Englishwoman, he was patient and playful. "Just one more . . . ," she promised as she raised the camera. "That's what they all say," Baraka quipped. "I tell myself what we try to get them to tell the drug dealers: 'Just say No!'" Both the kitchen and vestibule, which leads into a sequence of small rooms, are ornamented by a variety of masks, sculptures, and other items of Africana. Every surface in the vestibule is covered by books, about African art, jazz, "the fiction of LeRoi Jones / Amiri Baraka," a copy of *Blues People* in Swedish. The only white face on view belongs to V. I. Lenin, who surges forward, fists clenched, in a giant poster in the kitchen, above a slogan in Chinese.

The one-act play *Dutchman* was in the midst of a revival at the Cherry Lane Theatre in the Village, the venue at which it was first staged forty-three years before. Baraka was due at the theatre at seven. The play is basically a two-hander, set in the carriage of a subway train. A young blond woman, Lula, teases an unassuming black man, Clay. When he responds, first with passion and then with a volley of LeRoi Jones's characteristic "rhetoric of rage," Lula stabs him to death.

"It still plays," Baraka said. "It still has a resonance that you might not expect from a play that is that old." When *Dutchman* opened in 1964, a writer in the *New York Times,* referring to Clay's angry speech, said, according to Baraka, that "if even one Negro thinks like this then America is in trouble." Baraka recalled the notice with his hiccupping chuckle. "But the real deal is that, unfortunately, there are so many truths that are still relevant. I think it captures an element of what America is, at its base."

Dutchman received its premiere during the same spring as James Baldwin's protest play *Blues for Mister Charlie,* based on the murder of the black schoolboy Emmett Till in Mississippi. "That's not a coincidence. That was part of the atmosphere. Even Lorraine Hansberry's play *Raisin in the Sun* was part of the same thing." He calls Hansberry and Baldwin "the mother and father of the black arts movement." This represents a shift in his view of Baldwin, whom Jones/Baraka attacked on several occasions, most notably in a polemical essay in *Home:* "If . . . Baldwin were turned white, for example, there would be no more noise. . . . Somebody turn [him]!" Later, the two were reconciled, and in 1987 Baraka was invited to deliver a eulogy at Baldwin's funeral. "*Blues* and *Dutchman* share a similar theme, in that the protagonists both get murdered . . . *for* speaking out. I think that is the period when the movement began to see a dichotomy, in the sense of what Dr. King was presenting—you know, turn the other cheek—and the Malcolm X development, to speak out about the actual inhumanity of white people to black people. And they got killed. So it's not just me—or Baldwin or Hansberry—picking things out of the air. With these plays, the intention was to release a lot of the interior monologue that's been going on in black America for a long time."

Baraka says that on reading the reviews of *Dutchman* after the first night he felt "this terrific feeling of responsibility, suddenly, because I saw that they would make me famous. They were talking so abusively about me that it couldn't be just a brush-off. Then I thought, if people are going to know me, I have to be responsible. I would have to say the things that I really felt."

Soon after fleeing the Village and the white man's gift of fame, Baraka fell under the neo-Africanist influence of Ron Maulana Karenga, the leader of US (as opposed to "THEM"). In his autobiography, he outlines Karenga's "Seven Principles or Nguzo Saba . . . to be memorized in Swahili as well as English. They were: Umoja (Unity), Kujichagulia (Self-Determination), Ujima (Collective Work and Responsibility), Ujamaa (Collective Economics), Nia (Purpose), Kuumba (Creativity), Imani (Faith)." Karenga believed that the practice of these principles by black people would "give them a new value system," Baraka writes, "which would make them revolutionary." Even everyday greetings were Africanized. Baraka, who followed the Karenga doctrine for eight years, describes how the traditional greeting and response, "What's happening? / Fine," were replaced on the streets around the Spirit House by "Habari Gani? / Njemi." Men shook hands, "with one hand on their arm and then pounded their right fist on their chest, something like Roman legionnaires." When Karenga passed, women were obliged to "submit," that is, "cross their arms on their breasts and bow slightly in an Afro-American adaptation of West African feudalism." Amina, the former Sylvia, drew the line at that, but embraced Africanization in other respects. "Sylvia Robinson and Everett L. Jones were married the first weekend in August 1967 by the Yoruba priest Nana Oserjeman in a Yoruba ceremony."

One of Baraka's early heroes was Miles Davis, who said of his own musical development, "I have to change. It's like a curse." Baraka has similarly felt the need to change, less from aesthetic compulsion than in obedience to political vision. *The LeRoi Jones/Amiri Baraka Reader* (1991), edited by William J. Harris in collaboration with the author, is divided into four periods, namely: "Beat . . . Transitional . . . Black Nationalist . . . Marxist." As Edward Dorn might have realized on opening *The Dead Lecturer* to find first the dedication and then the poem about choking friends, the changes have sometimes come too fast for readers to keep up. For all Baraka's admiration for William Carlos Williams, who he says gave him license to "speak in my own voice, to sound like me," and for Olson, probably the most difficult poet of the Beat/Black Mountain federation, Jones/Baraka's poetry is based on flimsier foundations. On the final page of his autobiography, Baraka describes himself as "full of animation and almost boundless energy," and the thumbnail sketch reflects the good and bad parts of him. The Cherry Lane revival of *Dutchman*— the play was written in a single night—suggested both the advantage and disadvantage of his impulsive way of working. The writer Gilbert Sorrentino said of Jones's early verse that the poet "thinks too fast for the words"; while the "boundless energy" is everywhere apparent, linguistic creativity often limps behind. Whitman and Williams strove to serve poetry itself; Jones, even before he sacrificed himself for Baraka, was in the grip of something more urgent: "Say what you mean, dig/it out, put it down, and be strong/about it."

"My own proclivities were to be understood by black people," he told me, following an expression of admiration for the historical and geographical excavations of Olson. "So whatever I learned from him would be just grist for the mill: 'I understand these things and this is what it means to us.' That's the line of demarcation in the sense of who I first was, a petty bourgeois black intellectual, going into the arena of black nationalism, and coming out the other side into a Marxist projection." Shrugging off criticism of his ideologically rigid writings, he responds: "The funny thing is that is what it's supposed to do. Artists are being bought like prostitutes, whether it's by universities or Hollywood or Tin Pan Alley, but the artist's role is to raise the consciousness of the people. To make them understand life, the world, and themselves more completely. That's how I see it. Otherwise, I don't know why you do it. The major poets of New Jersey have all suffered, whether it's Whitman, who lost his job for *Leaves of Grass,* or Williams, who was called a communist— for *Paterson!*—or Ginsberg, whose *Howl* was prosecuted, or myself. If you practice poetry the way I think it needs to be done, you're going to put yourself in jeopardy."

The publication of the autobiography in 1984, as he passed his fiftieth year, represented a watershed for Baraka (the final chapter is called "To Sum Up"). During the next two decades, he was made Professor of Africana Studies at SUNY-Stony Brook, lectured at Columbia and other institutions, and accepted grants from the Rockefeller Foundation and the National Endowment for the Arts. In 2001, he was inducted into the American Academy of Arts and Letters. He has been active in local arts projects, housing schemes, poverty programs, and education. In addition to the Black Arts Repertory Theatre in Harlem, which marked his breakaway from Greenwich Village, he founded the Spirit House and, more recently, Kimako's Blues People, a monthly arts salon held at home. In the late 1960s, he was instrumental in establishing the Afrikan Free School, which offered a range of alternative classes, from self-defense to "doctrine," as well as basic instruction. During these years, he was also occupied with raising five children.

The invitation to act as Poet Laureate of New Jersey in 2002 represented a logical development of Baraka's aspiration to be poet to the people. The two-year appointment came with an annual stipend of ten thousand dollars. By the time of his official investiture, he had already written his poem about the September 11 attacks on New York City and Washington, D.C., "Somebody Blew Up America," and had "sent it around the world on the Internet, so it was familiar to a sector of at least the literary world before all the fuss began. I had gotten a couple of complaints about it, but it wasn't until I became state poet laureate that I started getting attacked—which I resented, because it was a lie. And it seemed to me that the poem showed that. All you have to do is read it."

"Somebody Blew Up America" rehearses a range of familiar concerns—from white supremacy and the oppression of colored peoples across the globe to more local issues such as "Genius Awards to Homo Locus Subsidere," a reference to the MacArthur awards to artists (Baraka's nomination was allegedly vetoed by the late Saul Bellow, a member of the jury). The prominent theme of the poem is the ruthless instinct of the powerful for political advantage and the blindness of the public at large to "terrorists" in their own midst: "Who invaded Grenada / Who made money from apartheid / Who keep the Irish a colony / Who overthrow Chile and Nicaragua later," and so on. The lines that have attracted widespread charges of anti-Semitism, first from the Anti-Defamation League, then from the governor of New Jersey, James McGreevey, and eventually commentators in the news media, were these:

> Who knew the World Trade Center was gonna get bombed
> Who told 4000 Israeli workers at the Twin Towers
> To stay home that day
> Why did Sharon stay away?

They are followed by the refrain that runs throughout, "Who, Who, Who." The poem is polemical and interrogative—it was written, like much of Baraka's later work, to be read aloud—not to mention burdened by logistical impossibility (there were not four thousand Israeli workers employed at the Twin Towers), but Baraka insists that nothing in it justifies the charge of anti-Semitism. The word "Jew" is not used, and while the poem does suggest a conspiracy theory involving Israel and the United States, it does not hazard a solution. The names of dozens of other countries and political figures also occur, all in the form of rhetorical questions. "It might have been raising questions about Israel, but that's just the usual defense against criticism: every time you say something about Israel, you're an anti-Semite."

Governor McGreevey demanded that Baraka apologize and resign his position as poet laureate and, when he refused to do either, the governor took the extraordinary step of abolishing the post. Baraka instigated legal action against the state, "for attacks on my character and violation of the First Amendment. Not to mention the fact that they owe me ten thousand bucks." In 2004, the saga took an unexpected turn when McGreevey resigned as governor, following allegations of corruption unrelated to the Baraka affair. He admitted to having had an affair with a man, unknown to his wife, to whom he had shown political favor. "It just shows you, the man he was having an affair with was an Israeli national." When I asked if he thought that fact might be related to McGreevey's antipathy to him, he was caught by a fit of laughter. "May-bee!"

In 1980, Baraka published an article in the *Village Voice*, "Confessions of a Former Anti-Semite," in which he "repudiated" his excesses from the heated days of the late 1960s. The title (which not he but a *Village Voice* editor chose) ought to have pleased his two Jewish daughters by Hettie Cohen.

Baraka expressed fear that the charges made by the Anti-Defamation League over the 9/11 poem would stick. "See, I have to carry that with me. Forty years from now, some fool will say, 'Baraka, the anti-Semite.'" Forty years ago, he wrote a poem, "Black Arts," calling for "dagger-poems in the slimy bellies/of the owner jews"; another, "For Tom Postell, Dead Black Poet," contains the infamous lines, "I got the extermination blues, jewboys/I got the hitler syndrome figured." In "Confessions of an Anti-Semite," he disavowed these poems "thoroughly," adding, "anti-Semitism is as ugly an idea and as deadly as white racism." In my presence, his concern, for that moment, seemed genuine. It made me think that each change to which he pledges himself eclipses from view the former selves, whose actions and words may then be forgotten. In a poem called "The Liar," included in *The Dead Lecturer*, by LeRoi Jones (from "The Transitional Period," according to the *Reader*), he wrote:

When they say, "It is Roi
who is dead," I wonder
who will they mean?

I reminded him of the white liberal woman who had asked at a meeting in the 1960s what she and others like her could do "to help." Baraka had replied: "You can help by dying."

"That reaction came from being in Greenwich Village while all this was going on, and feeling guilty about that, then trying to be supermilitant. That white woman, I would talk to her about the need to be active. It's not a question that should be just dismissed like that." Even the polarizations of race, which for so long determined his politics, have found a new conception. "You can't be an American without being related. Now first of all you've got to admit that. Baldwin used to say, I'm only black 'cos you're white. That was his criticism of the fraud of racial discrimination, when racial integration, quite clearly and visibly, has been going on for hundreds of years. There's no black people and no white people. So the question is: Why are you doing this? What kind of advantage does this carry?"

It was time to head for the Cherry Lane Theatre. Baraka invited me to travel with him. He put on his green tweed coat and hat against the cold and waited by the door for his regular driver. He had been trying to call him during our talk, to ask him to arrive earlier than arranged, but his calls had met with no response. From Newark Penn Station, the Path train would whisk us to Christopher Street in the Village. The driver was at most five minutes late.

"Where is he? . . . that motherfucker . . . he laid this same shit on me yesterday morning." The level of fury rose as his youngest son loaded books into a holdall to be offered for sale at the theatre. "You watch you don't mess up them books. Where *is* that. . . . Exact same shit!"

Within the next minute or two, the car pulled up before the front lawn. Once settled in the backseat, Baraka greeted the driver congenially. He laughed as he told me about nodding off during two separate showings of the film *Pirates of the Caribbean*. On the train, he expressed regret at having missed an all-day program of six plays by one of his favorite dramatists, J. M. Synge, staged during the previous summer at Lincoln Center by the Druid Theatre Company of Galway. "Sixteen hours it lasted. You go in for the whole day. I love the thought of that. . . . A whole day of plays."

PART III

Syncopations

At the end of the Second World War, in the midst of the threat of destruction by the atomic bomb, the "outsider" replaced the soldier as the credible romantic hero. In Europe, this daredevil of repudiation was called an "existentialist" (whether or not he or she had any adherence to tenets of recognized existential philosophy); in the United States, a little later, they would be known as "Beat."

The authors grouped together as the Beat Generation started out as youngsters tempted to steal a little of the fire of blacks, mostly as it sparked off of blues singers and jazz musicians, but also from style-artists—hipsters—and drifters. Big Bill Broonzy's "Lonesome Road Blues," Leadbelly's "Midnight Special," Bessie Smith's "Chicago Bound Blues," were local anthems long before the opening pages of *On the Road* set the tone for a mostly white, university-educated generation.

Not all the writers in this section have direct association with the Beat Generation, but they all come from Greenwich Village, so to speak, rather than the Upper East Side. If one were forced to isolate a common characteristic, it would be something like dissatisfaction with "the present order of things."

My reluctant understanding of the essential fakery of the position assumed by my first literary hero, Alexander Trocchi, dawned when I contrasted his self-anointed outsider status with that of Baldwin and Wright—excluded men desperate to get "in." Trocchi's solution to his dilemma of being a privileged, educated man in a free society that nevertheless disgusted him was to cross the ocean and take the Beat badge. Donleavy, a Bronx-born New Yorker, sailed in the opposite direction at about the same time and found himself affiliated with the Angry Young Men, publicly alleged to be cousins to the Beats. Thom Gunn was conscripted to The Movement, a poetry team corresponding to the mostly fiction-writing Angry Young Men. But in his absence—for he was in San Francisco, digging the rhythms of Snyder, Ginsberg, and Creeley (though his real heroes were disreputable Elizabethans, Ben Jonson and Christopher Marlowe). Membership of all literary groups is fluid, sometimes involuntary, frequently resisted by the member. Neither Gunn nor Edmund White could be said to be "Beat," but they are outsiders of a different kind and might have been beaten at certain stages in their lives, if not for the peculiar—why not say queer?—heroism of Allen Ginsberg.

FIFTEEN

High Peak Haikus

A PROFILE OF GARY SNYDER

Gary Snyder arrived on the San Francisco poetry scene, already in the lotus position, in the early 1950s. The main players there were Kenneth Rexroth and Robert Duncan, and among the conspicuous influences on the younger poets who became attached to them were the linking of poetry to everyday speech (and occasionally jazz), a tendency toward inclusive, "open" forms, and the elevation of spontaneity to an aesthetic value. In October 1955, handwritten posters appeared in the bars and cafés of San Francisco's bohemian North Beach district: "Invitation to a Reading. 6 Poets at 6 Gallery. Remarkable collection of angels on stage reading their poetry. No charge. Charming event." The poets that evening half a century ago were Allen Ginsberg, Michael McClure, Philip Whalen, Philip Lamantia, Rexroth as emcee, and Snyder, described by Ginsberg at the time as "a bearded youth of twenty-six, formerly a lumberjack and seaman, who had lived with the American Indians." Ginsberg added graciously that Snyder was "perhaps more remarkable than any of the others."

The Six Gallery reading has gone down in history as the first public performance of Ginsberg's poem "Howl." The task of following its apocalyptic declarations ("I saw the best minds of my generation destroyed by madness, starving hysterical naked") fell to Snyder, who admits to having doubted whether he could hold the suddenly stunned audience. He read parts of a long poem rooted in Native American folklore, "A

Berry Feast," about as far from "Howl" as it is possible to get, swinging between the Buddha and a black bear "married / To a woman whose breasts bleed / From nursing the half-human cubs." Snyder remembers the evening for "the feeling people had, by the time it was over, that it had been a historical moment. No question about it. From that time on, there was a poetry reading every night somewhere in the Bay Area. It launched the poetry reading as a cultural event in American life." Jack Kerouac, who was also present, drunkenly winding up the audience, later recalled Snyder as "the only one who didn't look like a poet." While the others were "either too dainty in their aestheticism, or too hysterically cynical," Snyder made Kerouac think of "the old-time American heroes." Three years later, Kerouac capped his homage by publishing *The Dharma Bums,* a novel featuring Snyder as the mountain-climbing, haiku-hatching hero, Japhy Ryder.

Snyder might still be taken for a lumberjack rather than a poet. He wears boots and a cap, keeps a multipurpose knife looped on to his belt (nowadays next to a cell phone), and spends a large part of each day outdoors, working with his hands. In the 1960s, he was part of the alternative literary movement that spread across the United States and Europe. Seamus Heaney recalls first reading Snyder's early poems "in a little anthology of Beat poets published in London. By the time I met him in person, at a party in Berkeley in 1971, I had caught up with the work he had published since. He was togged out in jeans and a rough cotton shirt. You could easily imagine him hunkering under a stone wall on the Aran Islands."

Snyder and his wife, Carole, live with their frisky poodle pup in a single-story house he built, with professional help, in the foothills of the Sierra Nevada, four hours' drive northeast from San Francisco. Deer peep through the foliage at the visitor on the three-mile unpaved road to Snyder's ranch. On a walk in the surrounding pine and black oak forest, he points out claw marks on a tree trunk made by a bear—the same bear, perhaps, that features in a recent poem, eating all the pears from a fenced-off tree by the house. A wildcat dispatched his chickens. Until recently, the family had only an outside lavatory some fifty yards away, which, he says wryly, "could be dangerous in the mornings"—pumas also lurk among the pines, though seldom seen—but the Snyders now have the luxury of an inside bathroom with a polished wooden tub. He called the place Kitkitdizze, a local Wintun Indian word for the surrounding low ground cover bush, also known as mountain misery. "We had our hands full the first ten years getting up walls and roofs, bathhouse, barn, the woodshed. I set up my library and wrote poems and essays by lantern light." Kai, Snyder's eldest son, was a child when work on the house began in 1969. He has memories "of heat and dust and a lot of people working, and me getting underfoot." In the beginning, says Kai, now in his late thirties, "all our water had to be pumped by hand, which my dad did every day for about forty minutes. It was good exercise, I guess. All the cooking was done on a wood stove, and our heating was produced by the same method. It was like a nineteenth-century lifestyle in lots of ways." A new wing was added when Snyder received a Bollingen prize (fifty thousand dollars), for "lifetime achievement in poetry," in 1997. He now has a telephone line, though no television aerial, and is hooked up to e-mail, whereby he communicates with a worldwide literary and ecological network of friends. "We are off the electrical grid," he says, not without pride, "but have a stand-alone power system, involving solar panels and generators. We cut our own firewood from the down and dead trees. And of course we keep things in stock, a pantry full of food, half a year's worth of rice." He serves tea in the Chinese manner, and for lunch Korean noodles, with local wine freely to hand.

In 2004, Snyder published his first collection of new poems in twenty years. Readers of *Danger on Peaks* soon find themselves in familiar territory: poems about work and nature, frequently with ecological and oriental overtones. A lifelong student of Buddhism, he lived in Japan for ten years during the 1950s and 60s, where he took the vows of a Zen monk. While serious about his Buddhism, he is undogmatic. The subject is sometimes treated with humor in his work. A poem that begins "The Dharma is like an avocado! / Some parts so ripe," moves on to "the great big round seed,"

Hard and slippery,
It looks like
You should plant it—but then
It shoots out through your fingers—
gets away.

Even when it goes unmentioned in the verse itself, the meditative tendency sits behind his work and nature poems. He writes about repairing a car with the same attentiveness he gives to Zen ritual. A Snyder poem about sweeping a path, or fiddling with the engine of a pickup, is about what it says it's about. "If somebody wants to find some moral interpretation, that's all right with me. But basically, yes, it's about repairing the car. Who needs more than that?" Some poems, such as "Getting in the Wood," are made up of the names of tools and accessories: "Wedge and sledge, peavey and maul, / little axe, canteen, piggyback can . . . / All to gather the dead and the down." The voice emerges from a clear gaze and a clear mind, qualities that have characterized Snyder's poetry since his first book, *Riprap* (1959):

Walking in February
A warm day after a long freeze
On an old logging road
Below Sumas Mountain
Cut a walking stick of alder,
Looked down through the clouds
On wet fields of the Nooksack—
And stepped on the ice

Heaney, to whom one of the poems in *Danger on Peaks* is dedicated, says: "From the start I trusted the unleavened quality of the poems, the materiality of what they started from, and liked them better the closer they hewed to sensation and the vernacular. And hearing him read strengthened my admiration. He wasn't in a hurry, not out to suck up to the audience or harangue them. The voice gave space and weight to the words, so that they back-echoed a bit." A poet of a younger generation, Glyn Maxwell, praises what he calls Snyder's "wide, gladdening openness." He believes the "laid-back, jotted-down tone of Snyder's verse masks an acute sensitivity to rhythm and assonance. He has a wonderful ability to convey the physical nature of a moment: 'Drinking cold snow-water from a tin cup / Looking down for miles / Through high still air.'" Heaney adds: "If a bricklayer's hand could speak, it might sound like early Snyder. If a buddha backpacked in northern California, he too might sound like Snyder."

Recently turned seventy-five, Snyder is wiry, his face weathered, with eyes that reminded Kerouac of "an old Chinese sage." Sleepy some of the time, they widen with curiosity and frequently crease with mirth. The remoteness of the hundred-acre ranch is such that Carole, who is Japanese, is excited at the prospect of "meeting someone new," but the Snyders live in a widespread community of about forty families, "each place pretty self-sufficient, though we all cooperate and lend each other things." Kai recalls that he and his brother "walked to school, about forty-five minutes through the woods to a one-room schoolhouse. The kids were a mix of original redneck population and the new wave of people who were coming back to the woods to try to live more in touch with nature and in a more sustainable way. My best friend at school was the son of a logging family, very conservative. His family kind of avoided my family. But they were good people."

Snyder is at pains to distinguish his way of life from "a back-to-the-land, countercultural, utopian image of living outside of society. That's all right if you're going to just go like Thoreau did for a year, and you can walk over to Emerson's for dinner. But this is more like what the farm and the ranch in the West is, where people live at a distance, with a certain amount of genuine sustainable skill, though for the time being our life depends on machinery—chainsaws, generators, grass-cutters, and so forth. Now, when I first came up here I didn't have any of that, and there may come a time again when I don't have it. And so there are other strategies, too." Kai emphasizes his father's attachment to "doing things in the old ways, using tools that are made locally, things that are made with an intimate understanding of the place where you live. It's about being rooted in a place, and also understanding that the world is changing very fast and that technologies may only be a transitory crutch, a substitute for a deeper understanding of how to live in a place."

The nearest shops are thirty miles away, in leafy Nevada City, a creation of the 1849 gold rush, now no larger than a sizable village. Greeted on all sides as he makes his way along the main street, reminiscent of Wild West film sets, Snyder has time for everyone while giving the impression he'd be unhappy anywhere but on his own patch. In a local bar, a large, hearty man recognizes him from a poetry reading at a farm almost forty years ago. His recollection of the event is perfect, while the poet's is hazy.

"Don't you remember, you signed the book to me and Ann?"

"I think I do remember," Snyder says.

"And don't you remember, the cow took a bite out of the book? And you signed it to the cow as well? And then the cow crapped on the book?"

"I must remember," Snyder says, unfalteringly polite.

Gary Sherman Snyder was born in San Francisco in 1930 and raised on a farmstead north of Seattle. His parents, Harold and Lois, were "semi-educated, proud, western-American-style working-class. My father's brothers all went to sea or worked in logging camps. My mother was from a railroad town in Texas, very much a feminist rebel." The Snyders owned a small dairy farm but required outside work to keep ticking over. When Snyder was a child, "there was no work for seven years." Family entertainment consisted of reading aloud in the evenings: "Robert Burns, Edgar Allan Poe—very musical poetry which caught my ear." Even as a small boy he was known for his love of nature. "I would go and cook and stay alone for a night or two, when I was just eight or nine years old, quite far from the house. At the age of fifteen, I became a mountaineer and began to climb all the peaks of the Pacific Northwest. The kind that require ropes and ice axes. Snow peaks. Volcanoes. Big ones." He read widely throughout childhood and adolescence, but "my first interest in writing poetry came from the experience of mountaineering. I couldn't find any other way to talk about it." The adventure of scaling summits blended with the aesthetic thrill of viewing oriental landscape paintings at the Seattle Art Museum, to inspire an approach to poetry that, while it has developed over the decades, has not altered fundamentally. In 1996, he published *Mountains and Rivers Without End,* a long poem begun forty years earlier.

After studying anthropology and literature at Reed College in Oregon, Snyder enrolled at the University of California, Berkeley, in 1953, to study oriental languages. He went on to translate poetry from Chinese and Japanese. His interest in East Asian culture and thought was spurred, he says, by "an ethical realization that the Judeo-Christian tradition gives moral value only to the human being. I discovered that there were other traditions, including Hindu and Buddhist and Native American, in which all biological life is considered part of the same drama, that the world is not simply a theater for the human being, in which everything else is just a stage prop. That became a very clear image to me." In the summer holidays, he worked as a fire-lookout in the Washington Cascade Mountains. "All through July and August. You take just the food you need for that time, and a radio." There he found the opportunity to practice meditation, study Chinese, and write his first surviving poems. Many years later, on Mount Sourdough, he discovered that a scribbled verse was still pinned to the lookout's cabin wall: "I, the poet Gary Snyder/Stayed six weeks in fifty-three/On this ridge and on this rock/ & saw what every Lookout sees."

He plays down his work as a translator; the best-known work is *Cold Mountain Poems*, by the eighth-century hermit Han-Shan, a T'ang dynasty dharma bum. The twenty-four versions, made in the mid-1950s, read as though straight from the pen of the young Snyder, already planning a life of wood-chopping and water-pumping, off the electrical grid:

Men ask the way to Cold Mountain
. . . there's no through trail
In summer, ice doesn't melt
The rising sun blurs in swirling fog.
How did I make it?

Most translations from Chinese and Japanese are "too wordy," he says. "The early translators would not believe what was in front of their eyes, which was very short lines. Arthur Waley's translations are outmoded now, though in their time they were helpful. Ezra Pound was a brilliant amateur, who by luck came up with a few good lines, but not many." The economy of classical Chinese poetry has influenced his own. "So much occidental poetry is full of religious imagery or mythological reference, both of which are absent from the Chinese. Chinese poetry is secular, logical, and unsymbolic."

An interest in Asian life and culture was "in the air" in San Francisco in the 1950s. "When I got into that scene I realized there were people thinking along similar lines and also doing similar things in poetry. Of course, there was a big Asian population in the city. The presence was palpable." Snyder points out that the San Francisco poetry renaissance was already advanced, in the work of Rexroth, Duncan, Jack Spicer, and others, before the subversive Ginsberg gang arrived from the east coast: "They just publicized it." Ginsberg died in 1997. While not averse to being classified as one of the survivors of the Beat Generation, Snyder stresses "that it's a historical term. Indulging a nostalgia for it is not interesting. People say: 'Are you a Beat writer?'—I get called a Beat writer all the time—and I say: 'I was at one time, briefly, but going by what I have done in the past thirty years, no.'" His writing, he says, "belongs in the nonacademic wing of contemporary American poetry. Beat is too limiting a word." The critic Marjorie Perloff, who has written widely on American poetry, says she never thinks of Snyder as a Beat poet. "His poetry has a directness and immediacy that appeals to young people. He started out as a follower of William Carlos Williams, using short, free-verse lines and colloquial diction, but as time has gone on he has shown himself to be first and foremost a nature poet in the Emerson-Thoreau tradition. The Beats were essentially urban, engaged in oppositional social activity, whereas Snyder's forte is an account of the relationship of man—and I do mean man, because Snyder is rather patriarchal—to his environment." Heaney feels that "he's right to resist the Beat label. He loves barehanded encounters with the here and now, but cares deeply for tradition. You might say he knows equally the workings of tanka and tanker. He keeps his ear to the ground, and listens more than he howls." Ginsberg remained a lifelong friend—in a late poem, he depicts himself reading Snyder's *Selected Poems* unselfconsciously while sitting on the loo—and was a partner in purchasing the land on which the Snyders live. Through the pines, Snyder points out a small house built by Ginsberg, now occupied by Snyder's younger son, Gen, a manual laborer. Kai is an environmental scientist; Carole, whom Snyder married in 1991, has two daughters: Mika, who recently graduated from law school, and Robin, a student, both in their twenties. (Carole Koda died in 2006.)

The last letters Snyder received from Kerouac, who died in a brokendown state in 1969, were ranting and insulting, but Snyder remains affectionate toward the man who mythologized him in a cult novel before he reached the age of thirty. "Jack was a dedicated person. As a Buddhist he had some very good insights. It was all mixed up with his French-

Canadian Roman Catholicism, but so what? It's hard to know why peo-ple self-destruct. They do so for reasons of deep and ancient karma, qual-ities of their character they were born with." As for the unwanted burden of being Japhy Ryder, "the only problem I have is that I have to keep reminding people it's a novel. There's a lot of fiction woven into *The Dharma Bums*. And I am not Japhy Ryder."

As the publicity surrounding the Beat Generation spread, Snyder typ-ically did his own thing and left for Japan. Settled in a bare room—"just a few books and a table"—in the Shokoku-ji Temple in northern Kyoto, one of several temple systems of the Rinzai sect of Zen, he acted as per-sonal assistant to a *Roshi*, or Zen master. "I spent my first year cooking breakfast and lunch for him and teaching him English. At the same time, I was studying Japanese and meditating for four or five hours a day." One week out of each month, he attended the local Zen monastery for intensive meditation, or *sesshin*, which means "concentrating the mind." In an essay, Snyder described the typical day: rising at 3 AM, dashing "icy water on the face from a stone bowl," then sitting cross-legged for lengthy periods. "One's legs may hurt during long sitting, but there is no relief until the Jikijitsu rings his bell." After a twenty-minute walking interval, the young monks resume their sitting. "Anyone not seated when the Jikijitsu whips around the hall is knocked off his cushion." Writing to a friend, Snyder quipped, "I wear me Buddhist robes & look just like a blooming oriental."

After a brief visit to the United States in 1959, he returned to Japan, this time with the poet Joanne Kyger. The pair were soon married (Snyder had previously been married briefly to Alison Gass). Judging by Kyger's *Japan and India Journals* (1981), conflicting expectations of life in Asia surfaced immediately. Kyger writes: "Shortly after arriving in Japan, Gary asked me, 'Don't you want to study Zen and lose your ego?' I was utterly shocked: 'What! After all this struggle to attain one?'" The jour-nals end with Kyger returning home alone. "He wouldn't let me keep a wooden spoon," she writes. In Snyder's new book there is a complimen-tary reference to Kyger's poetry. "I think we can say we are good friends now," he says.

It is a curiosity of Snyder's career that while his first full collections—

A Range of Poems and *The Back Country*—were issued by a London publisher, Fulcrum Press, in 1966 and 1967, he has barely been published in Britain since. His early work was welcomed by, among others, Thom Gunn, who wrote appreciatively on Snyder in more than one London journal. Snyder's British readership has had to depend mostly on American imports (readily available), which puzzles him. "There is more interest in my work in Germany, France, the Czech Republic." In the United States, some of his collections, such as *Riprap* and *The Back Country*, have never been out of print. *Turtle Island*, which won a Pulitzer Prize in 1975, is reprinted roughly once a year. Heaney and Maxwell lament the absence of British editions of Snyder's work. Maxwell says: "Perhaps he doesn't fit, as he's not seductively obscure or ringingly accessible. And his is a foreign landscape, a faraway country, really: America before us, without us, after us."

As a writer who, from the beginning, has yoked ecological concerns to literary values, Snyder is often asked about the high-consuming, short-attention-span hazards of modern existence. In short, what's wrong with the way we live, and what can be done? "I don't feel inclined to make the first humanistic, easy answer, which is: We must change our values. It would be foolish to put forward simple solutions. However, for those who can, one of the things to do is not to move. To stay put. That doesn't mean don't travel; it means have a place and get involved in what can be done in that place. That's the only way we're going to have a representative democracy in America. Nobody stays anywhere long enough to take responsibility for a local community." The George W. Bush–led U.S. government is "demonstrably bad" for the environment. "Under the Clinton administration, the Environmental Protection Agency was actually called on to defend and monitor the environment. The Bush administration made it clear it wanted the EPA to be on the side of industry. The fox is in the chicken run, and in this case the fox is the oil industry." With oil prices rising, he foresees an era of "turmoil and turbulence and probably dictatorships. People and subcultures who have the flexibility and know-how to slip through that will do so. So here is a Thoreauvian answer to the question, What is to be done? Learn to be more self-reliant, reduce your desires, and take care of yourself and your family."

SIXTEEN

Between Moving Air
and Moving Ocean

THOM GUNN AND GARY SNYDER

Thom Gunn's critical essays on modern American poets are filled with delight. Here is a brief sampling of his remarks on writers whom many of his English contemporaries have dismissed, if not ridiculed:

> Gary Snyder has worked to lay himself open to the feel, look, sound, and smell of things. Attentiveness becomes in him, as it does in William Carlos Williams, a form of moral discipline.

> Ginsberg's *Collected Poems* is an enjoyable book, informed by a constant energy of attack, by humanity of spirit and wild humor, and by aspirations toward ecstasy and vision that may recall to us earlier claims and prerogatives of poetry forgotten in the age of Larkin.

> I find more of Creeley's wonderful comedy early on . . . but essentially the poetry is still written with the same plain terse language and the same sure command over the verse movement.

> The *Opening of the Field* [by Robert Duncan] . . . seems to me one of the essential books for understanding the history of poetry in English over the last half century . . . it embodies the one really influential new theory of poetry advanced in our lifetime.

Gunn's essay on Snyder was first published in the little magazine *Agenda* in 1966, whereas the rest of these observations date from the 1980s. As Gunn admitted cheerfully in his review of Ginsberg's *Collected* (reprinted in *Shelf Life,* 1994), he "disapproved of Ginsberg's poetry a good deal . . . in the prim 1950s." He would have had the opportunity to read

"Howl," "America," "A Supermarket in California," and other of Ginsberg's long-lined invertebrates, in situ, as it were: when Gunn arrived in
California to take up a fellowship at Stanford University in 1954, all the
poets cited above were active down the road in San Francisco, or across the
bay in Berkeley. *Howl and Other Poems* was published in 1956, sparking
the second phase of what became known as the San Francisco Renaissance.
Yet Gunn had no contact with the movement. His "outraged sense of decorum," as he calls it, inhibited him from seeking out and participating in the
lively Bay Area literary scene, conducted variously by Kenneth Rexroth,
Lawrence Ferlinghetti, Robert Duncan, and Duncan's friend Jack Spicer. In
his first years out West, Gunn's mentor was the older, far more austere
Yvor Winters, of whom Gunn wrote that he lived in a world "where everything had already been decided in accordance with certain rules."

Gunn was not all that prim, of course. In addition to the fetishized
"gleaming jackets, trophied with the dust" of the Hell's Angels in "On
the Move," *The Sense of Movement* (1957) contained his own homosexual
admissions—less potent, certainly, than Ginsberg's "I'm putting my
queer shoulder to the wheel," but subtly present in the poem "The Alle-
gory of the Wolf Boy," and, less subtly, in "The Beaters" (the latter was
left out of Gunn's *Collected Poems*). *The Sense of Movement* was written
mostly in America, but the poet didn't speak often of American subjects;
when he did, the voice was unacclimatized. Take this verse from "Elvis
Presley":

> Whether he poses or is real, no cat
> Bothers to say: the pose held is a stance,
> Which, generation of the very chance
> It wars on, may be posture for combat.

Something of the shock that must have been caused by Elvis's first appearances is present here, but not the background against which he posed and
wielded his guitar. The context of the poem is not recognizably American;
it is composed of the violent tension and contradiction typical of the Gunn
of the period. The use of "cat" as an item of hip talk jars. It is a poem by an
English poet living in and observing America, but not yet at home there.

It was in his next collection, *My Sad Captains* (1961), that Gunn first exhibited an Anglo-American accent, specifically in Part II of the book. This section is frequently talked of as the place at which Gunn began to write in syllabics, as a way of making the eventual transition to free verse—a medium he believes ought to exert the same degree of pressure on language as the iambic pentameter. But the second part of *My Sad Captains* is equally notable for being the place at which Gunn's poetic voice took on a new inflection.

The title of the opening poem of the section, "Waking in a Newly Built House," is by itself suggestive of the departure, and its final stanza alerts us to the fact that Gunn, the knight of The Will, has settled on fresh terrain (it is also the first poem in which Gunn dispenses with capital letters at the beginning of lines):

> Calmly, perception rests on the things,
> and is aware of them only in
> their precise definition, their fine
> lack of even potential meanings.

Loosen up the syllabic articulations, and that could almost have been written by Gary Snyder. The poem which followed in sequence, "Flying Above California," was even more Snyder-like in theme; it continued the process of accommodating the adopted landscape in a mind brought up on English gray skies and neat parcels of greenery:

> Sometimes
>
> on fogless days by the Pacific,
> there is a cold hard light without break
>
> that reveals merely what is—no more,
> and no less . . .

By the time Gunn came to write "Flying Above California," first published in *Encounter* in 1961, he would have had the opportunity to read Snyder's book *Riprap*, which came out in 1959. When he wrote his essay on Snyder for *Agenda* in 1966, he praised "the cleanness of the senses . . . cleanness, exactness, adequacy are the first impressions that we have of the language and the rhythms." Of the opening poem of *Riprap*, "Mid-

August at Sourdough Mountain Lookout," Gunn wrote: "it is a poem of fact, not of metaphor or symbol; statement does all the work." The Thom Gunn of *The Sense of Movement* and the first part of *My Sad Captains* was not renowned for letting statement do all the work. Self-consciousness is the flesh and bone of the early poems. Yet his observations on Snyder could be applied equally to the author of "Waking in a Newly Built House," "Flying Above California," and many other poems since—that is, to the Anglo-American Thom Gunn. There is even a resemblance between the mental development of "Flying Above California" and that of "Mid-August at Sourdough Mountain Lookout"—"mental" rather than "intellectual," because the raison d'être of both poems is anti-intellectual and anti-self-conscious. Here is Snyder:

> Down valley a smoke haze
> Three days heat, after five days rain
> Pitch glows on the fir cones
> Across rocks and meadows
> Swarms of new flies
>
> I cannot remember things I once read
> A few friends, but they are in cities.
> Drinking cold snow water from a tin cup
> Looking down for miles
> Through high still air.

Compare Gunn's contemplation of

> valley cool with mustard, or sweet with
> loquat. I repeat under my breath
>
> names of places I have not been to:
> Crescent City, San Bernardino
>
> —Mediterranean and Northern names.

Snyder's poem comes about as close as it is possible to get to being a poem about nothing while still being interesting. He does not actually say, "so much depends upon . . . ," but the meditativeness which supplies the poem's tone implies it. Clearing the mind, the poet allows the jumble—cones, flies, the drink of water—to arrange itself in perspective. The aim of both poems is to regard "merely what is—no more, / and no less."

In his *Agenda* essay, Gunn also states that Snyder's rhythms grow naturally out of "a habit of accurate observation which imposes on the observer a humility before the world." The Gunn of *Fighting Terms* and *The Sense of Movement* was not known for that sort of humility, but in "Flying Above California" he comes closer than before to doing something characteristic not only of Snyder but of American writing in general: naming things, and allowing the names alone to stand as values and (with a good deal of behind-the-scenes effort from the poet) to do the work of the poem.

The successful modulation into an American key did not result in outright conversion. Gunn plays classical *and* jazz. For many of the anarchic revelations in *Moly* (1971), his summer-of-love celebration of drugs and personal freedom, he elected to write in traditional forms, and he has tailored his technique to fit the mood of his muse ever since. It is not surprising that he took several years to experiment with American, or Anglo-American, tones, for he rarely does anything in poetry without first testing it severely. Rhetorical flourishes are almost always banished as spurious; but the Anglo-American voice is authentic. Attentiveness to the sound and smell of the external world—light, nature, friends, household pets, neighborhood hustlers—is what most distinguishes the later poetry from the hard, shining meters that made Gunn such a powerful presence at the beginning of his career. It is more than an aesthetic shift. It is, as he said of Gary Snyder, attentiveness as "a form of moral discipline," a gradual and personal adaptation to a new world order.

SEVENTEEN Was That a Real Poem?

ROBERT CREELEY

In an essay written in 1967, Robert Creeley set out the limits of his particular type of literary nationalism. Placing himself apart from "such allusive society as European literature has necessarily developed," Creeley situated himself, by way of opposition, in "the condition of being American." As a poet, he wished to address "the intimate fact of one life at one time"—his own, naturally—in the context of that condition.

Creeley, who was born in Arlington, Massachusetts, in 1926, was well into a successful career by then, with several books of poetry and fiction to his name (including *Collected Poems 1950–65*, published in the United Kingdom), and his "nervous shudders"—a description once given to his poems—have not changed much in character in the years since. Among the first things to strike the reader of Creeley's poetry is how little he is concerned with any sense of the past. The "intimate fact" of the present moment is first and foremost his theme. No epochal echoes resonate between the lines of his poems, from the Old World or the New, and he makes claims on an unusually restricted range of literary reference. In *A Quick Graph* (1970), which brought together twenty years' worth of critical prose, the names of William Carlos Williams, Ezra Pound, and Charles Olson crop up on almost every other page, frequently to reiterate the point about "the condition of being American." These writers keep company, in Creeley's criticism, with a set of contemporaries, all of whom, one gathers, are the author's friends: Robert Duncan, Edward

Dorn, Denise Levertov, Michael McClure, Fielding Dawson, Allen Ginsberg, and so on through the Beat–Black Mountain roll call. The prominent mainstream poets of the era—Frost, Lowell, Berryman, Plath, not to mention MacDiarmid, Auden, Larkin, Gunn—rate scarcely a mention.

This exclusivity has come to seem like a type of engagement. Creeley has proved himself, in *A Quick Graph* and the essays that followed, to be fond of epigrammatic dicta, mostly to do with language and often involving its relation to his sense of nation and identity. For example, "the American," in contrast to the European, "must so realize each specific thing of his own—'as though it had never/happened before.'" In like mind, he is fond of quoting Olson's notion that the Americans are "the last first people." The sense of a poet engagé emerges strongly from an anecdote in the same essay from which all these remarks are taken ("I'm given to write poems"), involving Williams. According to Creeley, Williams once gave a "sharply contemptuous answer to the British English professor" who ventured to ask him "where he got his language from." Williams is said to have replied: "Out of the mouths of Polish mothers." Not very illuminating in itself—the point was to show that a "British English professor," with the assumed excess of cultural imperiousness that is crammed into the title, had been put firmly in his place.

Returning to Creeley's work, with Ekbert Faas's peculiar biography (*Robert Creeley*, 2001), I am struck not only by the limitations the poet has imposed on himself, but also by how distinctly he now seems to belong to a particular cultural moment, in which stress was laid on "process" in art, as often as not as a substitute for content. Creeley came of age in the first flourishing of abstract expressionism—subjectless painting; action painting; or, if you like, "process painting"—and many of the artists later became his friends. He has written about painting, in that elusive-allusive way of his, and theoretical statements made by artists are frequently invoked in his discussions of his own approach to poetry. For example, he strikes a deliberate echo of Jackson Pollock's well-known remark, which begins, "When I am in my painting," when he says, "In writing . . . one is *in* the activity"; and in a long and involved *Paris Review* interview, published in 1968—possibly the best introduction to Creeley and his work— he invokes statements by Pollock, Franz Kline, and Philip Guston, in order to say, in each case, "That was precisely how I felt about writing" (as he did, for instance, of Guston's remark, "You know when it's done when you are both looking at and involved with what's happening").

During the same period, in Creeley's circles, the Beat and Black Mountain schools, sons and daughters of Pound and Williams, the old (Old World) poetic practices were being cast out to let in new theories which demanded a minimum of acquired techniques. Validation was asserted by way of the poet's physiology. In an essay called "A Sense of Measure," Creeley wrote: "I want to give witness . . . to what I am as simple agency, a thing evidently alive by virtue of such activity." At its crudest, at the level of the most loquacious Beat poet, this desire to give witness to the fact of being "evidently alive" was a license to put down everything that came into the writer's head. At the more sophisticated end, where Creeley dwells, the new arrangement involved "breath" (primarily), field of vision, projection; "intensity of perception," to use Williams's words; "a series of tensions made to *hold* . . . through the poet," to cite Olson's. Creeley quotes Ginsberg saying that "Mind is shapely," seemingly confident that whatever a poet puts down will achieve shape by being generated by "a poet." These and overlapping criteria adopted from Duncan, Kerouac, and others compose the scaffolding which supports Creeley's work. To suggest that this theorizing, which comes up everywhere in his critical writing, is often vague and frequently self-absorbed to the point of solipsism, is to invite "sharply contemptuous" comment. You just don't get it. It was interesting, then, to find Faas relating the gist of a correspondence between Creeley and Williams, circa 1955, with comments from Olson thrown in, on the subject of "measure." According to Williams (in Faas's account), "without measure the line becomes chaotic." Creeley replied, quoting Olson, who had decided "that it was best to throw words like meter, measure, foot, and rhythm out of the window because they described a usage, not a fact of language. While endorsing Olson's view, Creeley added that, rather than measure, they needed some more general sense of the elements of poetic form. . . . Williams had grown tired of the discussion, advising that they forget the whole thing. Probably they were in essential agreement and were merely employing different terminologies."

Creeley's most famous dictum is, "Form is never more than an extension of content." He means it as a jazz musician might, in saying about his improvisation: The form is what you just heard. And indeed, one can imagine a jazz musician uttering the equivalent of Creeley's remark (from "A Sense of Measure"): "I have never explicitly known—before writing— what I would say." As I reread his work, I found him preoccupied by notions of "form," relating to art, of course, but also to love, to memory, and to the serendipitous drift of thought that binds them. A typical poem, in this respect, is "The Place," published in the late 1950s (in the collection *A Form of Women*). At first, the strange, obstructive lapses in grammar and punctuation may obscure the meaning, but on repeated readings, the tensions between the man and the woman, his thought and his feeling, the present moment and the already shaping snapshot of memory (a repeating Creeley theme), become clearer, and, to me, haunting. It is best to quote in full, as cutting off a part of the "content" corrupts the "form" of the whole:

What is the form is the grotesquerie—the accident
of the moon's light
on your face.

Oh love, an empty table!
An empty bottle also.
But no trick will go
so far but not further.

The end of the year is a division, a drunken derision
of composition's accident.
We both fell.

I fell. You fell.
In hell we will tell of it.
Form's accidents, we move backwards to love . . .

The movement of the
sentence tells me of you
as it was the bottle we drank?
No. It was no accident.

Agh, form is what happens?
Form is an accompaniment.
I to love, you to love:
syntactic accident.

It will all come true,
in a year.
The empty bottle, the empty table,
tell where we were.

This is Creeley at his best. At other places, the reader unfamiliar with his poetics is likely to find substantial quantities of his work either willfully confusing, to the point of incomprehensibility, or else ridiculously simple, not to say simple-minded. Creeley acknowledges that a good deal of his poetry takes its cue from a poem by Williams, "The Desert Music," which is quoted several times in the course of *A Quick Graph* (and elsewhere: Creeley's second volume of essays, *Was That a Real Poem,* 1979, depends largely on the same array of references). It includes the lines,

Only the poem!
Only the made poem, the verb calls it into being.

Since the mid-1960s, Creeley has appeared to take this increasingly at face value. You need look no further than his collection *Pieces* (1969). Readers uneducated in ideas about "form," "breath," and "measure" are likely to be left adrift by jottings such as this (untitled) one, which opens the book:

As real as thinking
wonders created
by the possibility—

forms. A period
at the end of a sentence
which

began *it was*
into a present, a presence

saying
something
as it goes.

The "something" is precisely what has just been said, guided by a theory of "forms," which are themselves held to be self-validating. The next part (also untitled) restates the old credo: "No forms less / than activity." These poems appear to take as their justification the idea that, as Creeley suggested to his *Paris Review* interviewers the year before *Pieces* appeared, "if you say one thing it will always lead to more than you had thought to say."

More—or maybe less. The friend who introduced me to the Black Mountain poets in the 1970s remarked that Creeley, whom he admired greatly, was "trying to disappear up his own poetry." This friend had not by then read *Pieces*, Creeley's most determined disappearing act, in which a line may consist of "etc.," a couplet of "so / so," or "—it / it—" (Creeley takes the liberty of quoting the last one in the title essay of *Was That a Real Poem*). *Pieces* is largely made up of fragments, many of which are about form; those that leave off the obsession are apt to sound like this:

The bird
flies
out the
window. She
flies.

Try another, from the same book:

Father
and mother
and sister
and sister
and sister

Here we are.
There are five
ways to say this

I quote more than one example of this whimsy, despite the threat of a "sharply contemptuous" response, because it doesn't seem enough to say "I don't get it." John Ashbery, himself sometimes called America's finest living poet, has in turn elected Creeley as "the best we have." Creeley has been showered with honors, awards, and fellowships, including an NEA grant, a Rockefeller, two Guggenheims, and, recently, a Lannan Lifetime Achievement Award (worth two hundred thousand dollars). No one should begrudge him any of it, but it is hard not to wonder: Is the rest of the world getting more out of "Father / and mother / and sister" than I am? Turning to *A Quick Graph* in search of clarity, you are apt to come across something like this: "I would mistake my own experience of poetry if I were to propose it as something merely *intentional*, and what men may imagine, either as worlds or as poems, it is not simply a *purpose* either may satisfy." That sentence can be forced to communicate something, with sufficient goodwill, but after grappling with one example after another of the same sort of thing, one is bound to recall a comment made in the course of the *Paris Review* interview. Asked, a mite crudely to be sure, about his "interest in possible readers," Creeley replied: "I cannot say that communication in the sense of telling someone is what I'm engaged with." The bland act of "telling" would be repudiated by most decent poets; but for Creeley the very consideration of a readership is associated with "some odd form of entertainment of persons one never meets and probably would be embarrassed to meet in any case."

None of this prepares us for Ekbert Faas, who presents probably the most unflattering picture of a subject you are ever likely to come across in a biography. Faas concentrates on the younger Creeley, taking the story up to about 1965, with a short chapter devoted to the years since. On the subject of literature (and music), first of all, Faas makes it plain that Creeley likes hardly anyone (except, of course, the friends and mentors already mentioned). Robert Lowell "he thought poorly of"; Robert Graves was "very damn dull, and slight"; Malcolm Lowry, author of *Under the Volcano,* is "pretentious and childish." In a letter to Olson (January 30, 1953), summarized by Faas, "he announced that he was not a humanist. And that Virgil was shit. He didn't think Rabelais was funny. He couldn't make Donne. Henry James was a horrible old bore. He hated Beethoven and had started to hate Mozart. Shakespeare? Too slow on the page."

This would be laughable, if there were not so much of it in Faas's biography, and if it did not emerge as the standard by which, as Faas tells the story, Creeley approaches most things in life. The very concept of pleasure—never mind "entertainment of persons"—is absent. There are, on the other hand, numerous accounts of the writer's belligerence, bullying, misogyny, and general awfulness. An anecdote involving his second wife, Bobbie, gives the tone: "They were driving along, Bobbie at the wheel. . . . Bobbie wouldn't let him drive in the drunken state he was in. So he started in on her in familiarly unnerving fashion. When needling failed to produce the desired effect, he suddenly leaned forward and spat into her hair." Friends are not spared. Duncan, when Creeley first encountered him around 1951, was "a prick . . . was not only a homosexual but had the gall to write like one." Denise Levertov, to whom Creeley was "physically attracted," nevertheless "repelled" him by her "self-confident bourgeois manner." Her husband, Mitch, "got on Bob's nerves." He has affairs with the wife of one friend, then another, and another, the most ruinous being with Kenneth Rexroth's wife, Marthe, in the mid-1950s. Ed Dorn refuses to allow him near Mrs. Dorn, but Creeley sleeps with her anyway. Many acts of violence are detailed, including an occasion when, according to an eyewitness consulted by Faas, he "all but strangled a clerk in a travel office"; the victim, a little shopkeeper, was "down on his knees . . . tearing away at the strangler's wrists," before being rescued by the same witness. The crime the clerk had committed was refusing to handle some luggage.

Robert Creeley ends with a previously unpublished hundred-page memoir, written by his first wife, Ann Mackinnon. It is a tale of quarrels, domestic violence ("I found myself on my back in bed with his hands around my throat") and life-threatening desperation. At one point, Mackinnon appears to have considered murder, dismissing it because of her relative physical weakness ("I could never kill Bob"). One evening when she slipped out of the house where they were living in Spain, "to escape continual scoldings," Creeley followed her to a cliffside: "he would only have to push me gently and I would tumble down the cliff to sure death." And so it goes on, until they are divorced and another wife takes her place (Bobbie, of the spat-upon hair).

Is Creeley really like this? And if he is, what motivates Faas to issue such an extended public shaming? He made contact with Ann Mackinnon only after completing his biography, which quashes the suggestion of a conspiracy. Still, the book should be approached carefully.

Faas writes in a pedestrian manner, is unenlightening about Creeley's poetry, and fails to quote at any length even from published correspondence, which is nevertheless held up as self-incriminating evidence (Faas seems unaware of the lawful status of "fair use" of quoted material). Creeley himself authorized the book in 1971, but in his acknowledgments, Faas mentions "a mystery": the reluctance or "downright refusal" of archives and institutions to give him access to documents. He adds darkly, "I can only guess at why this should be so. . . . To say more could only confound what this book may well bring into the open." This strange, vindictive, but still fascinating biography will no doubt bring it into the open, sooner or later—whatever it is.

> It will all come true,
> in a year.
> The empty bottle, the empty table,
> tell where we were.

EIGHTEEN

Fifty Years of "Howl"

Among the first people to whom Allen Ginsberg sent "Howl" for advice and criticism, when he completed the poem early in 1956, were his mum and dad. Louis Ginsberg was a poet of mild manners and modest abilities, whose neat stanzas were often to be seen in the poetry corner of the *New York Times.* "Howl" was as far from the kind of poetry he admired as it is possible to be, but he welcomed any indication of accomplishment in his troubled twenty-nine-year-old son. "It's a wild, rhapsodic, explosive outpouring with good figures of speech," Louis wrote to Allen in February 1956. But he remained uneasy at evidence of dangerous habits. "I still insist, however, there is no need for dirty, ugly words, as they will entangle you, unnecessarily, in trouble." There had been plenty of that already. At the turn of the decade, Allen had spent eight months in the Columbia Psychiatric Institute, New York, as an alternative to serving a prison sentence for receiving stolen goods.

Ginsberg's mother, Naomi, was in a mental hospital when she received her copy. "It seems to me your wording was a little too hard," she scribbled in a letter, practically the last words she ever wrote—she died the same day. "Don't go in for ridiculous things."

Between them, Louis and Naomi Ginsberg encapsulated the tone of the response that *Howl and Other Poems* would attract—from "rhapsodic" to "ridiculous"—when it appeared at the end of 1956. The little pamphlet, forty-four stapled pages, hardly the size of a postcard, was published by City Lights Books, Number 4 in the Pocket Poets Series over-seen by Lawrence Ferlinghetti and issued from his famous bookshop on Columbus Avenue, San Francisco. The poet and doctor William Carlos Williams contributed a short preface, lending the collection an air of respectability, but no mainstream publisher would have touched it. Ginsberg's extravagant, free-form verses were aesthetically off-putting to most editors and critics in the mid-1950s, but his language—his too-hard "wording"—was simply outside the law. To put things briefly in per-spective: at least two out of the last four Man Booker Prize winners (*The Line of Beauty* by Alan Hollinghurst and *Vernon God Little* by DBC Pierre) could not have been published in their present form before 1960. The same goes for many novels by Martin Amis and almost the entire output of John Updike and Philip Roth. Some writers devised ways of getting around the prohibition on four-letter words—Norman Mailer came up with "fug" to color the speech of soldiers in his 1948 novel *The Naked and the Dead*. Some, such as Henry Miller and Vladimir Nabokov, were con-tent to have their risky books published abroad, usually in Paris, where the Olympia Press and its offshoots rejected books *without* a high degree of sexual content. Most just avoided the problem.

Ginsberg's book contains the poem "America," which has the line, "America . . . Go fuck yourself with your atom bomb." Another, "Transcrip-tion of Organ Music," practically a prose poem, offers the recollection, "When I first got laid, H. P. graciously took my cherry," with the implication that both the speaker and H. P. were men. But it was the title poem that drew the most attention. The book was printed in England by the firm of Villiers, which shipped the first consignment to California without incident. This was the era of the beatnik, the poetry-and-jazz coffee bar, the late-night bookstore (City Lights) functioning as a literary talking shop, and *Howl and Other Poems* sold out right away. But 520 copies of the second printing were seized by U.S. Customs, on the grounds that the writing was obscene. In a remark much repeated in ironical tones, the Chief Collector of Customs said of *Howl*, "You wouldn't want your children to come across it."

And maybe you wouldn't:

> who let themselves be fucked in the ass by saintly motorcyclists, and
>   screamed with joy,

> who blew and were blown by those human seraphim, the sailors,
> caresses of Atlantic and Caribbean love . . .

Maybe you wouldn't want your feminist companion to come across it either:

> who lost their loveboys to the three old shrews of fate the one eyed shrew
> of the heterosexual dollar the one eyed shrew that winks out of the
> womb and the one eyed shrew that does nothing but sit on her ass
> and snip the intellectual golden threads of the craftsman's loom . . .

—the craftsman perhaps standing for the poet and his literary associates, almost all of whom were male ("America I'm putting my queer shoulder to the wheel"). And if your African American friends were inclined to wince at stereotypes, they might regard the scenario of a university-educated writer's chums "dragging themselves through the negro streets at dawn looking for an angry fix" as nothing more than an irritating piece of slumming.

The books arriving from England were impounded in March, but in late May the collector of customs decided not to proceed with the case—Ferlinghetti had had a further twenty-five hundred copies printed in the United States, to get around the legal technicality of importing obscene material—and the outlook appeared bright for the poet and his publisher. However, within a week, in a sting operation, two officers of the Juvenile Bureau of the San Francisco Police Department (SFPD) entered City Lights, where the "banned" *Howl and Other Poems* was now the main item on display, and made to buy a copy. When the counter assistant Shig Murao accepted money for the book and a magazine, *The Miscellaneous Man*, he was arrested for "peddling" literature likely to be harmful to minors. (Charges against *The Miscellaneous Man* were soon dropped.) This time, it was the turn of Captain William A. Hanrahan of the Juvenile Bureau to say of the poems, "They are not fit for children to read." The *San Francisco Chronicle* satirized the SFPD's lit crit by publishing a cartoon which showed an officer nailing a notice to the door of a bookshop—"All books must be fit for children to read"—while the bespectacled bookseller is bundled into a police van.

The opening line of "Howl"—"I saw the best minds of my generation destroyed by madness, starving hysterical naked"—is among the best-known in American poetry. It has become a catchphrase. In 1997, Anglia Railways used it as an advertising jingle, to plug a special deal on trains from London to Norwich: "I saw the best minds of my generation at Liverpool Street Station" (the Ginsberg estate politely put a stop to it). Ginsberg wrote Part I of the poem while living at 1010 Montgomery Street, San Francisco (the house is still there; no plaque). He later recalled that he had not intended to publish it, and therefore had "nothing to gain, only the pleasure of enjoying on paper those sympathies most inti-mate to myself and most awkward in the great world of family, formal education, business, and current literature." He felt free to commemorate the various assaults of madness, injury, death, and persecution that had befallen the "best minds" of his intimate circle in what they experienced as the repressive atmosphere of postwar America.

Most of the poem's long lines, or "strophes," begin with "who"— "who were expelled from the academies for crazy & publishing obscene odes on the windows of the skull"—and are traceable to actual events. In this case, "expelled from the academies" refers to Ginsberg's removal from Columbia University for writing "Fuck the Jews" on his bedroom window, in order to provoke the cleaner into washing it. Jack Kerouac, Neal Cassady, William Burroughs, Herbert Huncke all feature in the poem, in distorted form, as if under strobe lighting, as do minor Beat fig-ures such as William Cannastra, decapitated as he leaned from a New York train (who "fell out of the subway window"), Tuli Kupferberg, failed suicide, "who jumped off the Brooklyn Bridge this actually hap-pened and walked away unknown into the ghostly daze of Chinatown," and the poem's dedicatee Carl Solomon, whom Ginsberg had met in the Psychiatric Institute, "who were given . . . hydrotherapy psychotherapy occupational therapy pingpong & amnesia."

It may require an act of goodwill on the part of the reader new to "Howl" to stick with it all the way through, so strange are the language, imagery, and juxtapositions, much of it incomprehensible without the author's explanation (Ginsberg provided a set of annotations in 1986, published in the superb *Howl: Original Draft Facsimile*, edited by Barry Miles), but once you are committed to its unusual presence it becomes easy to like, to wonder at, to read repeatedly in search of new glimpses of meaning or memory pictures from the author's "associative flash" technique. It is not my favorite Ginsberg poem—"Kaddish," the thirty-six-page lament for his mother, is more emotionally extended and mature, less "hysterical naked"—but readers of poetry are inspired by the unexpected, and nothing more unexpected in 1956 than "Howl."

As the book was being seized by the SFPD, and Ferlinghetti was charged with publishing and selling obscene literature, Ginsberg was in Tangier with William Burroughs, helping to type the chaotic manuscripts of *Naked Lunch*, mentioned in the dedication of *Howl* as "an endless novel which will drive everybody mad"—as if there wasn't enough madness about the place. Burroughs had been briefly incarcerated in a mental hospital in New York and had cut off one of his own fingers. Later he was detained in a Mexican prison after shooting his wife in the head during a game of William Tell. Kerouac, another of the book's dedicatees, had been discharged from the navy when appearing to exhibit symptoms of "dementia praecox," schizophrenia. The others mentioned in the dedication were Neal Cassady and Lucien Carr, both of whom spent periods in prison, the latter for manslaughter (he later asked Ginsberg to remove his name from the book). This history fuels the poem: images of "madness," together with its cousins "visions" and "hallucinations," feature more prominently than the deviant sex that prompted Captain Hanrahan to position the forces of his Juvenile Bureau as a shield between the book and the "children."

When Ferlinghetti and Shig Murao arrived at the Municipal Court of the City of San Francisco on August 16 (the trial lasted until October 3), they must have groaned to discover that the judge assigned to hear the case was Clayton W. Horn, who had lately caused surprise by instructing five female shoplifters to attend a screening of the film *The Ten Commandments* and compose essays on its moral teachings in lieu of punishment. Judge Horn was a Sunday School teacher, but that would not necessarily make him well disposed to Ginsberg's "Holy! Holy! Holy! Holy! . . . The soul is holy! The tongue and cock and hand and asshole holy!"

The defense assembled a team of witnesses that included Mark Schorer, Professor of English at the University of California, and the poets Kenneth Rexroth and Robert Duncan. The prosecution attorney was Ralph McIntosh, a stolid philistine who turned out to be easy prey to the articulate spokesmen in favor of the book. Schorer was particularly eloquent, breaking "Howl" into component parts, explaining the nature of each and how they interacted. A book published by City Lights to mark the fiftieth anniversary of the case, *Howl on Trial,* contains transcripts of the court proceedings, which make absorbing reading. McIntosh asked Schorer if he understood what Ginsberg was on about. When Schorer replied, "It's not always easy, but I think so," McIntosh invited him to open his copy of the book.

> Q. Well, let's go into some of this. About the third line down, you understand what "angelheaded hipsters burning for the ancient heavenly connection to the starry dynamo in the machinery of night" means?
>
> A. Sir, you can't translate poetry into prose; that's why it's poetry.
>
> Q. What are "angelheaded hipsters"?
>
> A. That's a figurative statement: of "angelheaded"—I would say characters of some kind of celestial beauty . . . I'm not sure I can translate it in any literal way.
>
> Q. In other words, you don't have to understand the words. . . .
>
> A. You can no more translate that back into logical prose English than you can say what a surrealist painting means in words, because it's not prose.

McIntosh quoted a line from Part II of the poem, ending "Religions! the whole boatload of sensitive bullshit," and asked, "Couldn't that have been worded in some other way? Do they have to put words like that in there?" At this point, the judge intervened to say that it was "obvious that the author could have used another term; whether or not it would have served the same purpose is another matter." At that moment, Ferlinghetti surely sensed victory.

Judge Horn's verdict was largely reliant on a case which had reached the U.S. Supreme Court in the spring of the same year, *Roth v. United States,* in which it was established that literature was protected by the right to freedom of speech enshrined in the First Amendment of the U.S.

Constitution; but the case of Samuel Roth had involved photographic magazines with titles like *Aphrodite*. In applying the new standard to a book of poems, Judge Horn was setting a precedent for obscenity in literature cases to come (including the novel Ginsberg was currently typing, *Naked Lunch*, the subject of several trials). The measure of a book was not whether it was "fit for children to read," as both the Collector of Customs and the head of the SFPD Juvenile Bureau had claimed, but was to be gauged from its effect on "the average adult in the community." The test of obscenity was that "the material must have a tendency to deprave or corrupt readers by . . . arousing lustful desire to the point that it presents a clear and present danger of inciting to anti-social or immoral action." If a work had "the slightest redeeming social importance," it should be judged "not obscene." Obscenity was often in the eye of the beholder. Judge Horn summed up: "I conclude the book *Howl and Other Poems* does have some redeeming importance, and I find the book is not obscene. The defendant is found not guilty."

Howl was not the most significant of the obscenity cases clustered around the 1950s and early 60s, but it was one of the earliest, and as Nancy J. Peters writes in *Howl on Trial*, "over the next decade, a series of court decisions began to remove restrictions." Writing to Ferlinghetti from Amsterdam, on receiving news of the verdict, Ginsberg asked: "Is there chance of continuing the fight and freeing Miller, Lawrence, and maybe Genet? That would be really historic and worth the trouble."

Some of the people who read *Howl and Other Poems* would have owned a copy of the Henry Miller novel Ginsberg had in mind, *Tropic of Cancer*, but it would have been an illicit copy, smuggled from Paris, where it was first published in 1934 by Obelisk Press, the original ancestor of the Olympia Press. By Ginsberg's time, the Miller books—*Tropic of Cancer* was followed by *Tropic of Capricorn, Sexus*, and others, all unpublishable in the United States and Britain—were underground classics. In November 1949, the *New York Herald Tribune* reported the experience of a passenger on a transatlantic liner who came across a couple on deck apparently reading *Jane Eyre*, the covers of which concealed the texts of "Henry Miller's twin volumes, *Tropic of Cancer* and *Tropic of Capricorn*, neatly packaged by a Paris publisher."

When Barney Rosset of the New York firm Grove Press set out to challenge the customs ban against *Tropic of Cancer* in 1961, he found that the author had no wish to see his novel legitimized. As Rosset later summarized Miller's words, "What happens if you publish it and we actually win the case? In five years they'll assign it in college courses and no one will want to read it" (it took more than five years, but he was right). The Miller books really were banned by law, following the failure of a 1953 court case to overturn the customs prohibition. A vaguer definition of "banned" was used when publishers were afraid to publish a book with scenes of sexual activity, or booksellers to stock it, for fear of being prosecuted, or of a police raid. In this sense, but no other, *Lolita* was banned, as were Alexander Trocchi's *Young Adam* (to the author's satisfaction, his later novel *Cain's Book* was deemed obscene by a magistrate's court in Sheffield) and *The Ginger Man* by J. P. Donleavy.

Rosset did go to court over *Tropic of Cancer*, and succeeded, as he had in 1960 with *Lady Chatterley's Lover* (the Old Bailey trial, which altered the definition of obscenity in Britain, began the same year) and would do later with *Naked Lunch*. The fight for the freedom to publish "dirty, ugly words," and the sexual complexities they describe, was won. Even Louis Ginsberg came round, and he and his son appeared together on platforms in later life to read their poems, including "Howl."

It was not the end of censorship, of which there is still plenty about, including self-censorship. The new forms are less likely to involve sexual activity than sexual identity, or religious and ethnic sensitivity. In the *Howl* case, much was made of whether the "average adult" would use a four-letter word in "polite society." Many people still prefer not to, but among those who couldn't care less there might be a disinclination to use what is sometimes called "negative speech"—which could involve calling mature women "girls," or black people "colored" (or even "black"), or disabled people "crippled." Just as the definition of polite society has shifted since Ginsberg and Judge Horn's time, so have notions of what can be acceptably uttered in its midst. People who are at home with all kinds of sexual high jinks feel uneasy with the repeated use of "nigger" in Mark Twain's classic novel *The Adventures of Huckleberry Finn*. If the word were to be used in an unironic or uninstructive way here, it would certainly be censored, and no amount of protest would cause it to be restored.

More unsettling, perhaps because they are relatively new, and liberal (another word for "polite") society has not found comfortable ways to deal with them, are instances of religious censorship. In December 2004, the play *Behzti* by Gurpreet Kaur Bhatti was staged at a theater in Birmingham, in the English Midlands, but was forced to close—censored, in effect—by Sikh protestors claiming to be offended by its action and language. When Salman Rushdie deplored the threats of mob intimidation against the makers of the film *Brick Lane*, who intended to shoot scenes on location in East London, he was recalling the fight to keep his novel *The Satanic Verses* in bookshops, in the face of more violent suppression.

"Howl" still reads well, to a reader willing to be swept along by its apocalyptic imagery and its relentless rhythmic attack. The entire first part—eight pages in the City Lights edition, which continues to appear in a form that resembles the original book—is composed of a single sentence. It is an "event" poem, like *The Waste Land*, like Hugh MacDiarmid's *Drunk Man Looks at the Thistle*, like, in our own time, Christopher Logue's *War Music*, entering the language under its own terms. The occasional sloppiness—Ginsberg's annotations reveal that he was willing to sacrifice meaning for show—can be taken to add to the energy of the performance.

When he returned from Europe in 1958, to find himself the triumphant author of that ever-popular thing, "the book they tried to ban," as well as the assumed spokesman of the Beat Generation, Ginsberg gave his first recorded interview to the *Village Voice*. Why had he come home? "To save America. I don't know what from."

NINETEEN

Personal/Political

A PROFILE OF EDMUND WHITE

In a strip cartoon drawn by Edmund White's lover Hubert Sorin, published in a literary magazine in 1991, White is depicted reading aloud from one of his novels, a typically carnal passage: "Lou tried to turn me into the man, but I was too affectionate in a puppy-dog way. . . . 'You need to focus more on cock and ass,' Lou said. 'Pull out further and plunge deeper.'" In the adjoining frame, a member of the audience asks the author, "Do you intend to write the rest of your life?" to which White answers yes. The questioner then turns to the cartoonist himself: "Ah Ah Ah! Hubert it'll be your turn! I can't wait to read those spicy details!"

Sorin died of AIDS in 1994. If the questioner is still curious about his affair with White, the details may be found in the autobiographical novel *The Married Man*, published six years later, in which Hubert goes under the name Julien. About a hundred pages of the book are devoted to the harrowing spectacle of his disintegration, leading slowly to death in a Moroccan clinic at thirty-four. Readers who flinch at the memory of Emma's deathbed agonies in *Madame Bovary* are in for something far more protracted from *The Married Man*.

"I do believe sex is worth dying for," White once said—a view that could perhaps be held only by one who has watched so many die for and because of it. The wave of sex-related death that hit White's world in the 1980s is suggested by a sentence from Stephen Barber's biography *Edmund White: The Burning World* (1999): "Almost all of his closest friends and lovers in New York—David Kalstone, James Merrill, Bill Whitehead, Christopher Cox, John Purcell, among very many others—would die of AIDS in the decade following his departure for France." *The Farewell Symphony*, the novel preceding *The Married Man*, is a record of a community sickening to a plague, at first mysterious then dreadfully familiar. "I thought that never had a group been placed on such a rapid cycle," says the narrator, a barely disguised version of the author; "oppressed in the 50s, freed in the 60s, exalted in the 70s and wiped out in the 80s."

White exercises a survivor's detachment now, when discussing Sorin's death and the decade of loss that preceded it. "I think I'm very stoic. Death and dying are things that I'm used to," he says. "I felt like it was a subject that had been handed to me. In *The Farewell Symphony*, there is a Hubert figure, and there is a lot of humming and hawing about whether his story's going to get told. Finally, I decided it deserved its own book and wrote *The Married Man*." The humor and Jamesian social commentary of the first half of the novel, White says, "were a means of disarming the reader and softening him up for the kill. It seemed to me a way of getting around people's quite natural defenses. If you announce from the beginning that you're writing an AIDS book, then people just don't get around to reading that book." White felt that AIDS as a subject in literature "had become awfully kitschy—all those terrible plays by Larry Kramer and Tony Kushner, with angels and lovers who have deathbed marriages. Whereas the truth about AIDS was that it divides couples and destroys personalities. And of course it fills people with great resentment, because they're young and they have to die. So all of that was something I wanted to show."

Edmund Valentine White III was born in Cincinnati in 1940 to well-off Texan parents. His childhood experiences, to which he returns continually in his writings, were a mixture of the lurid, the sensational, and the dismal. Relations with both parents were complex, not to say bizarre. "I feel sorry for a man who never wanted to go to bed with his father," the White-like narrator says early in his most famous book, *A Boy's Own Story*; "when the father dies, how can his ghost get warm except in a posthumous embrace?" A few pages later, he is recalling fantasies of "seducing him, eloping with him." The recollection is given another air-ing, sixteen years on, in *The Farewell Symphony*, ornamented with explicit sexual imaginings. White's relationship with his mother was also unorthodox, involving massage duties and an elaborate foundation garment known as the Merry Widow—"a bra, a stomach-flattener, a butt holder-inner"—which her young son was conscripted to help her into and out of. White's sister, Margaret, has recalled how she would return home in the evenings to find "the two of them sleeping in Mother's bed together," which she found "disgusting."

Photographs of White, taken from the time of his early thirties to the present day, disclose a lurking sorrow in the folds of his eyes and mouth, but in person he is eager and funny. Once a heavy drinker, he is now teetotal. He has made reference in print to his annoyance at "being described as fat (or 'portly' or even 'matronly') in interviews." Taking a seat in a snug corner of the wood-paneled bar of the Hotel Lutetia, on the Left Bank in Paris, he recalls how he once interviewed Catherine Deneuve "at this very table. We started in English, then switched to French and her IQ jumped about ten points, but she spoke so fast I had difficulty understanding what she was saying." He runs through a roster of approving adjectives to invoke the great actress's charm, and a similar catalog is deployed by White's friends to describe him. The writer Andrew Holleran, author of the novel *Dancer from the Dance* (1986) and a founding member with White of the gay literary group known as the Violet Quill, describes him as "an extremely charming, wonderfully intelligent person, a man whose conversation will always give you something you didn't have before. He's a sort of lighthouse sending out beams of light." Barber calls him "insatiably curious. I've traveled with Edmund on a number of occasions from Paris to the south of France, on which he's coaxed a life history out of everyone within earshot, in addition to providing a discreet running commentary on all the beautiful men (and women) who pass through the train."

White's narratives are largely composed of social experiences, from the pleasures of dining with friends to the ecstasies of sex with strangers. Incidents that begin as anecdotes—such as Bruce Chatwin monologuing unstoppably at the dinner table—are later worked into personal essays, then stitched into novels. While admitting that his books reflect his own experiences more directly than those of most writers, White protests: "Part of my strategy in *A Boy's Own Story* and other novels was to try and normalize things a bit, because if I had made it as crazy as it really was, it would just seem like psychopathology and not like a representative story." His parents, he says, were "kinda nutty. My father was a misanthrope, who slept all day and stayed up all night so that he wouldn't have to see people. He ran a business with a large staff but would go there at night and leave things for them to do during the day when he wasn't there." White's mother was a child psychologist. "A lot of her friends were psychologists and psychoanalysts, and so my sister and I were in this milieu where people were encouraged to talk very frankly about their feelings. My mother was terribly invasive, all in the name of psychiatric honesty. It was a bad thing in some ways, but I do think it had the effect of making me interested in 'the truth' as a writer—more than beauty, more than having a shapely story." He has written yet again about his parents in his memoir, *My Lives*, "though I paint them in more extreme terms."

Keith Fleming, White's nephew, who as a teenager in the 1970s was partly raised by him in New York after White's sister divorced, published a book about his uncle, *Original Youth: The Real Story of Edmund White's Boyhood*. While Fleming has written kindly elsewhere about White, *Original Youth* is frequently unflattering. It dwells on "the artful solicitousness" of White's character. The novelist's sister is quoted as saying: "He charms everyone he's with but then he turns around and talks about you behind your back." The word *betrayal* is used throughout. White, who cooperated with his nephew in the preparation of *Original Youth*, is typically accepting of the book and speaks about it without resentment. "He interviewed all sorts of people, including the boy who lived next door, who said about our father, 'Oh, Mr. White was the most wonderful man who ever lived, he introduced me to baseball, he took me to concerts'—basically presenting this totally benign view of my father. So I'm prepared to believe there are other versions of him than the one I gave."

White lived in Paris for sixteen years, from 1983 onward, but has returned to New York. He emits a sense that Paris remains his spiritual home. He speaks French fluently, without modulating his singsong accent, and he has a formidable knowledge of the city's culture. A short nonfiction book, *The Flâneur* (2001), guides the visitor through the dense history of Paris with a light touch. The longest of his works is an eight-hundred-page biography of Jean Genet. White says he learned from Colette the habit of using himself as a character in his own books. However, White's principal hero in literature is probably Christopher Isherwood, who set the literary example he wished to follow, rather than that of writers such as James Baldwin or Gore Vidal. "Early gay novels such as *Giovanni's Room* and *The City and the Pillar* were not nearly as important to me as Isherwood's *A Single Man*. I mean, *Giovanni's Room* is a very beautiful book, but in terms of gay politics, if you care about that, it's not a very evolved book, because the idea behind it is, the only desirable men are straight men. And if they ever submit to your blandishments, they're worthless, because they're now gay. It's that self-hating attitude of the 1950s, which I knew when I was a boy." Isherwood's novel, on the other hand, was unapologetic. "It shows a gay man who has straight friends, and he's 'out' to them. He has problems, but in the way everybody else does. He's not this miserable homosexual condemned to a lifetime of suffering. That's an important distinction."

After obtaining a bachelor's degree in Chinese from the University of Michigan in 1962 (his interest in Chinese having grown out of an adolescent study of Buddhism), White moved to New York. He worked as a writer and editor at Time-Life on educational mass-market publications. One week he would be reducing an art historian's essay on the Renaissance to caption-sized chunks, the next simplifying the origins of the human race. He stayed until the end of the 1960s, keeping his after-dark life concealed from colleagues. His departure in 1969 coincided with the Stonewall riots in Greenwich Village, an event crucial to the making of modern gay identity.

Feminism, black power, and gay liberation are, to White, three points of an equilateral triangle, and he wears the term *gay* in the way others might brandish the badges of those crusades. In this way, he is a foundation writer of the personal-is-political movement—which he calls "probably America's greatest contribution to political thinking"—a teammate of authors who play in the colors of critical theory, all the way from Foucault (a friend) to Toni Morrison (another friend). It's a short hop from deconstruction to political correctness, and so it came as a surprise to White to find himself rejected by students as an old-white-man pariah at Brown University, where he taught in the early 1990s, for endorsing the alleged "objectification" of black subjects by photographer Robert Mapplethorpe (yet another friend). As White's nonfiction writings are studded with pieces on figures such as Yves St. Laurent and Elton John, it is easy to overlook his place as a theorist of the particular urgency of "writing gay."

Alan Hollinghurst, author of *The Line of Beauty*, which won the 2004 Man Booker prize, reviewed *A Boy's Own Story* when it appeared in the United Kingdom in 1983, in notably uncertain terms. He says now: "I see that I was disconcerted by it because it was such a radically new kind of gay book: it wasn't stirringly fatalistic, it wasn't obligingly erotic; it was palpably an account of a real gay life, in all its awkwardness, yearning, failure, and defiance. How often does it happen that a whole new area of human behavior becomes available to writers?" Hollinghurst was struck by "a fascinating tension" between the unidealized story and the "high finish" of the prose. "That I think was the lesson of the book for me, and was in my mind when I started writing my own first novel a couple of years later: that there was a need to tell the truth about gay lives, and a belief that those lives deserved the full richness of literary attention."

White's first published novel, however, was not a story of gay life. *Forgetting Elena* (1973) is a lyrical fantasia about a young amnesiac striving to rename the particulars of his inner and outer worlds. White had written several novels that remain unpublished, and twenty plays, of which only two were performed (one was *Blue Boy in Black*). Of his emergence into print, White says: "It sounds odd, but it suddenly occurred to me that a book should be well written. I hadn't really thought of that before. I was using writing as therapy. But with *Forgetting Elena,* because everything is transposed into other terms, it's more imagined. I saw the story as an artistic object rather than a confession."

White's fiction divides neatly into two halves. The better-known books, such as *A Boy's Own Story, The Beautiful Room Is Empty,* and *The*

Farewell Symphony, come with a direct narrative thrust. They read as if the author has written the reader a long letter. Then there are *Forgetting Elena, Nocturnes for the King of Naples,* and *Caracole,* which rise up from a deeper zone of imagination and have no noticeable traces of confession. Nicholas Jenkins, a literary critic and professor of English at Stanford, believes both Whites are present in each book. "As Auden said, every writer's personality contains a bit of Ariel and a bit of Prospero, a side that is hedonistic inventor and a side that is earnest truth-teller. At first glance, White's books seem to assemble neatly into two blocs, but in each case one half of White—it could be either—stands a little deeper in the shadows." One of the joys of reading him, according to Jenkins, "is to watch that hidden brother magisterially at work, sheltered behind his ostensibly stage-hogging sibling. At about the book's midpoint, you undergo a bewildering realization: Prospero is following Ariel's orders." White himself says: "I think I explore feelings and things that have happened in the past first on the level of fantasy and then on the level of reality. For example, I treated the whole subject of the New York intellectual world, and of raising my nephew, in very outlandish terms in *Caracole,* and then came back to the subjects, in a realistic way, in *The Farewell Symphony.* It gives you twice as much for your money."

When *Caracole* was published in 1985, several figures in the New York literary world thought they recognized portraits—unflattering portraits— of themselves. The late Susan Sontag, for one, was offended by seeing her reflection in the imperious, easily bored, readily offending figure of Mathilda. She and White barely spoke again. Other people were also offended, including the poet Richard Howard—"her protector," according to White. "They rejected me; I never rejected them. I thought they were pretty well disguised. For the Mathilda figure, I also had in mind Madame de Staël, but I guess people didn't see that. It seems kind of exaggerated to make such a fuss over a book that came out twenty years ago and sold three thousand copies. Susan and I tried to make up, but it didn't work."

Whether writing as a fabulist or a memoirist, White is the first to see that his strength does not lie in the intricacies of plotting. "My plots are scrapbooks," he admits in *The Beautiful Room Is Empty,* the sequel to *A Boy's Own Story.* He relies on memory and language to hold the reader's attention, writing at times with a prodigious lyric ease. An older man attempting a seduction is described as "someone crosshatched with ambiguity, a dandy who hadn't bathed, a penniless seducer, someone upon whose face passion and cruelty had cast a grille of shadows." A dazzling, self-assured young woman "acted as though she were royalty and being beautiful a sort of Trooping the Colour." When he puts his mind to the novel of manners, as in the first half of *The Married Man*, White is equally accomplished. And he lights up his pages with bright minutiae of daily life: of not quite having a voice to answer the telephone in the morning (and going through a do-re-me scale to warm up), of feeling out of place at lunch for wearing the wrong tie, of the sudden awareness that, to a bohemian sensibility, America means "not just New York City, not just Manhattan, but Greenwich Village."

However, sex between men provides the current of his straight-narrative novels, and sometimes the attention to "the truth" has scandalous results. It is hard to imagine a publisher today risking a novel that opens with a five-page account of a youth sodomizing a delighted twelve-year-old girl. *A Boy's Own Story* opens with such a scene, only both principals are male. The novel goes on to chart the boy's sexual territory, leading him away from his eccentric home life, and ends with the shocking betrayal of a teacher to whom he had offered himself for sex. Though the subject matter and treatment of *A Boy's Own Story* were new at the time of publication, White sees his breakthrough novel as fitting into an American tradition of boys' own stories. "It may come from American-style religions, where you're supposed to bear witness, which are always very convulsive and revelatory of the self."

While his writings from the early 1990s onward reveal a fear of the ponderous waistline and a panicky reliance on cologne, White has every reason to celebrate his longevity, for it is over twenty years since he discovered he was HIV-positive. As one friend or lover after another perceived the "morning auguries" of the onset of AIDS, White reasonably expected to be soon counted among them. "I'm sure I've been positive since 1979 or 80, because those were the years when everybody was coming down with it. I didn't have a regular lover at the time, and I was extremely active sexually. We didn't know about safe sex, because we didn't know about the viral nature of it. But I turned out to belong to a minuscule group, about five percent, who are called nonprogressors. It means you don't get worse. I've never taken any medicine for it. It was only about four or five years ago that I realized I probably wasn't going to die of AIDS, because there were many people who would hang on for ten years and then suddenly die. But now it looks like I'm condemned to live. In the end, I'll probably have to call Dr. Kevorkian or something."

He claims not to dwell under the accumulated shadows of his departed friends, though he is proud of being "one of the six people who founded the Gay Men's Health Crisis, which is now the largest AIDS organization in the world. I think I accept these things better than other people do, which may make some people think I'm heartless." Jenkins believes it would be a mistake "to limit our sense of White's significance as a writer to his role as a major chronicler of the AIDS crisis. We miss out on so much of White's art if we attribute a mainly documentary character to his books." Holleran points out that "at the start he resisted that role as a matter of principle, but in writing his autobiographical fiction he eventually could not avoid it. His own life forced it on him."

In recent years, White has had "a sort of reunion" with his sister, Margaret, who came out late as a lesbian and lives in Chicago with a brood of adopted children, all of whom were born with AIDS. "She has this wonderful family, from the age of twenty down to zero, one from Ho Chi Minh City, one from Addis Ababa, and so on." The return to the United States was motivated largely by the wishes of his partner, Michael Carroll, an American writer twenty-five years his junior. "He got fed up with living in France. He wanted to launch his own career, and to him Paris just felt like a dead end. It was a case of choosing Paris or choosing him, so I chose him." Two or three times a week, White travels by train to Princeton, where he is director of the creative writing program. He finds America an "irritating" place to be, but likes the university and enjoys the company of students, who have not put him through a similar ordeal to the one he experienced at Brown over Mapplethorpe. "I think the whole political correctness thing has come and gone now. I'm more PC than my students. I'll be worrying that I've ruffled their feathers, when they don't even know what I'm talking about."

He feels living in America has affected his writing in small ways. "Minimalism has really caught on—a journalistic minimalism, talking in bite-sized units for the MTV generation, that short-attention-span thing. It all seems to me to make long novels, literary novels, with lots of gray paragraphs, look sort of odd. The Updike style begins to seem terribly heavy, terribly dated. I think my writing's punchier than it used to be, so it's had a good effect. I can't imagine writing a novel like *Caracole* now— that all came out of living in Paris and reading and thinking about world literature." Barber believes New York will make him "more coolly concentrated. When Edmund left, all his friends were still alive; by the time he returned they had almost all vanished, together with the sites in the city to which he had been attached. He has had to recreate New York from scratch. I think that process has made his writing more inventive, and more focused. He wrote much of *A Boy's Own Story* in fits of hard drinking, and later novels were often written in fragments between one European city and another. I think the concentration that New York generates in Edmund will yield some great work."

White nevertheless describes himself as "the most disorganized writer I know." He writes quickly and in short bursts, sometimes going a month without doing any work, indulging his "compulsively sociable" side instead. He claims never to rewrite, "or even to blot anything out. I start very slowly . . . and then it's a kind of crisis . . . everything's an emergency . . . and I always have to make money, so I go faster." He writes in longhand, which he describes as "much more technologically advanced than the computer, you can take it on a train and into cafés," and then dictates from notebooks to "this rather sniffy secretary I have, who types it all up. And he disapproves of everything I do. I'll think, 'Oh, I can't say that to Patrick.' Or else he'll say severely, 'She had brown hair in the last chapter.' He has great taste and so I censor and rewrite stuff as I dictate it, to suit him really."

TWENTY

To Beat the Bible

A PROFILE OF J. P. DONLEAVY

In the summer of 1954, J. P. Donleavy wrote the letter that would determine the course of his life. The recipient was Maurice Girodias, proprietor of the Olympia Press in Paris. "Dear Sir, I have a manuscript of a novel in English called 'Sebastian Dangerfield.'" The book, later renamed *The Ginger Man*, had been rejected by more than thirty publishers, partly on account of its at times baffling stream-of-consciousness narrative, but more because of its ribald content. "The obscenity is very much part of this novel," cautioned the author. But he took care to add that "extracts . . . have been published in the *Manchester Guardian*."

Recent productions of the Olympia Press at the time included *Watt* by Samuel Beckett, *The Thief's Journal* by Jean Genet, classic works of erotica such as *Fanny Hill* and novels by Guillaume Apollinaire and Georges Bataille, all in English. At the time, Girodias was considered to be a publisher of risqué books of literary quality (the most famous of all Olympia publications, *Lolita* by Vladimir Nabokov, was soon to follow) but not cheap pornography. However, the latter was about to become his specialty. He bought Donleavy's novel for £250 and included it in his latest list, the Traveller's Companion Series, with titles such as *School for Sin*, *White Thighs*, *The Whip Angels*, and *Rape*, all advertised at the back of *The Ginger Man*, which itself bore the recommendation "special volume." Donleavy collected his £250 in cash from a middleman in a dubious Soho bookshop. "When I discovered that the novel was published in this pornographic series," he says, with as much feeling now as ever, "I realized I would never have any reputation, that the book would never exist in any real form—it was just a piece of pornography. It wouldn't get any reviews. It was a total nightmare."

On receiving his first copies in the post from Paris, Donleavy smashed his fist "with all my might upon the cover of the book." He swore that "if it were the last thing I ever did, I would redeem and avenge this work." He took his revenge. It was not to be his final act, and it required more than twenty years of litigation, begun when Girodias sued him for breaking their contract. The process ended—in a coup so stunning that even his tormentor had to applaud—with Donleavy owning the Olympia Press.

A slim, neat man with white hair and beard, Donleavy is remarkably agile for one approaching eighty. "He's a man of instant trust and credibility," says his younger brother T. J., a painter and sculptor, who lives in New York. "He doesn't stand for any shenanigans in general conduct. When he has a feeling for someone, it's about honesty. When we were boys he was always quick to defend anyone who was being bullied. Size wouldn't mean anything to him." Donleavy lives in Levington Park, a country house on two hundred acres near the town of Mullingar in the Irish Midlands. The house presents a bare, stony front to the world, with little hint of the farmyard and the warren of corridors and rooms spread out behind. In one room stands what he claims is the only fireplace of fossilized marble in Ireland; in another is a swimming pool. Across the meadows is Lough Owel, which is mentioned in the "Calypso" section of *Ulysses*. It is said (though it is hard to prove) that James Joyce slept at Levington Park while his father was on business in Mullingar.

Donleavy likes the Joyce connection. He has lived here since 1972. He separated from his first wife, Valerie Heron, the mother of his eldest children, Philip and Karen, in the 1950s. Karen is a successful ceramicist, while Philip works in film. Later, Donleavy married Mary Wilson Price, who has since remarried into the Guinness family, and a further two children, twins Rebecca and Rory, were born. For company, he has a herd of Hereford cattle, a pair of cheeky farm cats, a man who helps with the cows, and a secretary who helps with most other things. He must be the only living author to have placed a lonely hearts advertisement in one of his own books (*An Author and His Image: The Collected Short Pieces,* 1997): "Slightly reclusive but anxious to get out more, gracefully older fit man . . . requires pleasantly attractive younger lady of principle." His rectangular living room is a homely clutter of grand piano, peeling plaster, old newspapers, and memorabilia, including several photographs of himself affecting a more severe attitude than he has in person. A few Christmas cards remain on display into summer. Billy Connolly, who once acted triumphantly in a Donleavy play, sends one every year. "I can't stand to throw them away," he says, laughing at himself as he does frequently, "especially those with photographs of people's children and so on. You feel if you throw them away something dreadful might happen." The walls are hung with colorful paintings by J. P. and T. J. Donleavy.

James Patrick Donleavy, "Mike" to his friends, was born in Woodlawn, New York City, in 1926, the son of Irish immigrants. His father had studied for the priesthood and on arriving in the United States, as Donleavy puts it, "didn't have a pot to piss in." His mother was taken to New York by "a very rich Australian uncle." When Donleavy flew across the Atlantic to study sciences at Trinity College, Dublin, at the end of the Second World War, his mother was able to provide an allowance so he could live in style with rooms and "a white-coated servant who would serve tea in the afternoons and Madeira." He moved to London in the early 1950s, then to the Isle of Man, where his first wife's family lived, but later returned to Ireland to enjoy the tax regulations advantageous to writers and artists. Donleavy's accent, which he described long ago as "rather choice English . . . which when it slips has an even better one underneath," is nevertheless sturdily New York at its foundations. "He was quite well off and a bit reclusive even then," recalls Anthony Cronin, author of the classic memoir of Dublin literary life, *Dead as Doornails.* "He was a presence. He was rather striking looking, with hawkish features and a little beard, which would be unusual. You couldn't say he was part of the literary scene, though there was talk of a big novel about Dublin. But everybody was talking about writing a big novel."

At Trinity, Donleavy first set himself up as a painter (his debut show was in Dublin in 1950, the most recent in London in 2002), and it was while still a student that he began to write *The Ginger Man*. Critics have ranked its hero, Sebastian Dangerfield, with the Angry Young Men and even the Beat Generation, but he has no obvious social purpose other than to bed as many women as possible, between visits to a giddying variety of pubs. Everything goes wrong for Sebastian, yet everything somehow turns out right. Near the end of the novel, on a visit to London, he notices a servant draw back the curtains in a large house, and cries out: "That's good to see . . . I haven't seen such wealth for years. Not for years. And I need it. Need it." Donleavy points out that Sebastian is someone who is "waiting to come into his estate." Most readers, however, "are overwhelmed by this other picture of the man as a poverty-stricken, low-life type, which is false."

Sebastian was based on a friend of Donleavy's at Trinity, Gainor Stephen Crist, also an American. Cronin recalls Crist as "a gent. Bowler-hatted. He carried a stick, an actual cane. A very charming fellow, very intelligent, with no artistic ambitions." Crist was "kind of gentle," Cronin says, whereas Sebastian exudes violence. "I think Donleavy attributed some of his own qualities to Gainor, and therefore to Dangerfield. I wouldn't have recognized Dangerfield as Crist, but like all fictional creations, it departed from life." Crist is thought to have died en route to America in 1964. Apparently a cross marks a grave in Santa Cruz de Tenerife, in the Canary Islands, but to Donleavy his disappearance is "a mystery, a great mystery. I haven't solved it yet." Ten years ago, near Grafton Street in Dublin, Donleavy saw a half-familiar figure across the street, "and he was making these nervous, fidgeting movements with his fingers. And I thought: that looks like Gainor Crist. I walked on, and then I stopped in my tracks. My God, I said to myself, no one who knew Gainor Crist ever saw him dead. He had a lot of problems, with his marriage and so on. He may just have decided to disappear. And I later found out that one of his favorite songs was a ballad with the line, 'Don't bury me in Santa Cruz.'" But according to reports around the time of his disappearance, Crist had the DTs and was suffering from pneumonia. "It's an interesting theory," Cronin says of the notion that the original Dangerfield lives on in Dublin, "but it's more interesting that Donleavy should think of it."

The Ginger Man still reads well today, once one becomes accustomed to its headlong rush of style, its frequent verbless sentences, the switch of tenses and the manic swing between first and third persons as it lunges to catch the protagonist's babbling thoughts: "Sebastian went looking for aspirin. The house looks unusually empty. The closet. Marion's clothes are gone. Just my broken rubbers on the floor. The nursery. Cleaned out. Bare. Take that white cold hand off my heart." In other places, the prose hops along alliteratively, with hints of Joyce and Dylan Thomas. Many chapters end with a snatch of verse, a habit that began in Donleavy's first book and became his signature tune. At the close of the novel, he signed off plaintively:

> God's mercy
> On the wild
> Ginger Man

Forty years later, in his memoir, *The History of the Ginger Man*, he wrote:

> When you find a friend
> Who is good and true
> Fuck him
> Before he fucks you

Although the novel was banned in Ireland until the 1970s, the novelist John Banville discovered a copy of the original Paris edition as a teenager in Dublin in the early 1960s. "I haven't read it since," he says, "but I greatly admired it then. What struck me most forcibly about the book was not the humor or the sex, but the sense of sweet and delicate melancholy that clings to the pages. I thought it that rare thing in a novel, a genuine work of art. Would I feel the same if I were to reread it now? I don't know. It's too big a risk to take."

Donleavy has written twelve novels since *The Ginger Man*, and a dozen other books and plays. He is destined to be forever associated with his first book, and appears content that it be so. In conversation, he is apt to refer to it simply as "the book," or even "the manuscript." He has adapted it as a play, written a screenplay (though no film has been made), composed *The History of The Ginger Man* (1994), and in *What They Did in*

Dublin with The Ginger Man (1961) has given a separate account of the play's brief run in Ireland before it was hounded from the stage after three nights by a combination of press and clergy.

"I knew I had to write a book that was the best in the world. It was as simple as that. Brendan Behan told me, 'Mike, this book is gonna beat the Bible' . . . Well, you know, people say these things." Behan was the first person to read *The Ginger Man* and to offer an evaluation. "I was away for a few days and he broke into the cottage where I lived and found the manuscript in my studio. He plumped his own manuscript next to it, *Borstal Boy*, and wrote editorial suggestions all over my pages. When I got back I found all my shoes were missing. When I saw the manuscript of *Borstal Boy*, I knew who had been there. The nerve! He even autographed the thing. But then I began to look at his comments, and I ended up following every single suggestion. People didn't take Behan seriously, because of his behavior." If *The Ginger Man* hasn't beaten the Bible, it has provided Donleavy with his house and his acres; the book has never been out of print.

During the legal marathon with Maurice Girodias, it was said that both sides were funding their campaigns with profits from the novel. "I never set out to ruin Girodias," Donleavy says. "He was always the aggressive one. He sued me because I wanted to have the book published properly in England. It's ironic that I should sit here owning him." It happened like this: When Donleavy sold the rights to publish the novel in Britain to a small London firm, now defunct, called Neville Spearman, Girodias argued that no such entitlement was provided by the terms of their agreement, and took him to court. Twenty years later, the two parties were still suing each other, under the guise of phantom companies— Donleavy was "The Little Someone Corporation"—with no end in sight. Girodias, having declared himself bankrupt, not for the first time, was preparing to buy back the title of his beloved Olympia Press at an auction in Paris. Donleavy learned of the sale and sent his wife to France with a large sum in cash. When bidding went over eight thousand dollars, Girodias ran out of money. The mysterious woman (as Girodias saw her) made a final bid, and the Olympia Press belonged to J. P. Donleavy. In an interview not long before he died in 1991, Girodias called the story "fabulous. Much better than the book, actually." Donleavy says that Girodias wrote to him afterward, offering to buy back the company. "He said if you don't want to do it, just tear up this letter."

The poet Christopher Logue, who had several books published by the Olympia Press (including *Lust* under the pseudonym "Count Palmiro Vicarion"), visited Donleavy in his house in Fulham in the 1950s. "I looked at the books. They were law books. On copyright. There were no other books in the house." Most of the books in the living room at Levington Park today are by Donleavy, and most of those are various editions of *The Ginger Man*. In his memoir, *Prince Charming* (1999), Logue recalled Donleavy nursing an obsessive grudge, while Donleavy remembers Logue asking him not to be too hard on Girodias. Donleavy adds: "I am not someone who takes revenge lightly. But there was no doubt that I was not going to let anything be done to that book that was detrimental. That is why I'm a different kettle of fish to most authors. I've never had anything happen in my life, from the literary world, in the way of a pat on the back or encouragement or anything else. All I've ever known are lawyers and litigation and attacks from every source possible."

When Donleavy's second novel, *A Singular Man*, was delivered to Atlantic Monthly Press, the Boston firm that was eager to publish it, some senior employees recoiled at the sexual content, which is more explicit than that of *The Ginger Man*. They informed the author of their wish to withdraw from the contractual agreement. Donleavy responded with a letter stating his intention "to institute proceedings and to seek damages of not less than $375,000." He confides that the insertion of an odd figure such as "75" is a good ruse when threatening damages—or, even better, "something like $375,236 and 41 cents." The Atlantic executives promptly affirmed their willingness to publish *A Singular Man*, "despite our confidence that we can win any lawsuit that might be commenced," and the novel came out on schedule in November 1963. T. J. Donleavy feels that the combination of literary life and legal action was "something Mike found very romantic. When it happens, everybody wants to know about it. But people don't have a lot of luck with him, when they take him on, because he's a very good lawyer. He's a logician. He could have been a chess master if he chose."

A Singular Man is the story of a recluse involved in all-consuming litigation with obscure parties whose only apparent purposes are postponement and obfuscation. On the opening page, the protagonist, George Smith, receives a legal letter headed "The Building. You well know which year." The message reads, in full: "Dear Sir, Only for the moment are we saying nothing." This is what Donleavy calls his "empirical letter," and he himself has written many over the years. After the Atlantic fiasco, the editor who had enticed him to the firm, Seymour Lawrence, felt obliged to leave and subsequently started his own company. "I became beset by doubts as to whether this venture would work out," wrote Lawrence, who died in 1994, "when one day Donleavy rang from London and gave me this advice: all you need to be a publisher is one room, one desk, one phone, and one author. I'll be that author." It was not until 1965, ten years after *The Ginger Man*'s insalubrious Paris debut, that Lawrence was able to publish an unexpurgated edition of *The Ginger Man* in the United States. In Ireland, T. J. says, "They'd find it in your luggage at Customs and just take it."

Invited to discuss the prose style that emerged fully formed in his first novel, Donleavy hesitates. "My big advantage is being practically uneducated, for a start, and my grammar being appalling. I grew up in a country where language is manufactured all the time, but something original did come out, I presume through the rewriting, when I began to see that the brain would unconsciously go to the first and third person. Being a writer is just catching your unconscious. Another thing is that my background at university was all science—bacteriology and so on—and that must have been an influence. Then I just focused on how to get the word off the page and into the reader's brain, as directly as possible." He claims not to have read Hemingway, for example—"not more than a page or two. I'm not literary in that sense of reading books." T. J. Donleavy compares his brother to Mark Twain, as a "great democrat," but adds, "he himself is not influenced by Twain. He wouldn't have been exposed to his books. I know he didn't read *Tom Sawyer* in his early days. He wasn't a literary boy, no way. He's a natural."

If *The Ginger Man* led to an early coupling with the kitchen-sink school of writing that was growing popular at the time of the book's appearance,

Donleavy decisively ended the association with his subsequent novels. After depicting the "limozine" life of George Smith, Donleavy began his elevation to the country-house world. Logue remembers him talking of a planned play, to be called simply *Wealth*. Darcy Kildare, who features in a trilogy of novels, beginning with *The Destinies of Darcy Dancer, Gentleman* (1977), continuing with *Leila* (1983), and concluding with *That Darcy, That Dancer, That Gentleman* (1990), romps around in a world of crumbling estates and horsey occupations. The hero of Donleavy's third novel, *The Beastly Beatitudes of Balthazar B* (1968), we learn in the opening paragraph, "was born in Paris in a big house on a little square off Avenue Foch. Of a mother blonde and beautiful and a father quiet and rich." These characters are pampered by a retinue of devoted servants and hopelessly loving, seductive nannies. In author photographs dating from the 1960s, Donleavy is typically shown buttoned up in a tweed suit, with plus-fours and a knobbly cane. In *An Author and His Image*, which shows his dry humor to good effect, he remarked that "the only people with time to waste in my company and at the same time willing to be pleasant to me have been persons who have had private incomes." His second wife, whom he met when she auditioned for a part in the stage adaptation of *A Singular Man*, bred horses at Levington Park, and organized hunting parties. "So that got me into that world," Donleavy says. One of his oddest and most entertaining books is *The Unexpurgated Code* (1975), a "manual of survival and manners" aimed at those who aspire to social climbing but are feeling unsteady on their feet. Short sections, with titles such as "Upon Being Excluded from Who's Who" and "Name Changing," give counsel: "The world's richest families often have the names best suited to you and, with imaginatively selected Christian names, they will not only immediately make you sound better than you look but make people think they like you."

Donleavy's working methods are idiosyncratic. He writes a passage in longhand, which then goes to his secretary, who works in a different part of the house (on some days they don't encounter one another). She types it up and returns it to him. "Then I will write around that and it goes back to her, and then I paste the pages one over the other, until the sheets get very long. I have to lay them out on the floor. I want to see where each thing is, in each draft. It can be a terrible business. Soon I'll have to move into another room."

He has lived in Ireland off and on for almost sixty years, yet he feels that the people, described in *The History of The Ginger Man* as a "small inbred population of highly active begrudgers," have not been kind to him. As a result, he says, he can't read the Irish papers. "I think that the policy in Ireland has been almost unbelievable. I know people who have arrived in Dublin from America, and gone into a pub, and they'd hear, 'Oh Donleavy, he died last year.' There was a lot of this." Cronin feels he is mistaken in believing the Irish have it in for him. "He's always been quite well received. It's just that he doesn't see that many people nowadays." According to Logue, "he doesn't really cultivate human relationships. And he's rather proud of it. But I think geniality has grown on him over the years." Donleavy is apt to frown at his own reclusive habits. "I think it's a bad thing. Sometimes I don't go beyond those gates for two weeks at a time. You only get by having people to visit. Touch wood, I seem to have kept a lot of my old girlfriends, and they tend to come on visits, so I'm not always here alone. But it isn't good."

Following the success of the film *Young Adam,* adapted from the novel by Alexander Trocchi, he found himself obliged to defend his publishing property. *Young Adam* is an Olympia original, published under the pseudonym "Frances Lengel" in 1954. (Trocchi was also the author of some of the pornographic potboilers advertised at the back of *The Ginger Man.*) Donleavy contends that the book's copyright rests with him. "It's a situation I could never have foreseen, that I might have to go to court to protect the works of the Olympia Press."

Meanwhile, there is the farm to be worked, the Ginger Man industry to oversee—an entrepreneur in the United States has named a string of pubs after it, for which privilege he pays a royalty—and his good physical condition to keep up. In the living room, above the peat fire, pride of place is given to a photograph of Joe Louis knocking out Max Schmeling in 1938. The referee, visible in the picture, was Arthur Donovan, Sugar Ray Robinson's boxing coach. Donovan also coached Donleavy, so that the novelist and the legendary middleweight have in common "a left hook so fast you can't even see it." Donleavy gets up out of his fireside chair to demonstrate. "My right is just as fast, and all combined I can do seven-and-a-half full punches in one second. I'm faster now, probably, than in my earlier days."

TWENTY-ONE The Making of a Monster

ALEXANDER TROCCHI

Cain's Book, Alexander Trocchi's drug-related mastercrime, is a novel to give to minors, a book to corrupt young people. It has been banned, burned, prosecuted, refused by book distributors everywhere, condemned for its loving descriptions of heroin use and coarse sexual content. Trocchi died in London in 1984. Since completing *Cain's Book* a quarter of a century earlier, he had written hardly anything. It's not difficult to see why. *Cain's Book* is more than a novel: it is a way of life. The book is autobiography and fiction at once, the journal of a fiend, a stage-by-stage account of the junkie's odyssey in New York, an examination of the mind under the influence, a rude gesture in the face of sexual propriety, a commentary on literary processes and critical practices, a chart for the exploration of inner space.

Trocchi moved with the Burroughs/Kerouac pack on roads newly charted in the 1950s; but he wrote with a sophistication shared by none of the other Beats. He was more keenly attuned to Literature and therefore could refuse its terms more conscientiously. In Glasgow, ten years later, we dipped into the mythology of the Beat Generation, borrowing what we needed and adapting it to suit our brand of Celtic Hip. Trocchi appeared to us a colossus, bestriding a narrow world, forging his own myths. And he was one of ours. Only a Scot could formulate an epigram so calculated to outrage the native temperament as "It is difficult to explain to the underprivileged that play is more serious than work." Or, taking different aim, "My friends will know what I mean when I say I deplore our contemporary industrial writers. Let them dedicate a year to pinball and think again."

Even before *Cain's Book* was published in Britain in 1963, Trocchi was shaping his terror tactics. At the 1962 Edinburgh International Writers' Conference, he listened to the poet Hugh MacDiarmid promote his own work, denigrate everything English, dismiss all contemporary fiction out of hand, and proclaim Scotland's potential as an international force. When he had finished, Trocchi got to his feet and replied first by saying that the best modern poetry had been written by novelists anyway, then dismissed the work of MacDiarmid and his clan as "stale, cold porridge. Bible-clasping nonsense. Of what is interesting in Scottish writing in the past twenty years or so, I myself have written it all."

As a stunt to publicize a writer still unknown in his own country, it was quite a success. Trocchi's neatly phrased hyperbole grabbed the front pages of the Scottish press, and he was invited on television as a "self-confessed drug addict." As the debate continued in the columns of the *New Statesman*, MacDiarmid denounced Trocchi as "cosmopolitan scum," which only enhanced his reputation further.

I don't doubt that Trocchi saw the humor in it all. He had written altogether nine books, but most of them were dirty books, which had appeared, under pseudonyms, in Maurice Girodias's Traveller's Companion Series published by the Olympia Press in Paris in the 1950s. Nevertheless, there is a finger of truth in his words to the Edinburgh conference, for Scottish prose writing in the period 1942–62 has nothing to rival *Cain's Book*, which was published in Britain in 1963 (it had come out in the United States three years earlier), for style, intelligence, and formal originality.

.   .   .

Cain's Book provided a context. I first came across it in 1970, a nineteen-year-old literary minor living in the same streets where Trocchi had grown up some thirty years earlier. I refused to work. I was anti-university. I explored my "inner space" with the help of hallucinogens. Play is more serious than work. All you have to do is say it, and—well, isn't it so?

Our view of ourselves was as outsiders, escapees from society's snares, gentle outlaws. But Trocchi really was an outlaw, being a determined drug addict (there was also a rumor—true, I was to discover— that he had had to escape the United States, and the electric chair, in disguise, being wanted on a charge of supplying narcotics to a minor). How far can a man go, he wondered, "without being obliterated"? And he put himself forward as the guinea pig for his own tests.

To adopt the identity of the junkie was to refuse society's own narcotics: work, marriage, civic responsibility, family duty; it was to make oneself avant-garde, the anti-man; it was to escape the bounds of social consciousness, which deadened creativity, and take up residence in inner space. Trocchi went further. He implied that his was a moral position: "to think that a man should be allowed a gun and not a drug." Only incidentally did he invoke the orthodox intellectual justifications for drug use, claiming that he was "experimenting," or seeking to unlock concealed compartments of the mind. Of Aldous Huxley—the pioneer of controlled experiments—he cheekily wrote in *Cain's Book:* "He was a boyhood hero of mine, and I'm glad to see him on drugs at last." Trocchi barely countenanced the notion that his addiction could debilitate him physically, or erode his talents. On the contrary, he made heroin sound positively beneficial: "It's somehow undignified to speak about the past or to think about the future. I don't seriously occupy myself with the question in the 'here-and-now,' lying on my bunk and, under the influence of heroin, inviolable. That is one of the virtues of the drug, that it empties such questions of all anguish, transports them to another region, a painless theoretical region, a play region, surprising, fertile, and unmoral. One is no longer grotesquely involved in the becoming. One simply is." In addition to espousing original opinions on the drug laws (heroin should be "placed on the counters of all chemists . . . and sold openly"), and taunting taboos in general, Trocchi was an authentic literary craftsman. This concerned us more than the drugs, which my friends and I would have solemnly described at the time as an objective correlative for alienation in the novel.

Trocchi's erudition was among his most attractive attributes. He had been properly educated (he didn't let on that he had taken full advantage of the education system before opposing it); he knew Latin, read Baudelaire in the original, quoted Unamuno; he breathed out phrases like "the Aristotelian impulse to classify" as casually as blowing smoke rings. Trocchi's professor of philosophy at Glasgow University described him as the best student he ever taught. The junkie and pornographer Trocchi was also a philosopher, one who plays the old trick by asking you to consider the contradiction inherent in the statement, "This statement is not true." For the ingenuity of *Cain's Book*, the tease that draws you into it again and again, is that it questions its own processes at every turn, consciously undermining its own validity as a "novel," yet finally standing free as a work of art.

On my first copy, a picture of Trocchi's hollow-cheeked face glowered from the cover like a Glasgow hardman advertising his prison memoirs. I set off on a hitchhiking expedition through Europe, North Africa, and the Middle East, taking *Cain* with me, the alternative version, the lost book. At every opportunity, I preached its gospel to believers in the false gods of plot and linear narrative.

> In the pinball machine an absolute and peculiar order reigns. No scepticism is possible for the man who by a series of sharp and slight dunts tries to control the machine. It became for me a ritual act, symbolizing a cosmic event. Man is serious at play. Tension, elation, frivolity, ecstasy, confirming the supralogical nature of the human situation. Apart from jazz—probably the most vigorous and yea-saying protest of *homo ludens* in the modern world—the pinball machine seemed to me to be America's greatest contribution to culture; it rang with contemporaneity. It symbolized the rigid structural "soul" that threatened to crystallize in history, reducing man to historicity, the great mechanic monolith imposed by mass mind. The slick electric shiftings of the pinball machine, the electronic brain, the symbolical transposition of the modern Fact into the realm of play. (The distinction between the French and American attitude towards the tilt ("teelt"); in America and England, I have been upbraided for trying to beat the mechanism by skilful tilting; in Paris, that is whole point.)

The situation in Paris in the early 1950s, where Trocchi went after taking his finals at Glasgow University, was comparable to that of the 1920s: a catastrophic war had recently ended, the city was cheap for foreigners, and artists were attracted by its reputation for freedom from social and sexual restraints. London in the 1950s was witnessing the evolution of Angry Young Man, but in Paris there were Sartre, Camus, Cocteau, and Trocchi's mentor, Beckett . . . not to mention Richard Wright, James Baldwin, Chester Himes, and others. Compared to this, Glasgow offered square sausage and the work ethic.

Basing himself in a cheap St-Germain hotel, Trocchi founded the literary magazine *Merlin*, publishing Ionesco, Genet, and others. Collection Merlin, an imprint of the Olympia Press, was the first publisher of Beckett's novel *Watt*, in 1953, and later issued the English version of *Molloy*.

When Trocchi quit the Left Bank scene and sailed to New York, it was ostensibly in pursuit of a woman, but the move had another significance. Greenwich Village, not St-Germain des Prés, was the proper backdrop for his new drama. His leave-taking from literary society—and society at large—was fully planned. "I reject your entire system," he wrote in a letter of the time; "I am outside your world and am no longer governed by your laws." He found a job as a scow captain, shifting cargo on the Hudson and East Rivers; now he was living on the margin both while at work—his days were spent mostly on water—and at play. It was on the scow that he drew together the notes which had accumulated in Paris and elsewhere and formed them into *Cain's Book*.

Trocchi writes of himself in the novel (as Joe Necchi) stepping between cities, luggage in hand, one suitcase packed with notes and scraps of text. Quotations are given in *Cain's Book* from "Cain's Book," passages which do not appear in the main body of the novel. It took a long time to fall into place, but in 1959 it finally did so. On the last page, Trocchi writes as if discussing another book entirely: "as soon as I have finished this paragraph [I intend] to go into the next room and turn on. Later I shall phone those who have kindly intimated their willingness to publish the document and tell them it is ready now, or as ready as it ever will be."

I wish that Trocchi's bold remarks to the Edinburgh Writers' Conference could be said to be pertinent still—"Of what is interesting . . . I myself have written it all"—but he wrote nothing of moment before his death from pneumonia in April 1984. All play and no work? It makes a dull twenty-five years, and for a writer as talented as Trocchi—"the most brilliant man I've met," Allen Ginsberg called him—a pitiful waste.

What happened? There was the corroding effect of the drugs, of course. There was also the revolutionary movement, project sigma, to which Trocchi devoted a large part of the 1960s. The aim of sigma was "the invisible insurrection," a takeover by the culturally enlightened of the "grids of expression and the powerhouses of the mind." Based by now in a West London flat, and with a body of support that included R. D. Laing, Michael McClure, John Arden, and Robert Creeley, Trocchi planned not the coup d'état of Lenin and Trotsky, but what he called a *coup du monde,* a gradual assumption of control by "the creative ones everywhere." In his manifesto, Trocchi set out sigma's aims:

> We have already rejected the idea of a frontal attack. Mind cannot with-
> stand matter (brute force) in open battle. It is rather a question of per-
> ceiving clearly and without prejudice what are the forces that are at
> work in the world and out of whose interaction tomorrow *must* come to
> be; and then, calmly, without indignation, by a kind of mental ju-jitsu
> that is ours by virtue of intelligence, of modifying, of correcting, pol-
> luting, deflecting, eroding, outflanking . . . inspiring what we might
> call *the invisible insurrection.* It will come on the mass of men, if it comes
> at all, not as something they have voted for, struck for, fought for, but
> like the changing seasons.

The invisible insurrection seems very much of its period, and very far-fetched, now. Trocchi's prophecies—from the redundancy of the pub-lisher ("we must eliminate the brokers") to the collapse of the nation-state—are mocked by history. The idea of a cultural terrorist seems foppish. But if the project appears blurred by the psychedelic patterning (Trocchi envisaged "spontaneous universities" sprouting like mush-rooms across the globe), it also has a characteristic originality about it, and an imaginative ambition which is endearing at a time when under-ground movements mostly involve real terrorists with real guns.

Trocchi's admirers wondered why he was giving so much of his time to his manifestos and so little to literature. His London publisher John Calder (no doubt contemplating his coming elimination) expressed annoyance at the failure to capitalize (*capitalize!* Trocchi would have shrieked) on *Cain's Book*'s success and complained that no one really understood what sigma was all about anyway.

But the real question for the writer was: how to follow such a book? Trocchi's art was confessional, and you cannot make the same confessions twice. And while the novel is structured on a number of clever devices, one of them is timed to detonate at the very second at which its creator attempts to sneak back to conventional narrative. At all its stations, *Cain's Book* announces: "This novel is not a novel; such categories are hereby rendered defunct."

In short, there is a negativity in *Cain's Book* to which Trocchi could do little but succumb. "You write your future," a friend of mine once said, and the writing in *Cain's Book* is much taken up with the then-fashionable topic, the death of the novel. The novel didn't die, after all, but, following Cain, Trocchi's part in it did.

·   ·   ·

Trocchi never lost the desire to shock. Nor the ability. "If I'm not capable of satisfying my wife, for some reason, I've no objection to providing some young bull to pleasure her." Those were among the first words he spoke to me. His wife, Lyn, reading on the nearby sofa, looked up briefly from her magazine.

It was 1972 and I had lately become associated with a small magazine, published from Glasgow University, called *GUM*. When the editor suggested I interview a writer for his series, I mentioned Trocchi. We got his telephone number from the publishers, and on a wintry afternoon some two weeks later, Trocchi met me at the door of his Kensington flat. He was dressed in a shabby black t-shirt with short sleeves. I suspect now that he wore it on purpose so that I could see for myself the ski-track scars running down both snowy-white arms where the veins had collapsed. He was very tall with an enormous nose and a gray complexion, and the girl who came with me said later that she could smell evil about his person. He made her think of another notorious figure associated with Scotland, Aleister Crowley, the occultist and black-magician who was known as the Great Beast. Trocchi would not have refused the compliment.

My first impressions were more mundane. I was dismayed to learn that the Trocchis lived a fairly orderly family life. Lyn, an American, made inquiries about old friends in Glasgow, whom I knew in passing or by name. She wore dark glasses even though dusk was pressing at the windows. Trocchi himself prepared café au lait and recommended a pastry—just hot from the oven, he chimed. There were two nice boys present, Marcus and Nicky. When their father told the younger one to lower the volume on the television, the instruction was quickly obeyed. Painters had recently redecorated the flat, so that the woodwork gleamed. Before leaving Glasgow, I had conferred with my editor over what to do if invited by Trocchi to shoot up with him. The editor said I must accept. "It'll look great in the interview." Fat chance. The gulf between the person I had read about and the person before me now was wide, and it wrong-footed me: he was plumper and grayer than I had expected, and while he still liked to tickle the toes of the moral majority from time to time, he had gone soft on hard drugs.

Trocchi was still an addict—it was one of his gimmicks to ask you to wait while he gave himself a fix—but he would advise any young person against getting started, he said. I read him a passage from an article by Cyril Connolly, which had appeared in a recent *Sunday Times,* presenting the addict in a familiar way: "A striking observation is the anti-intellectual climate that prevails in the networks. All who have known someone addicted to drugs . . . will have remarked on the increasing indifference to reality, whether of the time of day . . . or reading, or any of the pleasures and passions, food, drink, love, sex, places of art or the acquisition of knowledge that makes life worth living." Trocchi made a partial defense of his stance by referring to Coleridge and de Quincey: "If nothing else, they were intellectually curious. But up to a point, it's true what he writes. What else can one say about it?"

I learned Trocchi's own version of his flight from the United States and the electric chair in 1961. One year after the Grove Press edition of *Cain's Book,* he was arrested and charged with supplying narcotics to a minor, for which the penalty in New York State at the time was death. The evidence was strong—a prescription bearing his name had been found in the possession of a sixteen-year-old girl—and made a conviction look likely. He was bailed out of prison with the help of an old friend from his Paris days, but once free he immediately got in trouble with the law again. This time it was for fixing up, with Lyn, on a station platform. Trocchi himself got away, but Lyn and their son Marcus were detained and taken to prison. Supported by people on the Greenwich Village scene, Trocchi obtained a false passport, slipped over the border to Canada, to be met by Leonard Cohen, and made his way back to England, where Lyn and Marcus later joined him.

He chose London not only because of his nationality but because it was a place where heroin was available to registered addicts legally, and without cost, on the National Health. In this way, in the 1960s, Britain controlled its minor drug problem. There was no need to hustle on the street, to mug or to steal, except for the few who, for some reason, could not register for prescriptions.

To this I partly attributed Trocchi's demise as a literary figure. While the easy availability of heroin comes as a relief to the junkie, it also cuts him off from the occupation which propels him from one day to the next. "The identity of the junkie was consciously chosen," Trocchi wrote with reference to his decision to go "far out," to make himself an outlaw in a society of conformers. But who ever heard of a state-subsidized outlaw? Much of the energy of *Cain's Book* derives from the excitement of scoring, of settling on a safe pad, of heating the spoon. Legitimized, this act is deprived of its drama. Only a kind of pathetic, undersubscribed theater remains. The junkie's determined "outsider" stance turns out to be a bit of a fake.

With Trocchi, there remained a literary style. In 1972, I was much inclined to look on the bright side, but I could get scant information from him regarding current and future projects. *Cain's Book* was over ten years old. "You must be finding it difficult to do a follow-up," I said, "having written a book about the inability to write a book." This drew from Trocchi the comment—which I carried back to Glasgow on the night train like a coconut—that I was "quite perspicacious." He was writing something called *The Long Book,* he said, and read a portion aloud to me. I listened hard—I really wanted to hear it—for the old brilliance.

.   .   .

Trocchi relished the notoriety which first his drug-taking and then the book had brought him—far more intoxicating than ordinary fame. A provisional title for *Cain's Book* was "Notes Towards the Making of the Monster," which, though charming in its way, reveals an off-putting self-consciousness. Real monsters, like real outcasts, are not self-made. The necessary condition of the outcast is that he cannot step in. The black man (for example) in downtown New York in the 1940s and 50s, trying to find an apartment, trying find a job, was an outcast in the way that a white, university-educated junkie can only imagine.

When a monster is self-loving and not self-loathing, he is inhabiting what Trocchi in his Paris days would have called a "false consciousness." He is probably more of a danger to others than himself. Trocchi had, in fact, created two monsters: one of them he could control, and he exhibited it before the public on a leash; as for the other, as time went on it turned on its master, savaging him and all around him.

Rereading *Cain's Book* after many years, I am struck by a morbidity in the relationship between sex and drugs, and sometimes death. Whereas he never waxes lyrical over women, Trocchi forges a poetic mythology of junk, which fills the space marked "love" in the novel: "I remember Jody saying: 'When we do make love, Joe, it'll be the end!' The end-love, she meant, the ultimate.—Like an overdose, Jody?" And again: "I thought of Jody, and of how plump she is from eating too many cakes, of the soft wad of her belly, of our thighs without urgency interlaced, of her ugly bitten hands . . . into which she drives the needle each time she fixes. 'That's your cunt, Jody.'" At other times, Trocchi dwells on the separate parts of women's bodies like a lecherous mortician: "the flaccid buttocks like pale meat on the stone stairs"; "this first sex shadowy and hanging colourless like a clot of spiderweb from the blunt butt of her mound"; "her belly dangling like an egg on poach"; "the skin close, odorous, opaque, yellowish, and pitted almost like Pumice-stone"; "a French woman's vitals would be sweet to the taste, while with those of an Englishwoman one risked being confronted with a holy sepulchre, a repository for relics"; and plenty more in the same vein. In *Cain's Book,* from which all those quotations come, the most affectionate liaison (apart from one with a man) is with Jake, a woman with one leg cut off above the knee. Necchi desires her genuinely, but at the same time he cannot help whipping back the sheets and saying to the reader, *Look what a monster I am.*

Trocchi's Divine Marquis mode is even less gorgeous in his pornographic books: *Helen and Desire, Thongs, White Thighs, School for Wives,* and others. It may be that artists reveal themselves more in their moments of lowbrow frivolity than, as they might like to think, at times of high-minded seriousness; what is shown up by Trocchi's obscene writing can be unappealing in the extreme.

He told me that the books were written for money to help keep the magazine *Merlin* afloat, but added that he considered them to be "serious enough within their own limits." Each book contains some good passages, particularly the extraordinary *My Life and Loves: Fifth Volume* by "Frank Harris" (1954), which is about two parts Harris mixed with three parts Trocchi and is so stylistically convincing that it was later published as part of a "complete" edition of Harris's work (much to others' mirth but Trocchi's annoyance, since he received no royalties). The issue at stake is not sex, but the violence which sex in Trocchi's pornographic books conceals. In this passage from *Thongs* (1956), sex is hardly visible at all, appearing instead in the guise of power and pain: "My father would mark her, a small cross cut with a razor on the soft inner surface of her left thigh; his cattle. . . . Everyone knew about the mark. Fourteen women in the Gorbals had been cut already. Normally my father kept the woman for about two months afterwards. Then they were free to go. The men of the Gorbals fought each other to marry a marked woman." The monstrosity was not confined to the printed page. Joe Necchi in *Cain's Book* does not actually say that he is responsible for turning Jody on to heroin, nor any other member of the novel's grotesquely fascinating cast of junkies, but it is a fact that in life Trocchi did just that, leading people to a "far out" place, from which many could not return. When he met his second wife, Lyn Hicks, she was a twenty-one-year-old from Hicksville, New York. Within months of meeting him, she was hooked, and six months after their wedding in Mexico in 1957 she was hustling outside casinos on the Las Vegas boulevards, one more way to earn money for junk. In his biography of Trocchi, *The Making of the Monster,* Andrew Murray Scott tells us that at other times "she danced in a sleazy nightclub wearing silver spangles the size of half-dollar pieces gummed to her nipples and black satin stretched over a tiny piece of cardboard at her crotch." Trocchi told friends that on at least one occasion he had "cooled out of a bust" by having Lyn offer herself to a policeman in the back of a police car. Whether this is genuine monstrousness, or mere bravado, it cannot be waved away by a gesture in the direction of the old outrageousness. Lyn died in London in her thirties, having tried unsuccessfully to kick the habit many times.

If Trocchi himself by now seems ripe for dismemberment, not just by feminists but humanists of every sort, we might ask the question: What made the monster? What lay behind Trocchi's destructiveness? What is the key to his psychopathology? A clue can be found in an interesting diary jotting uncovered by Andrew Scott and quoted in his biography, concerning the funeral of Trocchi's mother, who died when Alex was sixteen: "the last vital link with existence [was] cut. Lowered into a grave that was my extinction. Men and women in black. Brothers. Aunts. Uncles. Lingered on the green slope like quavers on a musical score. Sixteen at the time. And my father said to me: 'You will never see your mother again,' like a drain running out. But she continued to exist. Her death was my direction." The picture has the force of a dream, a vivid summary of the dreamer's existence, which appears to him as his fate. The relatives motionless on the grass, and the insensitive father, are less alive to the boy than the corpse now underground.

This revelation about his mother connects in highly suggestive ways with self-portraits in Trocchi's published writings. For example, in *Cain's Book* there is an unexpectedly tender moment in which Joe tells how much he enjoyed "brushing my mother's hair to make it beautiful," when a child. "I never knew my mother when young and, they said, beautiful and sometimes when I passed my hand over her hair I was invaded by a sense of outrage that she was not young and beautiful to have me."

That "have me" is awfully ambiguous, and it becomes even more troubling once it is recalled that this passage follows hard on one in which the narrator explicitly ties his liking for the red hair to a subsequent revulsion at the thought of her red pubic thatch. These associations are then made concise, in a formula that links the "red sex" to a fear—which duly became reality—of losing his mother's love: "Only the mute knowledge of her constant loving me was as vivid as the seditious thought of her red sex." This mother is both loved—for her selfless loving—and loathed, for her private sexuality.

At this point, we turn back to Trocchi's first novel, *Young Adam,* to the part near the opening in which the narrator—also Joe, also living on water, though on a barge and not a scow—discovers a female corpse floating in the canal. As Joe describes what he has found, one detail in particular stands out: "As I leaned over the edge of the barge with a boathook I didn't think of her as a dead woman, not even when I looked at her face. She was like some beautiful white waterfungus, a strange shining thing come up from the depths. . . . But it was the hair more than anything; it stranded away from the head like long grasses. Only it was alive, and because the body was slow, heavy, torpid, it had become a forest of antennae, caressing, feeding on the water, intricately." If this already gives off a whiff of necrophilia, the place is positively reeking once it emerges, in the second half of the book, that Joe himself is responsible for the woman's death. Wrap it all up together with further quotations from correspondence, such as "the conquest of a new female, especially a beautiful one, was closer to hate than to love" (from a letter to a woman Trocchi had hoped to marry), and one would feel confident quoting back to him his own judgment on his mother's departure—"her death was my direction"—and concluding, Yes, you were right.

Death was to be directed to Trocchi's house with an accuracy, and a swiftness, that he could not then have foreseen. But it appeared to some people, even in Paris days, that the celebrated charisma was toxic. Sometime around 1980, hoping to spark a few illuminating anecdotes about one Left Bank trooper from another, I mentioned his name to James Baldwin. "Trocchi?" Baldwin snapped, the nostrils flaring as the great eyes bulged. "The junkie? I hate him. *I hate him.* Tell him that from me!"

.   .   .

If I never did, it was because I still felt that one good book, while it cannot excuse everything, gets you away with quite a lot. I kept in touch with Trocchi, off and on, over the years that followed our first encounter, more than once asking him to contribute to another magazine I was editing, the *New Edinburgh Review.* I had no success. The last time I saw him, in 1981, he again met me at the top of the stairs, sleeves rolled up. "I'm just about to give myself a fix," he said. "Can you wait?"

This time I was alone, and although it would have enhanced my sense of the occasion to have glimpsed an evil aura about his still remarkably large and hardy frame, it simply wasn't there. "My family's dying all around me," he said, a vulnerable and affecting grin pulling at his lips. Not long after Lyn's passing, their elder son, Marcus, had lost a three-year battle with cancer. He was eighteen. A woman friend from New Zealand had moved in, and he spoke fondly of her attempts to impose order on his flat, though to me the place looked a shambles. "I must sort all this out," Alex murmured, gazing with the visitor's eyes at the papers and envelopes, books and wooden sculptures, paint boxes and odd detritus that littered the floor. The way he said it told you he never would.

"I am a cosmonaut of inner space," Trocchi had once proclaimed. Inner space was all that remained to him. Between complaints about difficulties in getting his books relaunched in London, he spoke frustratedly, for once, of his addiction. Heroin, the young champion, had long since turned old tyrant. As much as anything, he missed the freedom to travel abroad. Alex was a francophile, but the English Channel was hard to cross. "You have to make arrangements about drugs and all that. Ach, it's a drag."

By this time, he was running a second-hand bookstall in Kensington High Street. We went there together, and I bought three modern

American first editions (by Baldwin!), kindly sold to me at token prices. Then he took me to his afternoon drinking club, where he ordered us the Scotsman's favorite tipple, a glass of whisky with a beer chaser. "A hauf-an-a-hauf, Jim-meh!" Alex said to the uncomprehending barman, and chuckled as if he and I were sharing a family joke.

Such moments, together with his knowledge of antiquarian books and stamps (in which he also traded), were to me curious and poignant little reminders of his "insiderness," of the tameness of the monster. For years he was forgotten in Scotland, and *Cain's Book* has hardly ever been readily available in bookshops. It was while writing an article in which I cited *Cain's Book* as one of our country's three best postwar novels—the other two, Archie Hind's *Dear Green Place* and Alasdair Gray's *Lanark*, also feature artists who cannot finish their work—that I heard he was dead. Twenty months afterward, his younger son, Nicky, climbed on to the roof of the empty Kensington flat and threw himself off. Like his late brother, he was eighteen.

I am horrified to discover—both because of the Trocchi tragedy and for my own failure to be "perspicacious"—that my callow interview with the great man for the university magazine in 1972 ended with the words: "Trocchi's book is about living. . . . Most of all, that is what *he* is about: life." I know what made me put that down. Trocchi the cartographer, the flag-planter, opened frontiers for fellow travelers. He went far out, and then further—he went so far out that inner space swallowed him up.

TWENTY-TWO

Travels with RLS

One evening in the spring of 1880, Robert Louis Stevenson dropped into the bar of the Magnolia Hotel in Calistoga, at the head of the Napa Valley. There was little more to the town than the springs, the railway station, and the enticement of a fortune to be made from mining gold or silver. The West was still wild. Inside, someone asked Stevenson if he would like to speak to Mr. Foss, a stagecoach driver; Stevenson, always alert to the suggestion of travel, said yes: "Next moment, I had one instrument at my ear, another at my mouth, and found myself, with nothing in the world to say, conversing with a man several miles off among desolate hills." It was "an odd thing," Stevenson reflected, that here, "on the very skirts of civilization," he should find himself talking on the telephone for the first time. Later, he adapted the incident for use in a novel. "May I use your telephone?" asks Mr. Pinkerton in *The Wrecker* (1892), possibly the earliest occurrence in literature of that polite request.

Stevenson and his wife, Fanny, were in the middle of their honeymoon, spent mostly in an abandoned California silver mine. Throughout his life, Stevenson preferred to circumnavigate civilization, with its increasing reliance on contraptions, and steer toward the rougher fringes. Wherever we catch sight of him—tramping in the Highlands of Scotland or shivering in the Adirondacks or sailing in the South Seas, where he feasted with kings and cannibals—Stevenson is self-consciously turning his back on the Victorian idol, progress. In similar spirit, he chose the past more often than the present as a setting for fiction. His most popular novels—*Treasure Island, Kidnapped, The Master of Ballantrae*—are set in a semimythical realm, where the fire of adventure catches on every page. Stevenson loved the sound of clashing swords; he didn't want them getting tangled up in telephone wires overhead.

Yet, though he might try to avoid it, Stevenson was destined to be a modern man. He was born 150 years ago in Edinburgh, into a family of civil engineers, esteemed for its technological genius. His grandfather, also Robert, was Britain's greatest builder of lighthouses, and his graceful towers continue to guide sailors today. Three of Robert Senior's sons followed him into the profession, including R.L.S.'s father, Thomas, who made his own mark in the field of optics. Among his various inventions are louver-boarded screens for the protection of thermometers (these are still in use) and the marine dynamometer, which measures the force of waves.

It was expected that Louis would enter the family business in turn, and a great wringing of hands greeted his announcement to the contrary. He told his father that he wanted to be a writer, which Thomas Stevenson regarded as no profession at all. We can imagine the consternation in the solid bourgeois drawing room when Stevenson's letters arrived bearing pleas such as "Take me as I am . . . I must be a bit of a vagabond." This was written in his final year at Edinburgh University, and a vagabond was precisely what the graduate set out to be: long-haired, careless about food though never without tobacco, walking through France or planning an epic ocean voyage; a far cry from the offices of D. & T. Stevenson, Engineers. He was forging the template for generations of college-educated hobos to come. "I travel not to go anywhere, but to go," he wrote in *Travels with a Donkey* (1879). "I travel for travel's sake. The great affair is to move." Compare that with Jack Kerouac, as he climbed into a car with Neal Cassady three-quarters of a century later: "We were leaving confusion and nonsense behind and performing our one and noble function of the time: *move.*"

Stevenson would not be an engineer, but he left his own lights, in Scotland and across the world, by which it is possible to trace his unceasing movement. No other writer, surely, is as much memorialized by the words "lived here" as he is. There are five houses with R.L.S. associations in Edinburgh alone, not to mention the little schoolhouse he attended as a child and the lavish gardens opposite the family home in Heriot Row, where he played and, the fanciful will have you believe, first acted out the quest for *Treasure Island*. I have shadowed Stevenson up to the northeast of Scotland, where he tried his hand at being an apprentice engineer, back down to the Hawes Inn at South Queensferry, where David Balfour is tricked into going to sea in *Kidnapped*. It still serves rum and ale. There are landmarks in Switzerland, on the French Riviera, and on the Pacific islands where the adventure of his final years took place among a peculiar clan of relatives and natives.

Recently, I stumbled across a place where Stevenson lived briefly in London: Abernethy House. Now a private dwelling, it was once a lodging house. It stands in a secluded corner of Hampstead, where no cars and few pedestrians pass by, and which seems little changed from Stevenson's day. He stayed here when he was twenty-three. High up on a hill, and separated from foggy London by farms and heath, Hampstead was kind to Stevenson's tubercular lungs. It left a healthy impression on him, let's say; and Abernethy House left its mark, too, for Stevenson wrote an essay, "Notes on the Movements of Young Children," about a scene witnessed from his bedroom window. His friend Sidney Colvin, who was also staying at Abernethy, called the essay "merely an exercise," but it is among the first pieces in which we hear the mature, intelligent voice of the writer he would become. One day, Colvin found Stevenson entranced by the sight of some girls skipping rope in the street below. The youngest was particularly appealing: "The funniest little girl, with a mottled complexion and a big, damaged nose, and looking for all the world like any dirty, broken-nosed doll in a nursery lumber-room, came forward to take her turn. While the others swung the rope for her as gently as it could be done . . . and playfully taunted her timidity, she passaged backwards and forwards in a pretty flutter of indecision, putting up her shoulders and laughing." The description is capped by a typical note: "Much as I had enjoyed the grace of the older girls . . . the clumsiness of the child seemed to have a significance and a sort of beauty of its own."

Ethereal traces of R.L.S. are to be found elsewhere in Hampstead. I cannot pass the old pub, Jack Straw's Castle, without seeing the dog that Stevenson met there in 1874, "looking out of a gate so sympathetically that it has put me in good humor." And it was while standing on Hampstead

Hill one night that he gazed down on London and imagined a technological miracle of the future, "when in a moment, in the twinkling of an eye, the design of the monstrous city flashes into vision—a glittering hieroglyph." He is anticipating the effects of electricity and a time when the streetlamps would be lighted "not one by one" by the faithful old lamplighter, but all at once, by the touch of a button. Not for him improvements in optics, and his father's "azimuthal condensing system"; give him the flickering gas lamp and the "skirts of civilization" any day.

Lamps of one sort or another occur frequently in Stevenson's writing. In addition to this essay, "A Plea for Gas Lamps," there is another, "The Lantern Bearers," and his poem for children, "The Lamplighter," which celebrates an old custom: "For we are very lucky, with a lamp before the door, / And Leerie stops to light it as he lights so many more." Then there is the memoir he wrote in California, while waiting for Fanny to extract herself from her unhappy first marriage, in which he describes how, when a child and sick, his nurse would take him to the window, "whence I might look forth into the blue night starred with street lamps, and see where the gas still burned behind the windows of other sickrooms." And the lights shine again, with a subdued glow, in the obituary he wrote of his father in 1887. Thomas Stevenson's name may not have been widely known, yet "all the time, his lights were in every part of the world, guiding the mariner."

A year later, Stevenson chartered the schooner yacht *Casco* and became a mariner himself, sailing circuitously through the South Seas for Samoa. With his mother in tow, as well as his wife and stepchildren, he had, in a sense, entered the family business at last. By then, a very modern cult of celebrity had grown up around the author of *Treasure Island* and *Strange Case of Dr. Jekyll and Mr. Hyde,* and Stevenson found it difficult to evade admirers and the press. After his death in 1894, Fanny recalled how they set out from Tahiti, where they had been living in contented isolation, and set their sails for Hawaii. When they reached Honolulu, "the change from our simple, quiet life to the complications of civilization . . . proved confusing to a degree almost maddening." There were crowds of visitors at the door of their cottage, numerous letters to be answered and—there it goes again—"the almost constant calls to the telephone."

CODA Boswell and Mrs. Miller

A MEMOIR OF TWO TONGUES

When James Boswell took the low road from Scotland to London in 1762, to seek his fortune and eventually to write *The Life of Samuel Johnson,* he required no passport to cross the border; but as he went, he imagined his whole being receiving the stamp of improvement. Boswell's overwhelming purpose in life was to better himself; in order to do so, he was ready to slough off the rough Scots "Jamie," and admit the politer, anglicized James. In London, however, Boswell encountered an unexpected and unwanted reminder of home on the southern air. "Mrs Miller's Glasgow tongue excruciated me," he wrote in his *Journal* for March 17, 1763. "I resolved never again to dine where a Scotchwoman from the West was allowed to feed with us."

The Scotchwoman from the West must have made an awful din. Boswell suggests a genteel table upset by a barking ruffian. We notice that, while he "dines," Mrs. Miller "feeds." It comes as a surprise to learn that Mrs. Miller was the wife of Thomas Miller, Lord Advocate of Scotland, the country's highest-ranking legal figure. She would have been considered, and would have thought herself, a member of the gentry. Boswell's annoyance and embarrassment tell us that it was common for respectable society figures in mid-eighteenth-century Scotland to speak a form of what is called Older Scots, a generic designation for the dialect tongue that wags across time, from the Middle Ages to the present day. Boswell himself could only have avoided sounding like Mrs. Miller by making a positive effort not to.

How, exactly, does Mrs. Miller speak? She says "aff" for off and "oot" for out; "ben the hoose" to mean indoors, and "greetan" for weeping. Mrs. Miller gets wired intae her dener, while Boswell and the others are carefully keeping their elbows off the table. She uses idioms and peculiar grammatical constructions which he has been taking pains to expunge for years: "Ah doot Jamie canny tell a rich wumman bi a puir," she thinks, sensing Boswell's snobbish contempt. "He haes a face on him aye that wad soor milk." Catching his angry eye, she cries out, "Dinna fash yersel'," before turning back to her "parridge," the common name she gives to the tastiest of dishes. To Boswell and the assembled company, Mrs. Miller seems incapable of grasping the difference between "those" and "they" (or thae), and equally incapable of pronouncing the flat *a*, so that references to those apples in the dish over there inevitably tumble out of her mouth as "thae aipples," no matter how she tries to prevent it happening. She speaks of the dish as "thon ashet yonder." She havers on about her "faither" and "mirra," and the "wee wean," her child, and "hoo i wiz glaiket but bonny forby." When she does use the flat *a*, it's in the wrong place: water, for example, drips off Mrs. Miller's tongue as "waa'er." Imagine these deviations spread across the entire field of speech, and you have some idea of the sound that "excruciated" Boswell.

Mrs. Miller cannot be allowed back to the table; if she should be, Boswell will refuse to join in. A few weeks earlier, he had reflected in his *Journal* that it would be wiser in future—more socially advantageous, he meant—to avoid contact altogether with the compatriots who arrived in London and came knocking on his door. Particularly those who embarrassed him by speaking in "the abominable Glasgow tongue."

I know Mrs. Miller well. I can hear her clearly. With a few shifts in flats and sharps, a slight increase or reduction in the incidence of glottal stops (try removing any hint of a *t* from "waa'er" and replacing it with an emphasis on the second syllable), her descendants in Glasgow speak today as she did two and a half centuries ago. Mrs. Miller's speech reflected the natural West of Scotland way of talking; it was Boswell, powdering his palate from a compact of airs and affectations, who was trying to groom himself to "talk suddron" (southern). It was fashionable

among some, though not all, Scottish ladies and gentlemen of the day to
do so. Boswell came from a well-to-do family of landowning lawyers
from the rural Southwest and attended Glasgow University. He had
taken lessons in elocution in Edinburgh from Thomas Sheridan, father of
the playwright Richard Brinsley, and he would have been familiar with
the little books of "Scotticisms," published in the 1750s and 60s, containing alphabetical lists of words and phrases that Scots in public life were
advised to avoid, especially when indulging in commercial or social
intercourse with their English or foreign counterparts. Mrs. Miller's
offense, on being "allowed to feed" at a polite table in London, was to
disregard the presumed linguistic etiquette.

Boswell's objections make him sound like a boor and even a traitor.
But he was less of a snob than he might seem. His attachment to the great
natural democrat Dr. Johnson was genuine and philosophically
grounded, and his feeling for Scotland was deep. Eventually, he married
a Scotchwoman from the West and lived with her in Edinburgh, in the
East. However, his severe attitude toward the Glasgow tongue is just as
familiar to someone who was born and brought up in the city, as I was,
as the tongue itself. The two ways of speaking may be separated into
"Glasgow" and "Glesca," after the different pronunciations of the city's
name. The tongue has divided families, neighbors, and neighborhoods; it
has drawn a notional segregation marker through the city. A refined
Glasgow speaker might go out of his way to avoid contact with a Glesca
speaker. Each would recognize the social standing of the other as soon as
they opened their mouths. Mr. Glasgow might treat Mr. Glesca and his
"patter" ("paa'er") as a topic of couthie humor, a kind of Caledonian
minstrelsy, which is calculated to amuse; similarly, the Glesca man can
only bring himself to pronounce the official name of his city, "Glasgow,"
in a pointed, comical way. To attempt it in ordinary conversation would
be to invite ridicule from his friends. The Glasgow man probably believes
(without having given it much thought) that the other who says "Glesca"
does so out of an inability to pronounce "Glasgow." It is possible that
neither is aware that the "lower" pronunciation reflects the medieval
spelling of the city's name; in the fourteenth and fifteenth centuries,
Glasgow was "Glescu" and must have been pronounced that way by the
Boswells and Mrs. Millers alike.

The linguistic division, which developed fully around about 1600 with the Union of the Crowns of England and Scotland, has also split individuals. There is no better illustration of the double-sidedness of the Scottish tongue than the national poet himself. For both his daily life and his poetry, Robert Burns had two dialects: Older Scots and Standard English. Sometimes he employed them both in a single sentence, or poetic couplet, as in the well-known lines, "The best-laid plans o' mice an' men / Gang aft agley." Like many Burns poems, "To a Mouse" is written in a combination of Scots and English, but the dominant flavor is Scots, even when dialect vocabulary is used scarcely—"Wee, sleekit, cowrin, tim'rous beastie." The same was true of Burns's everyday speech. To the neighboring farmers in Ayrshire (Boswell's county, as it happens, some fifty miles southwest of Glasgow), Burns spoke like this:

> I'm sitten down here, after seven and forty miles ridin, e'en as forjesket and forniaw'd as forfoughten cock, to gie you some notion o' my landlowper-like stravaguin sin the sorrowfu' hour that I sheuk hands and parted wi' auld Reekie. . . .
>
> I hae daunder'd owre a' the kintra frae Dumbar to Selcraig, and hae forgather'd wi' monie a guid fallow and monie a weelfar'd hizzie—I met wi' twa dink quines in particular, ane o' them a sonsie, fine fodgel lass, baith braw and bonnie.

Yet he was capable of adopting a cultivated manner when circumstances required it. For the men and women with whom he socialized in the drawing rooms of Edinburgh ("auld Reekie"), on whom he sometimes was forced to depend financially, he adopted a different voice altogether: "I cannot bear the idea of leaving Edinburgh without seeing you—I know not how to account for it—I am strangely taken with some people; nor am I often mistaken. You are a stranger to me; but I am an odd being: some yet unnamed feelings; things not principles, but better than whims, carry me farther than boasted reason ever did a Philosopher." The letter in Scots, dealing with one of Burns's favorite subjects (the "twa dink quines" might elsewhere be described as two comely wenches), is to the poet's friend William Nicol, a schoolmaster; the other, written in the same year, 1787, is to Agnes McLehose, a more genteel-sounding Scotchwoman from the West than Mrs. Miller, with whom Burns conducted a brief courtship.

Scots has numerous regional variations, of which Burns's Ayrshire and Mrs. Miller's Glesca are only two. All are related, and all forms of Scots are likewise linked to standard English. The use of Scots for day-to-day purposes was still common in the time of Burns and Boswell. Two hundred and fifty years before that it was universal. For the past century and a half, however, Scots has been declared dead, or regarded as petering out—or else it is in the throes of a revival. Robert Louis Stevenson, born into a middle-class Edinburgh family in 1850, picked up a fair sprinkling of Scots from servants and gardeners, which he put to spirited use in poems and letters, and occasionally in short stories such as "Thrawn Janet"; but he was aware as he did so that he was indulging a linguistic form of nostalgia. Stevenson recalled his grandfather, born a year or two after Burns's effusions, as "one of the last, I suppose, to speak broad Scots and be a gentleman." The country folk of present-day Ayrshire, tuning into *EastEnders* and *Friends,* and conversing via the transatlantic line with their emigrant cousins in North America, no longer talk to one another as Burns did to Willie Nicol, nor do they use much of the vocabulary that gives poems such as "To a Mouse" and "Tam o' Shanter" their distinct fiber. There is, in a sense, less space for the dialect; the distances that separate groups of people have shrunk, and we are apt to address our neighbors in a language we trust they will understand. Yet Scots is still alive. It is current in ways that may be barely noticed. Boys and girls in the streets of Glasgow today, for example, would find the idiom of this sixteenth-century ballad quite familiar; should you be passing by, you might hear them speak in a way that is close to it:

As I was a-walkin all alane
I spied twa corbies makkin a mane.
The tane untae the ither did say-o:
Whaur sall we gang tae dine the day-o.

In ahent yon auld fell dyke,
I wot there lies a new slain knight.
And naebody kens that he lies there-o
But his hawk an' his hound an' his lady fair-o.

"Doubles" or "doubling" are often evoked in discussions of Scottish literature, with reference made to Stevenson's *Strange Case of Dr. Jekyll and Mr. Hyde* and James Hogg's *Confessions of a Justified Sinner,* and even to poems like "Tam o' Shanter," which inhabit a split-level reality—this world, and the world of ghaisties, witches, and warlocks into which Tam stumbles. Indeed, "doubling" is an actual feature of the language in which a large portion of Scottish literature is composed. There is a formulation, originally made by the poet Edwin Muir but so often cited as to have become a commonplace, that modern Scottish writers who make use of the dialect feel in one language (Scots) while they think in another (English).

The conflict between the two elements continues to occur in Scotland today. It was played out in my family living room on the south side of Glasgow in the late 1950s and early 60s. We were a typical working-class family with typical aspirations to be more middle class. I was carefully brought up to speak properly (or, as the people who don't speak properly say, "speak polite"). But in my mid-teens, as part of a private revolution, I began a linguistic migration back to the Older Scots. I didn't know then that that was the name of the dialect which I heard all around me ("As I was a-walkin, all alane"); there must have been something in the rougher way of talking that suited my adolescent storm. My parents took the position, let's say, of Boswell, whereas I found myself cast as Mrs. Miller. The process coincided with my falling in with a new crowd of friends, who came from a poorer, notorious area of Glasgow, the Gorbals. There was nothing in my friends' behavior to deserve the stamp of notoriety, but geography is itself the marker of repute in most big cities, and Glasgow is no exception. Each evening, to the alarm of those who cared for my welfare and my future, I walked past the neatly trimmed hedges of our street and strolled into the world of tenement closes, pens, yards, and dunnies. And, like Boswell but in reverse, I exchanged my tongue on the way. Leaving my jacket at home and pittan oan ma jaiket; leaving Glasgow and daun'erin owre tae Glesca.

It is not unusual for teenagers to have one language for the playground and another for the classroom, or as in this case, one for the street and another for the living room. Here the scene was dramatized into a choice between dark and light, like the choice Tam o' Shanter faced as he rode home on his gray mare Meg after an evening sat "bousin at the nappy." My mother, like most of the mothers around about, had barely heard of Boswell; but she knew all about "the abominable Glasgow tongue." By gentling their vowels, and those of their children, my parents were doing what generations of lowly folk had done before: they were trying to "get on," or in Boswellian terms, to make themselves welcome to feed at the table. The streets of Glasgow were crowded with people who had not got on. They were poor, they were out of work, they drank too much and had troublesome dealings with the law, and frequently with everyone else who came near them. It seemed they could not even negotiate the vowels and consonants of the language, the Queen's English, with proper competence. *Who'll give you a job when you speak like that?* It was held up before us as a character failure.

There were respectable people who said "grun" when they meant *ground*, who couldn't shape the "ou" in *house*, or the "ea" in *dead* and *bread*, but said "hoose" and "deid" and "breid"; who said "hame" for *home*; who had difficulty in completing simple words, such as *of, all, Dad* (o', a', Da'), and could not master the pronunciation of *blind*, but had to settle for "blinn" instead. But mostly they lived in the country, like my mother's adored Uncle Willie, a shepherd on a Highland farm, where a Scots tongue was regarded as a "hertsome" thing. In the country, the broad Scots accent sounded healthier, just as the cream and the eggs that came straight from the farm onto our breakfast table tasted better.

If these acceptable Scots speakers were not country folk, they were elderly, rooted in old ways and the nineteenth century, like Grandma and Grandpa. It is an oddity of the linguistic politics I am discussing that when my sisters and I went to visit our grandparents, born within the lifetime of Robert Louis Stevenson, we were greeted by the auld tongue. "C'wa ben the hoose," our grandmother would say on our arrival. A light fall of rain she'd call a "smirr," or a "smirrie rain"; wet children were "fair drookit." If she should "jalouse" a cold, she gave us loathsome brandy. Like many of her class and generation, her speech, though principally English, dawdled naturally and frequently amid the Older Scots. She said "gang" for *going*, "havers" for *nonsense*, called boys and girls "chiels and quines," called a drain a "stank." If it was "dreich" outside, it was "a scunner" to her. Many of the words from Burns's vocabulary would have come naturally, and still do to large numbers of Scottish people: "bide" for *live,* for example; "thole," to endure. Grandma would never have heard of Hugh MacDiarmid, the greatest twentieth-century practitioner of Scots, but she would have understood his verse:

> Mars is braw in crammasy,
> Venus in a green silk goun,
> The auld mune shak's her gowden feathers,
> Their starry talk's a wheen o' blethers,
> Nane for thee a thochtie sparin',
> Earth, thou bonnie broukit [neglected] bairn!

Meanwhile, my elder sisters were being sent to an elocution teacher to comb out as many *tholes, bides, dreichs,* and *drookits* from their speech as possible. They pranced around the house saying, "How—now—brown—cow" in theatrical fashion. Boswell, recalling his own youthful instruction from Thomas Sheridan, would have smiled on them.

My mother and Boswell had a formidable range of good intentions in their armory. They included education, respectability, worldly acceptance. On our side, Mrs. Miller and I (though I did not yet realize it) had literature. Only much later did I realize that the language spoken by my friends in the Gorbals, by Grandma and Grandpa and Uncle Willie with his shepherd's crook, and by the chiels and quines in Ayrshire and throughout Scotland was not corrupt at all. Each regional variation, including the Glesca dialect, was derived from the Older Scots, the language used by the great fifteenth-century "makaris," William Dunbar and Robert Henryson. The boys and girls in the neighboring streets, who said "thae aipples," did not do so out of an inability to pronounce "these apples," or because they found it an embarrassment to "speak polite," as when prodded by teachers to say "Glasgow" instead of "Glesca"; they were simply, unwittingly, carrying on the Older Scots idiom which centuries of elocutional refinement had failed to smooth out. "Doon," "gaun," "grun," "dinnae," and a thousand other features of present-day Glasgow speech are retentions from a way of talking that was once common to all the people of Lowland Scotland (as "gotten" and "the fall," no longer used in English English, are retained in the American). "Thae aipples yonder, lyan oan the brae ahent the dyke, are sweit and bonie" is a sentence which my Gorbals comrades and the poet William Dunbar (1460–1513) would understand, as one. "Those apples on the hill, over there behind the wall, are sweet and delicious" is not.

Do I "feel" in Scots, despite thinking in English? On occasion, yes, especially to accommodate certain rushes of skepticism or joy that I take to be native. Or to express anger, or engage with children and animals. Scots words are apt to make a particular appeal to me, and Scots poetry, in the higher range, pleasures me like no other. Dunbar was quick to insist that he was a lesser poet than Chaucer, but Dunbar's poetry speaks to me in ways that Chaucer's never does and never could. It finds the familiar in me. The language of Dunbar's poetry, and that of certain colleagues writing five hundred years later, comes across as something half-remembered, like a first language since superseded. When I arrive at Glasgow Central Station these days, a wave of recognition breaks over me as I step off the train. The speech in the air around me carries experiences which, though I might not have realized it till then, were obscured by the invisible wall that separates Scotland from England.

When I went south to live in London, at the age of thirty, I admit it, I did a Boswell. I straightened out my tongue. It had never been "abominable"—at least not since those adolescent days—but it had what others were pleased to refer to as a "lilt." When I heard myself speak on a tape recorder or on the radio, I would be surprised at how strong my accent was. But gradually it faded. It happened without my noticing. I didn't shoo it away, or plot my advancement among the London literati by honeying the knobbled surfaces and thistled joints of my syllables. I excuse this fact, when people remark on it (invariably to my annoyance), by telling myself that my voice is mimetic by nature, that my tendency is to sound like those by whom I wish to be understood, that my Scots voice hasn't gone away, it's just concealed beneath these southern clothes. Thae suddron claes.

The paradox—our own family paradox—is that while my accent traveled southward, that of my parents went back in the opposite direction.

In recent years, my father, in particular, would announce "ah cannae thole it," usually in reference to a politician or something else that he found "a right scunner." He never talked like that in the days when I was being persecuted for the company I kept. He would have said of the politician "I can't stand him," that he found him annoying. In his last years, living at the lower fringe of the Highlands among people who speak a mild modern form of Scots, he found his vowel sounds drawn back to the streets where he had grown up—not that far, it so happens, from the stamping ground of my notorious Gorbals cronies. I noticed a certain self-consciousness as he modulated into this voice, often for my benefit, but also a pleasure, a relaxation, at being reacquainted with his older tongue.

My mother would have no qualms about sticking with the "Glasgow" way. But one day, during my father's last illness, when he responded to doctor's orders by failing to take his medicines when he should have, threatening to go out when he shouldn't, and generally behaving obstinately, she sat down in her usual chair with an air of great weariness and turned to me. "*Thrawn*, I think is the word," she said. Her precision took me aback. *Thrawn* means, literally, twisted or crooked, but it has a more common figurative sense, which is not hard to see: difficult, stubborn. *Thrawn* was indeed the word. I believe I had never heard her use it before. She must have been saving it up.

As for Boswell, several years after his abomination of Mrs. Miller he was back in London, having in the meantime returned to Scotland to marry and set himself up as a lawyer. An entry in the *Journal*, March 30, 1772, finds him in a Covent Garden coffeehouse with Johnson, contemplating the idea of moving his practice south for good (he never did). "Mr. Johnson is not against it; and says my having any Scotch accent would be but for a little while." Here he gives himself away. Almost a decade after having seen off Mrs. Miller, despite his lessons in "pronunciation" from Thomas Sheridan, Jamie is still talking native.

TEXT: PALATINO
DISPLAY: UNIVERS CONDENSED LIGHT 47, BAUER BODONI
COMPOSITOR: BOOKMATTERS, BERKELEY
PRINTER AND BINDER: MAPLE-VAIL MANUFACTURING GROUP